CONAN®

SHADOWS OVER KUSH

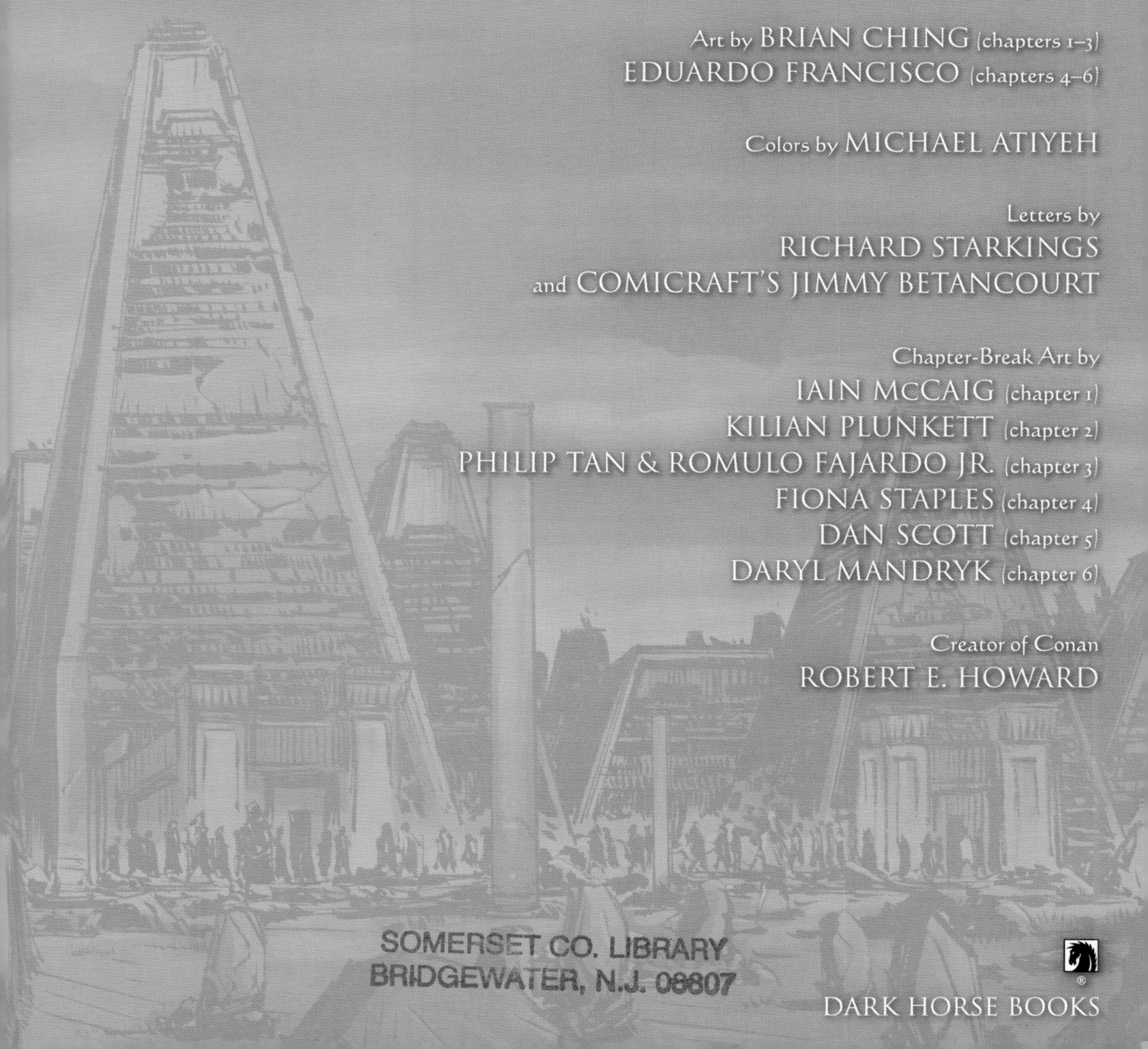

Writer FRED VAN LENTE

Art by BRIAN CHING (chapters 1–3)
EDUARDO FRANCISCO (chapters 4–6)

Colors by MICHAEL ATIYEH

Letters by
RICHARD STARKINGS
and COMICRAFT'S JIMMY BETANCOURT

Chapter-Break Art by
IAIN McCAIG (chapter 1)
KILIAN PLUNKETT (chapter 2)
PHILIP TAN & ROMULO FAJARDO JR. (chapter 3)
FIONA STAPLES (chapter 4)
DAN SCOTT (chapter 5)
DARYL MANDRYK (chapter 6)

Creator of Conan
ROBERT E. HOWARD

DARK HORSE BOOKS

Publisher MIKE RICHARDSON   Designer KAT LARSON   Digital Production CHRISTIANNE GOUDREAU   Assistant Editors ROXY POLK and AARON WALKER   Editor DAVE MARSHALL

Special thanks to JOAKIM ZETTERBERG at CONAN PROPERTIES.

This volume collects issues #1–#6 of the Dark Horse Comics monthly Conan the Avenger series.

Published by Dark Horse Books
A division of Dark Horse Comics, Inc.
10956 SE Main Street
Milwaukie, OR 97222

DarkHorse.com

International Licensing: (503) 905-2377
To find a comics shop in your area, call the Comic Shop Locator Service toll-free at 1-888-266-4226

First softcover edition: August 2015
ISBN 978-1-61655-659-4

10 9 8 7 6 5 4 3 2 1

Printed in China

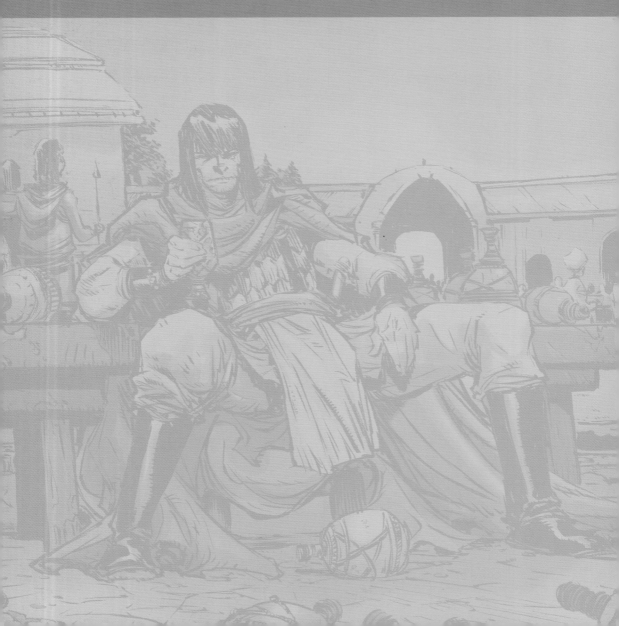

CHAPTER ONE

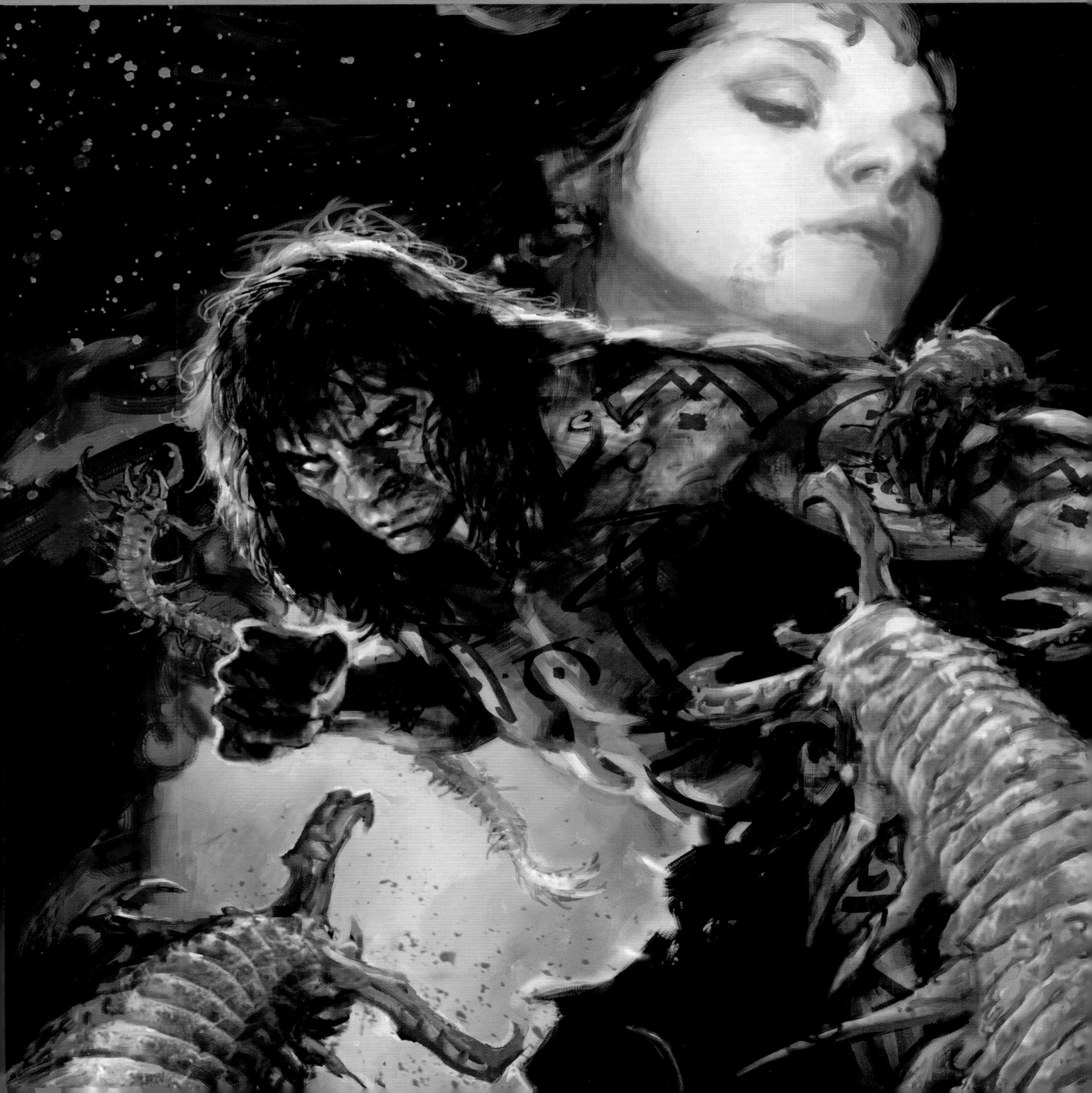

"*Wherever* he hides, I swear by our shared ancestors . . .
he will *not* escape me."

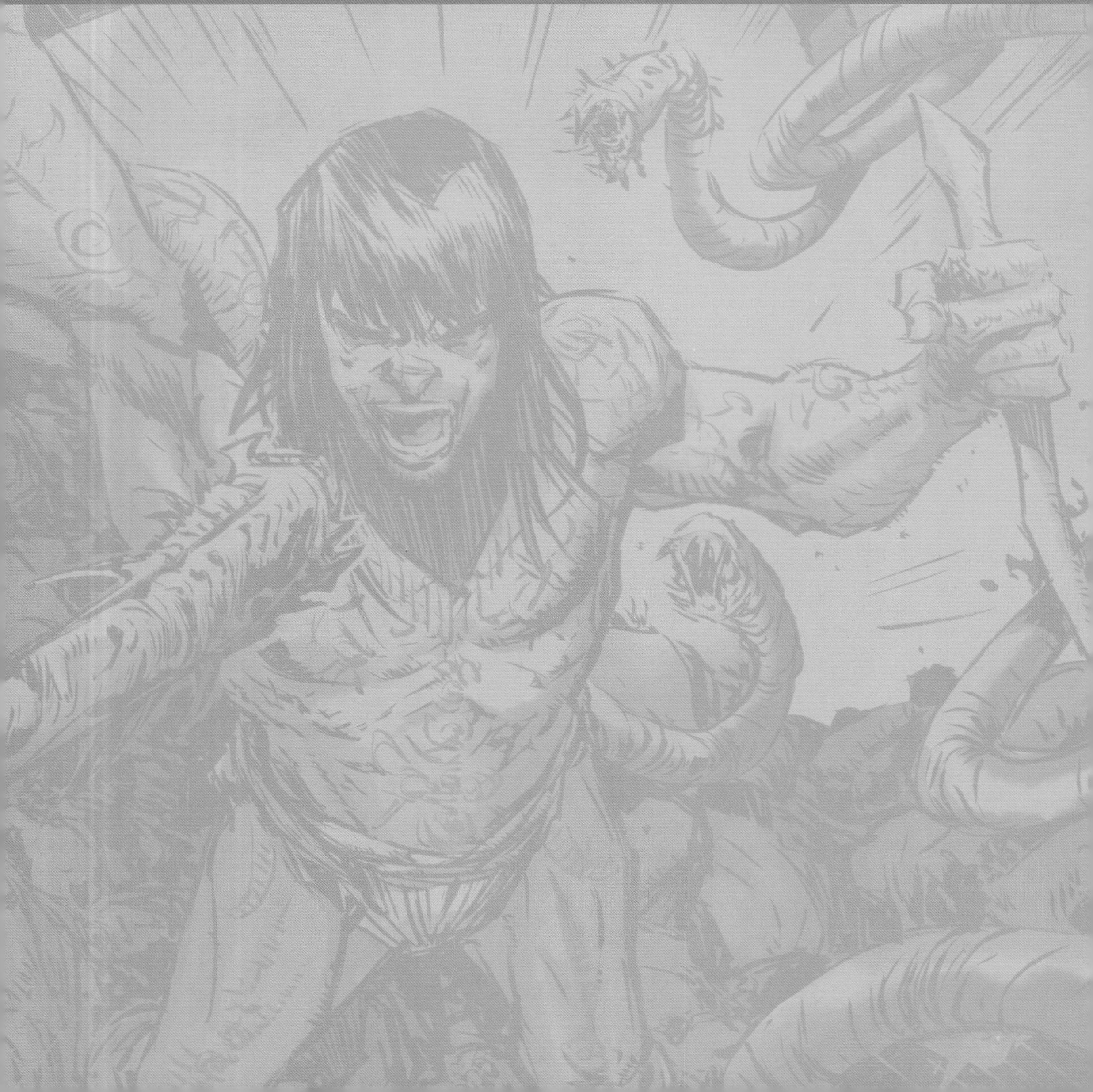

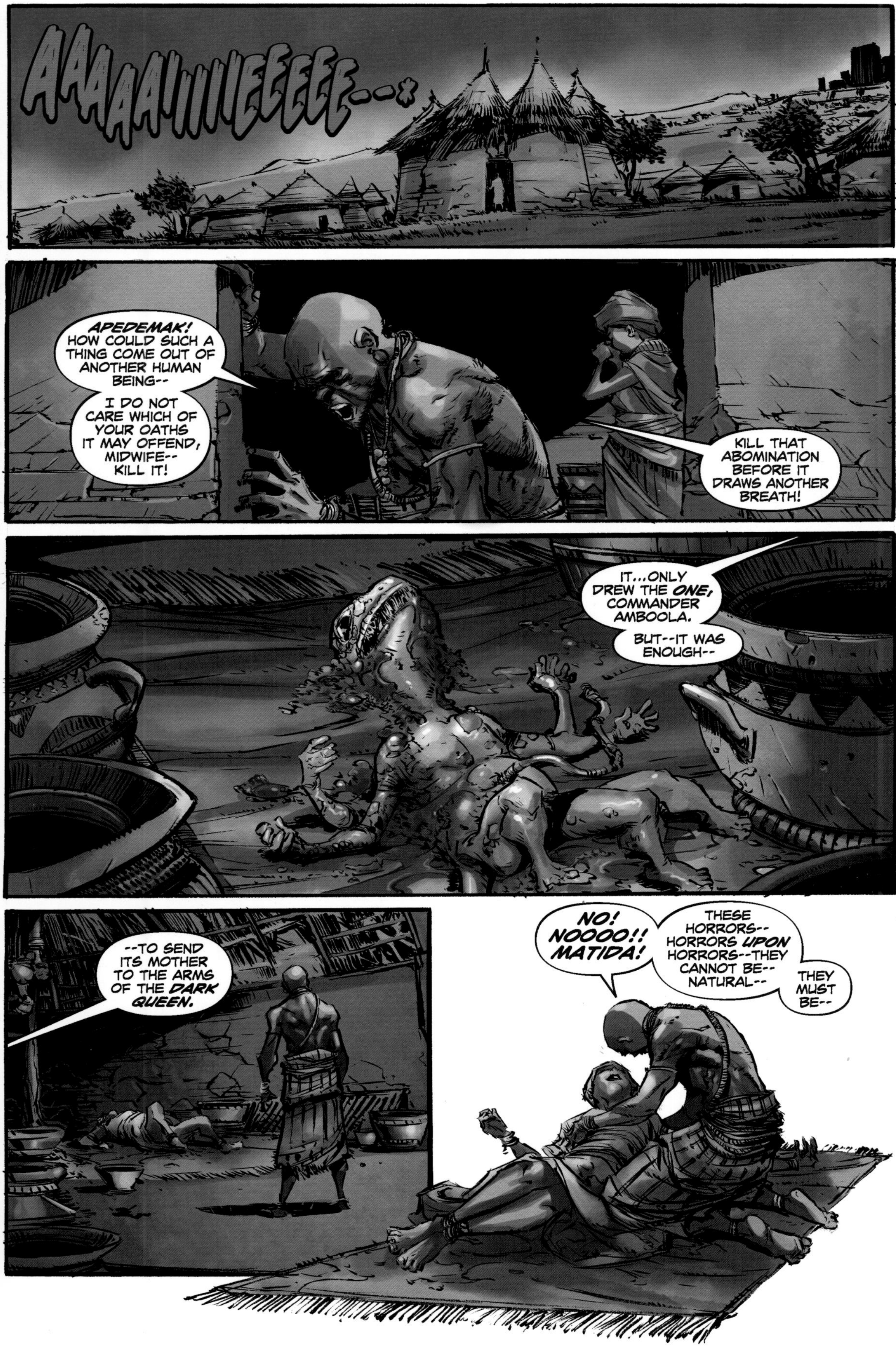

AAAAAIIIIIIEEEEE--*
APEDEMAK! HOW COULD SUCH A THING COME OUT OF ANOTHER HUMAN BEING--
I DO NOT CARE WHICH OF YOUR OATHS IT MAY OFFEND, MIDWIFE-- KILL IT!
KILL THAT ABOMINATION BEFORE IT DRAWS ANOTHER BREATH!
IT...ONLY DREW THE ONE, COMMANDER AMBOOLA.
BUT--IT WAS ENOUGH--
--TO SEND ITS MOTHER TO THE ARMS OF THE DARK QUEEN.
NO! NOOOO!! MATIDA!
THESE HORRORS-- HORRORS UPON HORRORS--THEY CANNOT BE-- NATURAL--
THEY MUST BE--

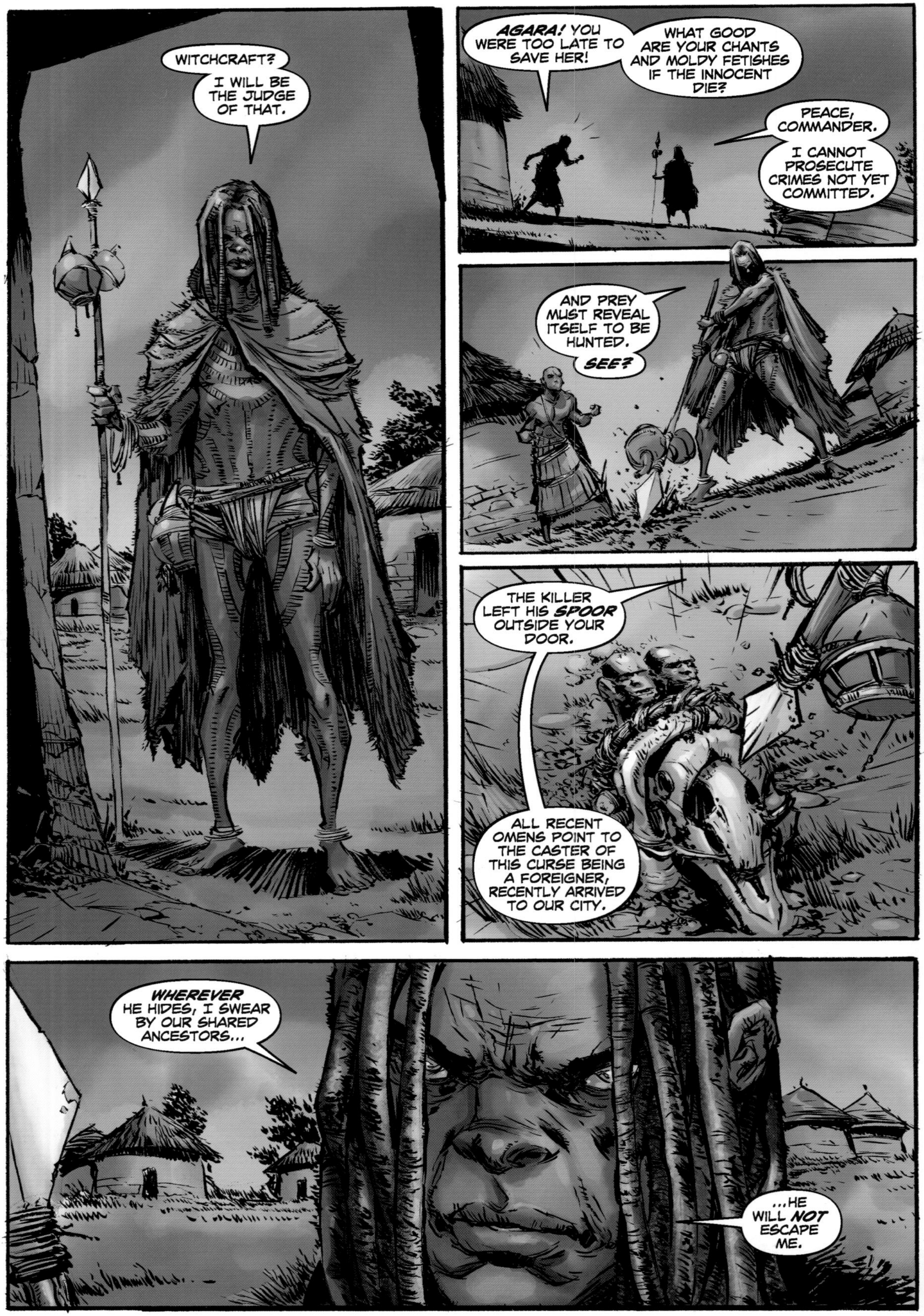
WITCHCRAFT?
I WILL BE THE JUDGE OF THAT.
AGARA! YOU WERE TOO LATE TO SAVE HER!
WHAT GOOD ARE YOUR CHANTS AND MOLDY FETISHES IF THE INNOCENT DIE?
PEACE, COMMANDER.
I CANNOT PROSECUTE CRIMES NOT YET COMMITTED.
AND PREY MUST REVEAL ITSELF TO BE HUNTED.
SEE?
THE KILLER LEFT HIS SPOOR OUTSIDE YOUR DOOR.
ALL RECENT OMENS POINT TO THE CASTER OF THIS CURSE BEING A FOREIGNER, RECENTLY ARRIVED TO OUR CITY.
WHEREVER HE HIDES, I SWEAR BY OUR SHARED ANCESTORS...
...HE WILL NOT ESCAPE ME.

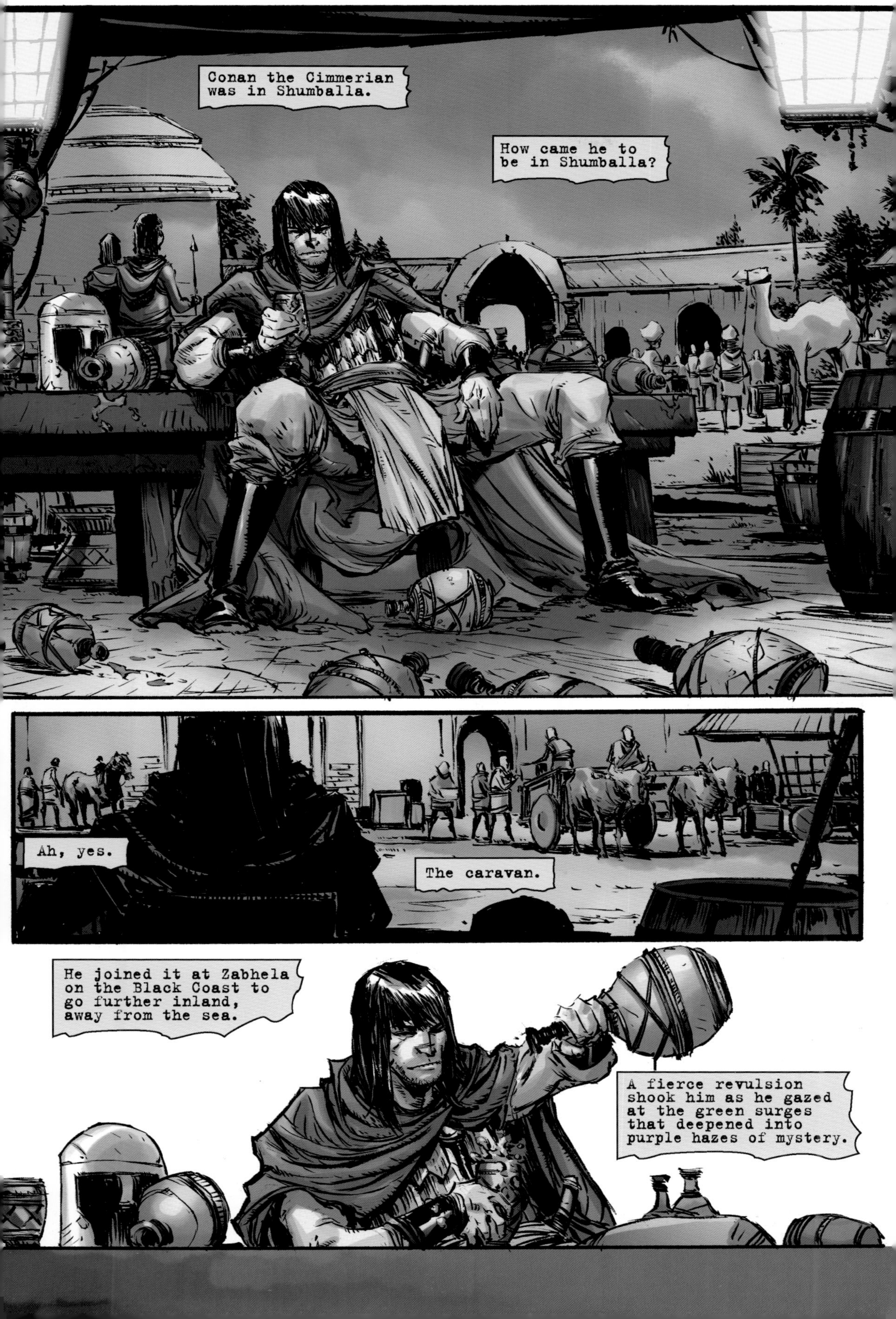

Conan the Cimmerian was in Shumballa.
How came he to be in Shumballa?
Ah, yes.
The caravan.
He joined it at Zabhela on the Black Coast to go further inland, away from the sea.
A fierce revulsion shook him as he gazed at the green surges that deepened into purple hazes of mystery.

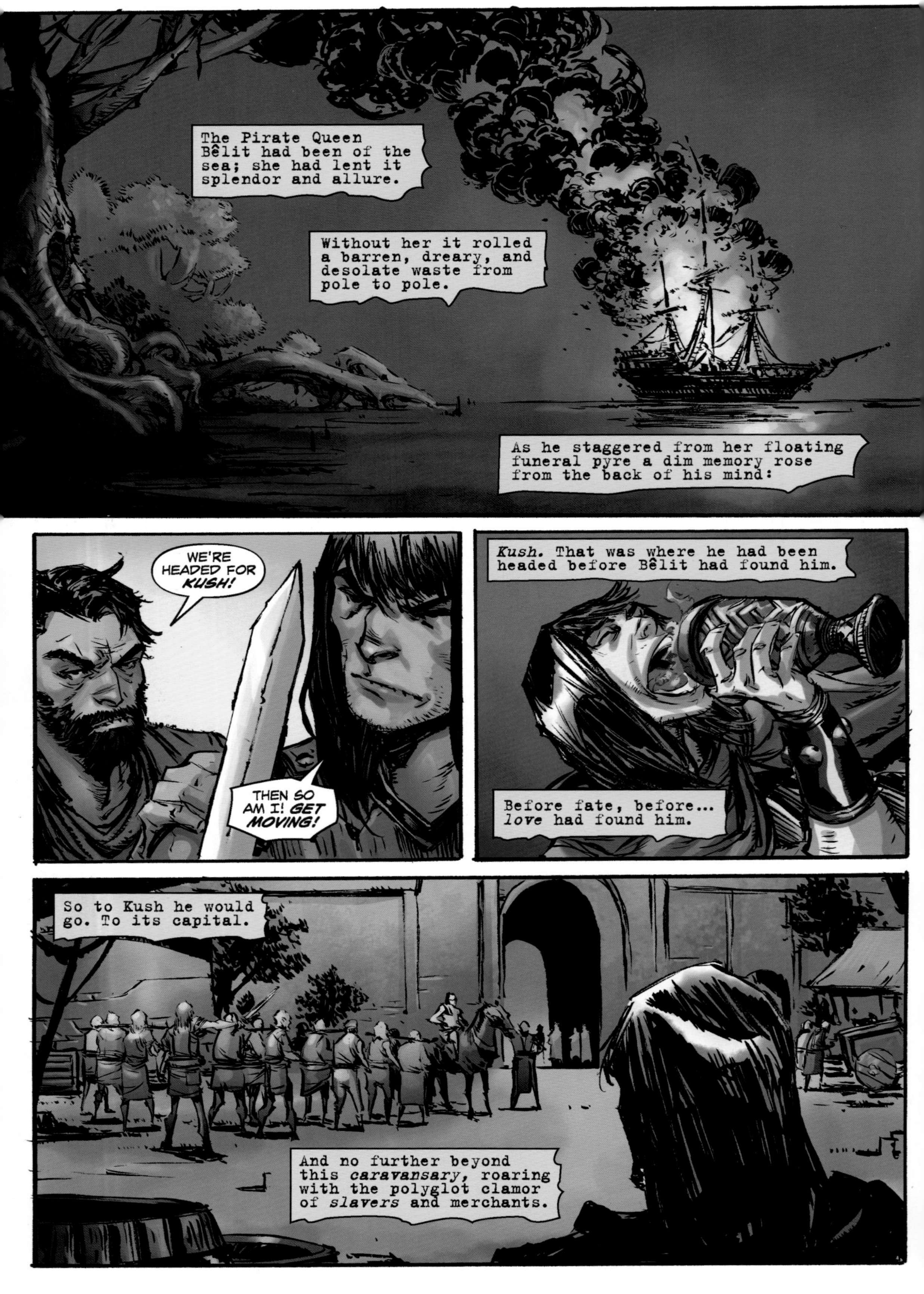
The Pirate Queen Bêlit had been of the sea; she had lent it splendor and allure.
Without her it rolled a barren, dreary, and desolate waste from pole to pole.
As he staggered from her floating funeral pyre a dim memory rose from the back of his mind:
WE'RE HEADED FOR *KUSH!*
THEN SO AM I! *GET MOVING!*
Kush. That was where he had been headed before Bêlit had found him.
Before fate, before... *love* had found him.
So to Kush he would go. To its capital.
And no further beyond this *caravansary*, roaring with the polyglot clamor of *slavers* and merchants.

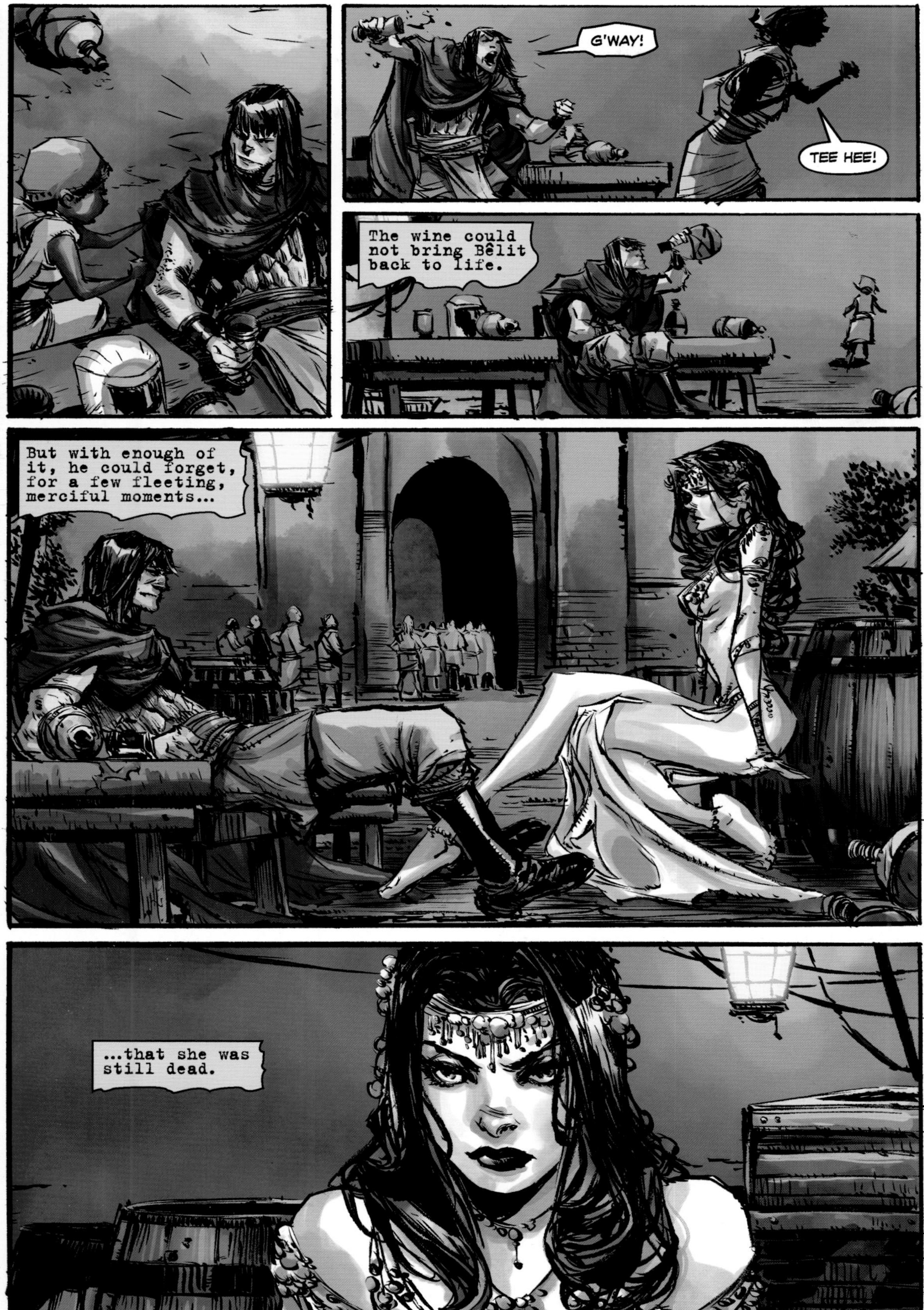
G'WAY!
TEE HEE!
The wine could not bring Bêlit back to life.
But with enough of it, he could forget, for a few fleeting, merciful moments...
...that she was still dead.

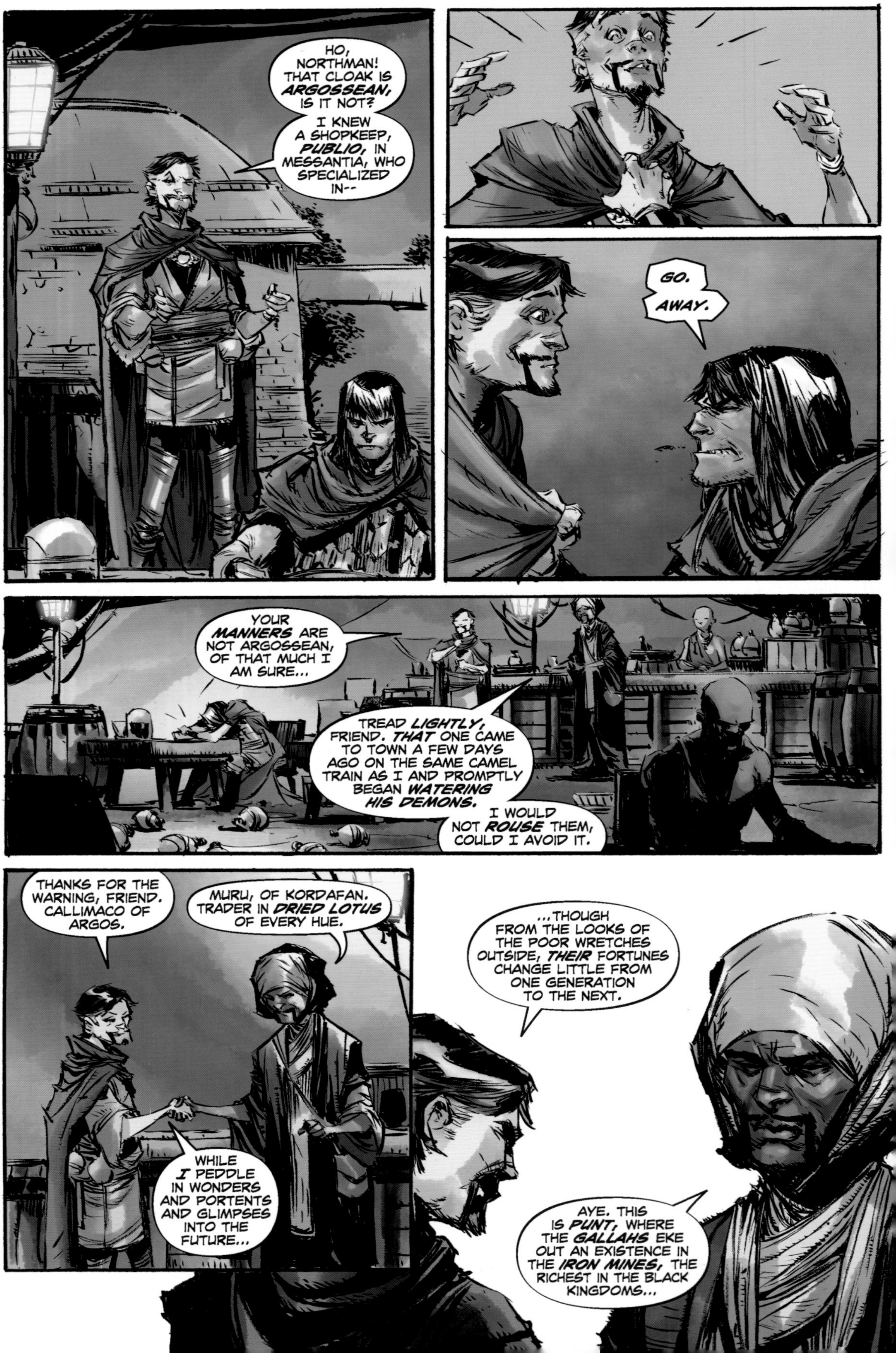
HO, NORTHMAN! THAT CLOAK IS ARGOSSEAN, IS IT NOT?
I KNEW A SHOPKEEP, PUBLIO, IN MESSANTIA, WHO SPECIALIZED IN--
GO. AWAY.
YOUR MANNERS ARE NOT ARGOSSEAN, OF THAT MUCH I AM SURE...
TREAD LIGHTLY, FRIEND. THAT ONE CAME TO TOWN A FEW DAYS AGO ON THE SAME CAMEL TRAIN AS I AND PROMPTLY BEGAN WATERING HIS DEMONS.
I WOULD NOT ROUSE THEM, COULD I AVOID IT.
THANKS FOR THE WARNING, FRIEND. CALLIMACO OF ARGOS.
MURU, OF KORDAFAN. TRADER IN DRIED LOTUS OF EVERY HUE.
WHILE I PEDDLE IN WONDERS AND PORTENTS AND GLIMPSES INTO THE FUTURE...
...THOUGH FROM THE LOOKS OF THE POOR WRETCHES OUTSIDE, THEIR FORTUNES CHANGE LITTLE FROM ONE GENERATION TO THE NEXT.
AYE. THIS IS PUNT, WHERE THE GALLAHS EKE OUT AN EXISTENCE IN THE IRON MINES, THE RICHEST IN THE BLACK KINGDOMS...

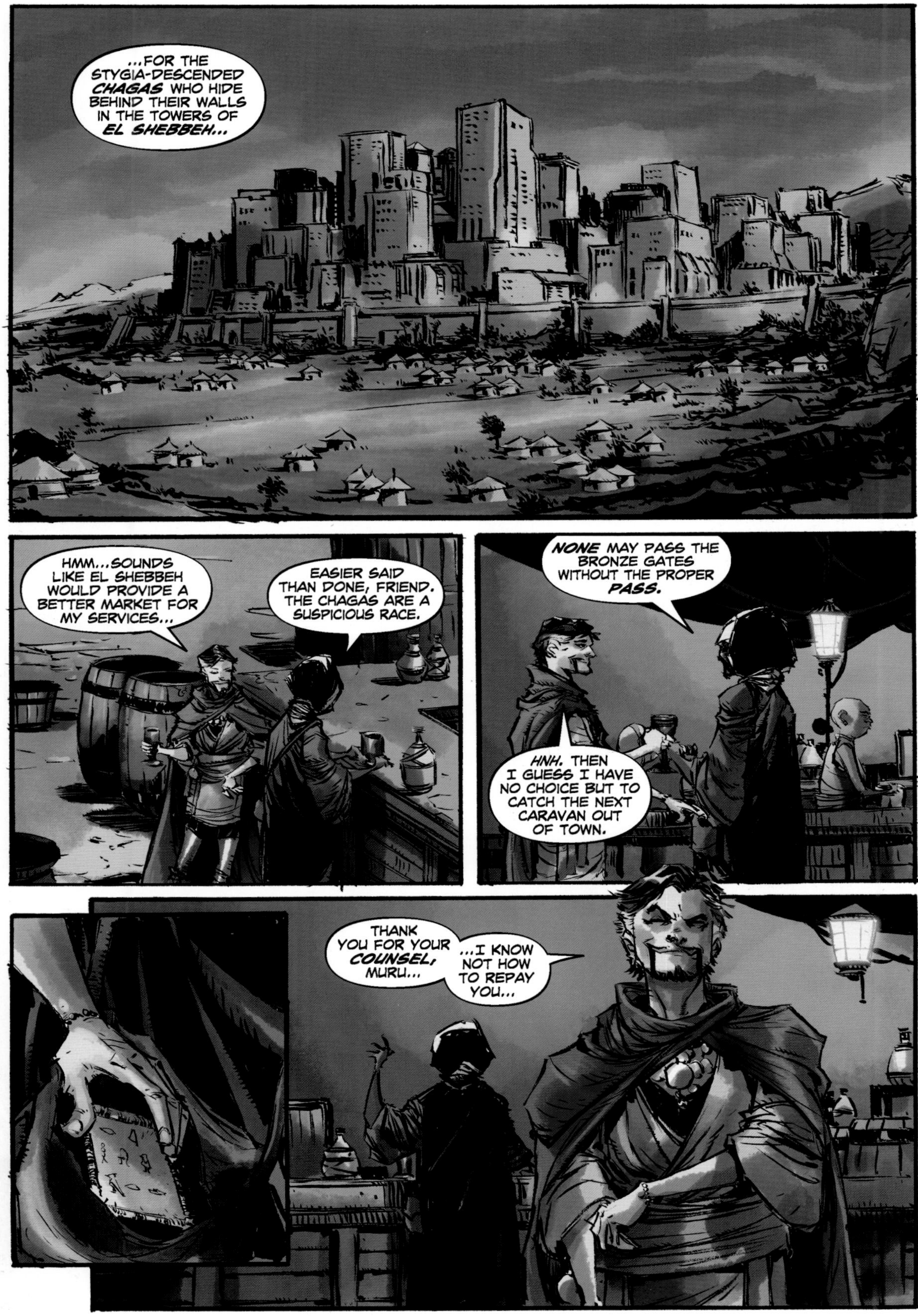
...FOR THE STYGIA-DESCENDED CHAGAS WHO HIDE BEHIND THEIR WALLS IN THE TOWERS OF EL SHEBBEH...
HMM...SOUNDS LIKE EL SHEBBEH WOULD PROVIDE A BETTER MARKET FOR MY SERVICES...
EASIER SAID THAN DONE, FRIEND. THE CHAGAS ARE A SUSPICIOUS RACE.
NONE MAY PASS THE BRONZE GATES WITHOUT THE PROPER PASS.
HNH. THEN I GUESS I HAVE NO CHOICE BUT TO CATCH THE NEXT CARAVAN OUT OF TOWN.
THANK YOU FOR YOUR COUNSEL, MURU...
...I KNOW NOT HOW TO REPAY YOU...

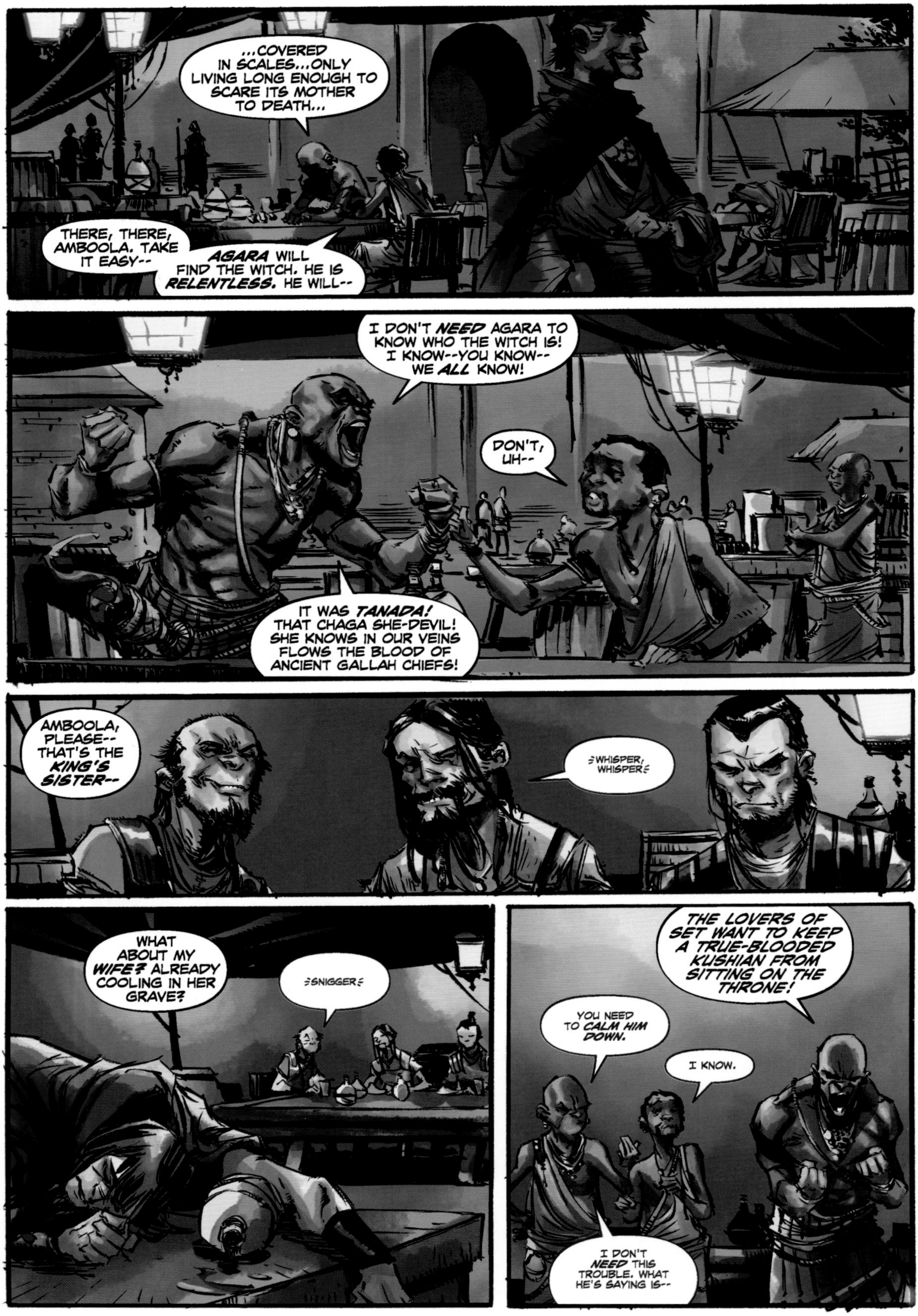
...COVERED IN SCALES...ONLY LIVING LONG ENOUGH TO SCARE ITS MOTHER TO DEATH...
THERE, THERE, AMBOOLA. TAKE IT EASY--
AGARA WILL FIND THE WITCH. HE IS RELENTLESS. HE WILL--
I DON'T NEED AGARA TO KNOW WHO THE WITCH IS! I KNOW--YOU KNOW--WE ALL KNOW!
DON'T, UH--
IT WAS TANADA! THAT CHAGA SHE-DEVIL! SHE KNOWS IN OUR VEINS FLOWS THE BLOOD OF ANCIENT GALLAH CHIEFS!
AMBOOLA, PLEASE--THAT'S THE KING'S SISTER--
WHISPER, WHISPER
WHAT ABOUT MY WIFE? ALREADY COOLING IN HER GRAVE?
SNIGGER
THE LOVERS OF SET WANT TO KEEP A TRUE-BLOODED KUSHIAN FROM SITTING ON THE THRONE!
YOU NEED TO CALM HIM DOWN.
I KNOW.
I DON'T NEED THIS TROUBLE. WHAT HE'S SAYING IS--

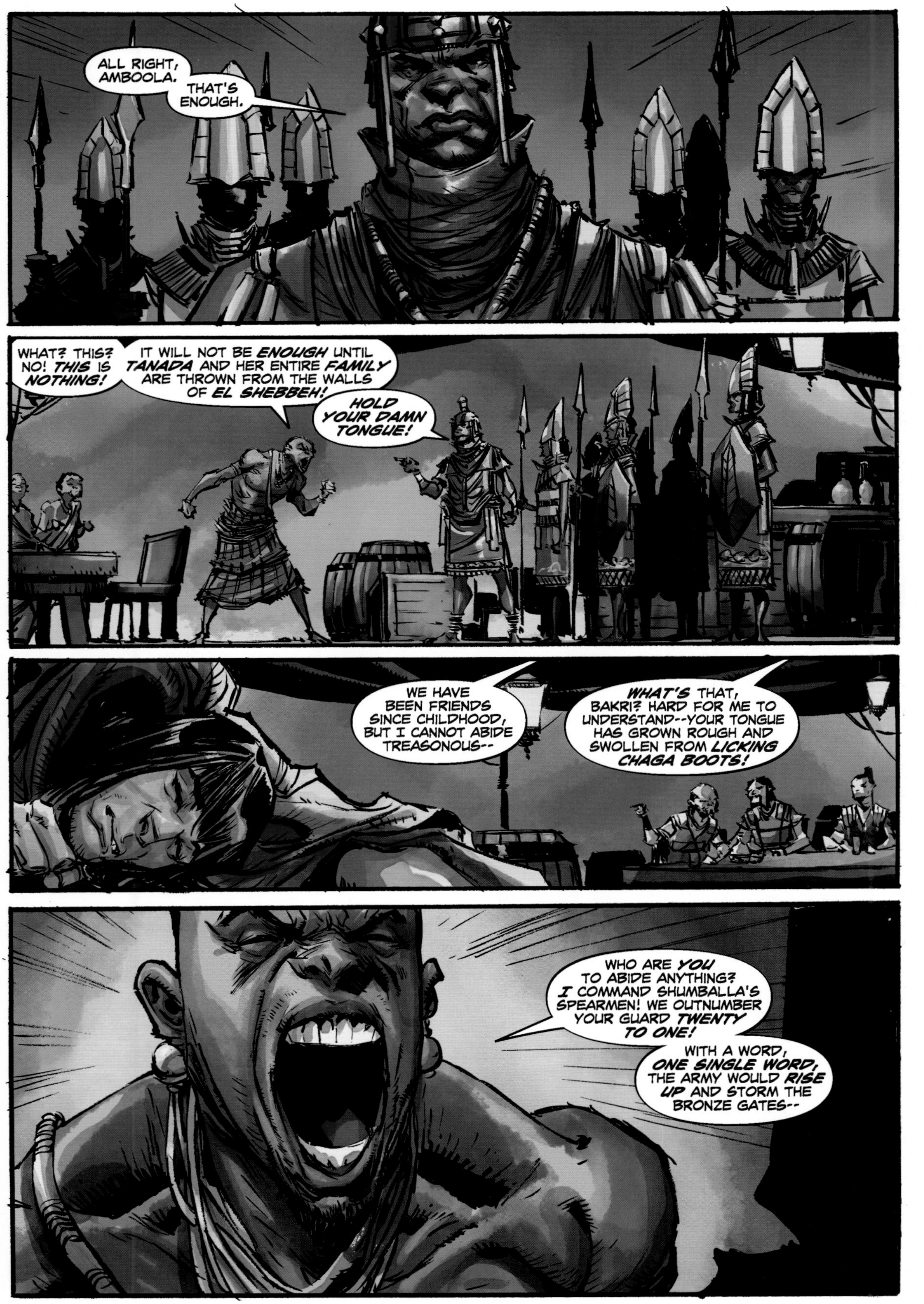
ALL RIGHT, AMBOOLA.
THAT'S ENOUGH.
WHAT? THIS? NO! THIS IS NOTHING!
IT WILL NOT BE ENOUGH UNTIL TANADA AND HER ENTIRE FAMILY ARE THROWN FROM THE WALLS OF EL SHEBBEH!
HOLD YOUR DAMN TONGUE!
WE HAVE BEEN FRIENDS SINCE CHILDHOOD, BUT I CANNOT ABIDE TREASONOUS--
WHAT'S THAT, BAKRI? HARD FOR ME TO UNDERSTAND--YOUR TONGUE HAS GROWN ROUGH AND SWOLLEN FROM LICKING CHAGA BOOTS!
WHO ARE YOU TO ABIDE ANYTHING? I COMMAND SHUMBALLA'S SPEARMEN! WE OUTNUMBER YOUR GUARD TWENTY TO ONE!
WITH A WORD, ONE SINGLE WORD, THE ARMY WOULD RISE UP AND STORM THE BRONZE GATES--

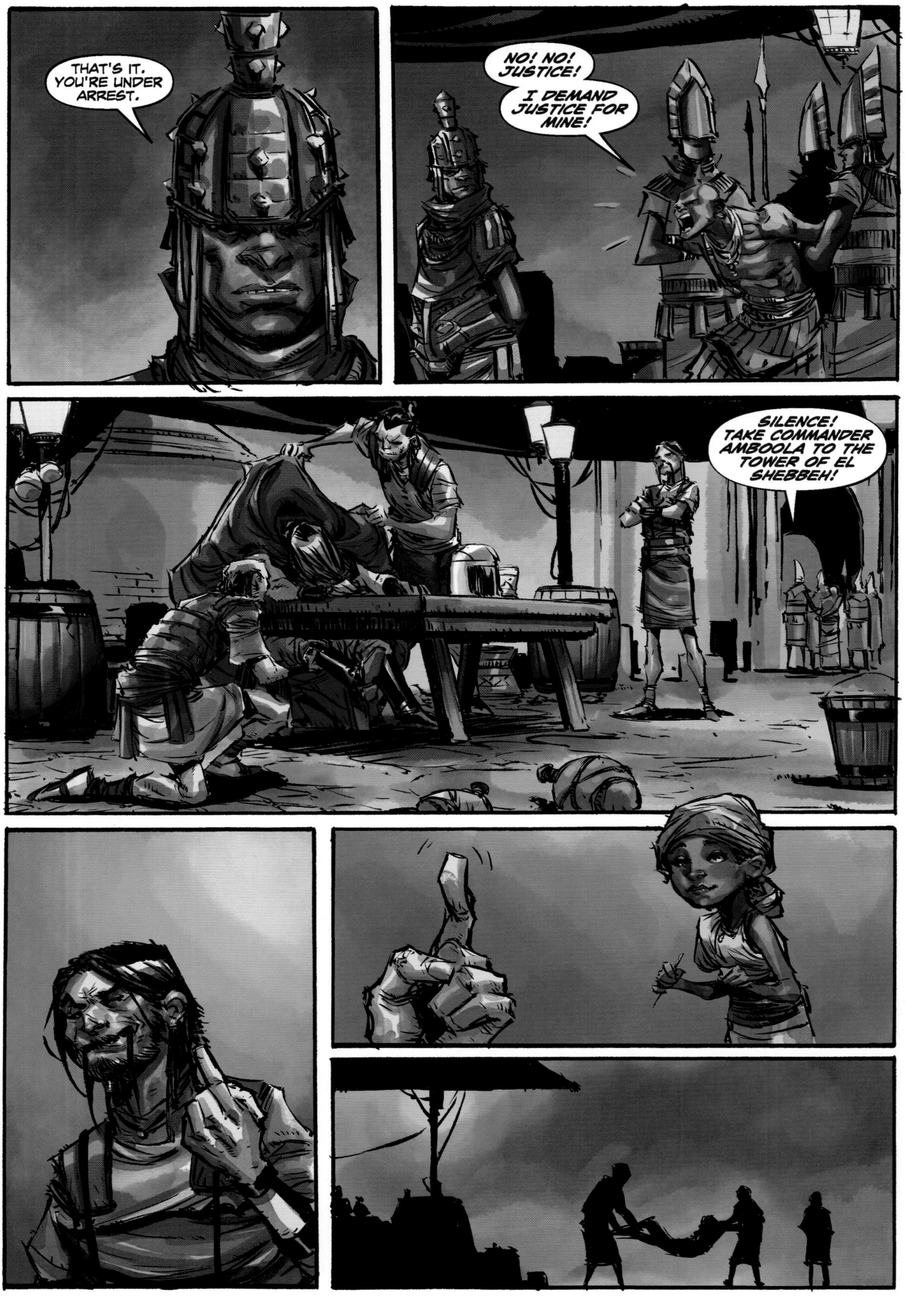
THAT'S IT. YOU'RE UNDER ARREST.
NO! NO! JUSTICE!
I DEMAND JUSTICE FOR MINE!
SILENCE! TAKE COMMANDER AMBOOLA TO THE TOWER OF EL SHEBBEH!

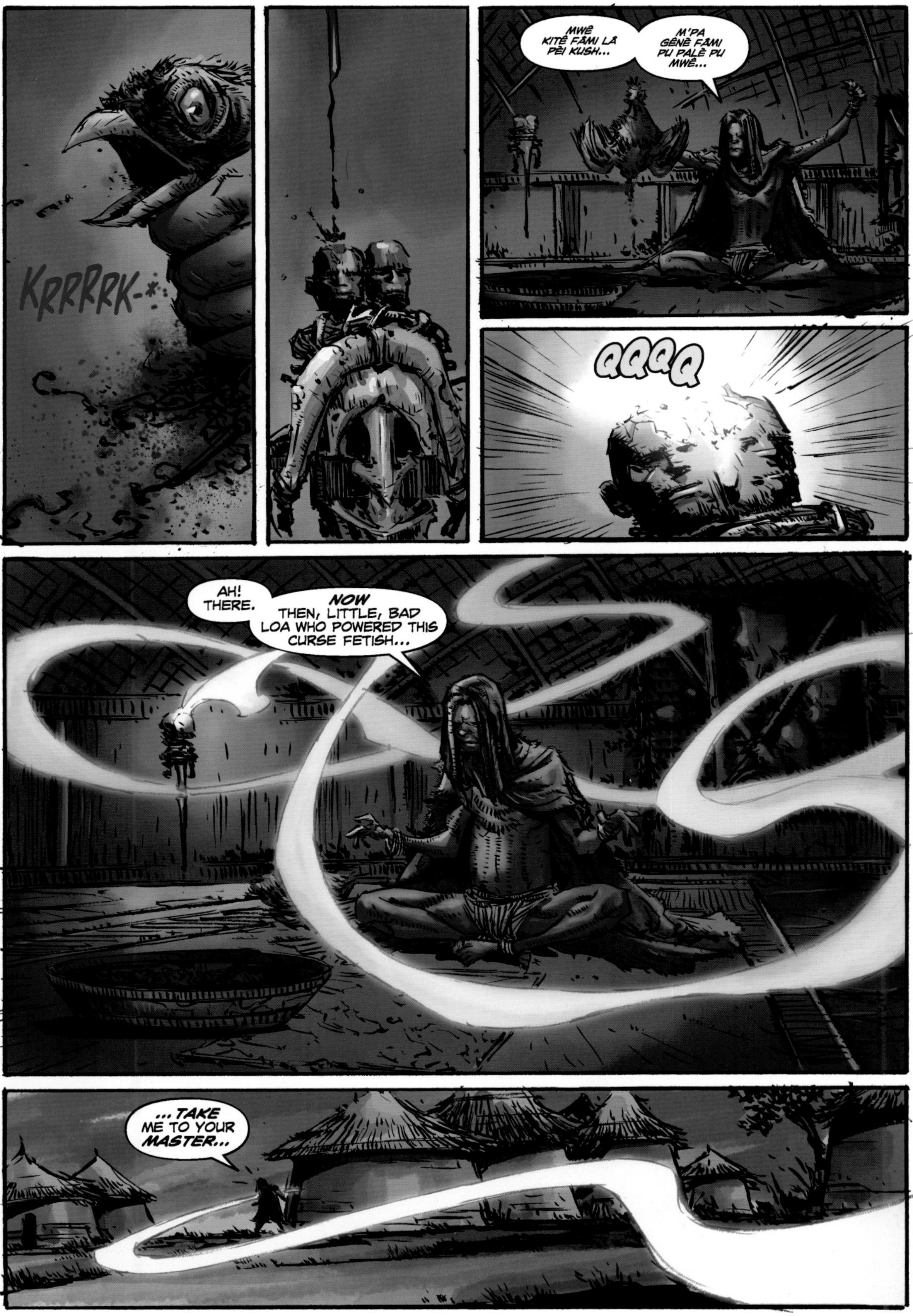
KRRRRK-*
MWÊ KITÊ FÂMI LÂ PÈI KUSH...
M'PA GÊNÈ FÂMI PU PALÈ PU MWÊ...
QQQQ
AH! THERE.
NOW THEN, LITTLE, BAD LOA WHO POWERED THIS CURSE FETISH...
...TAKE ME TO YOUR MASTER...

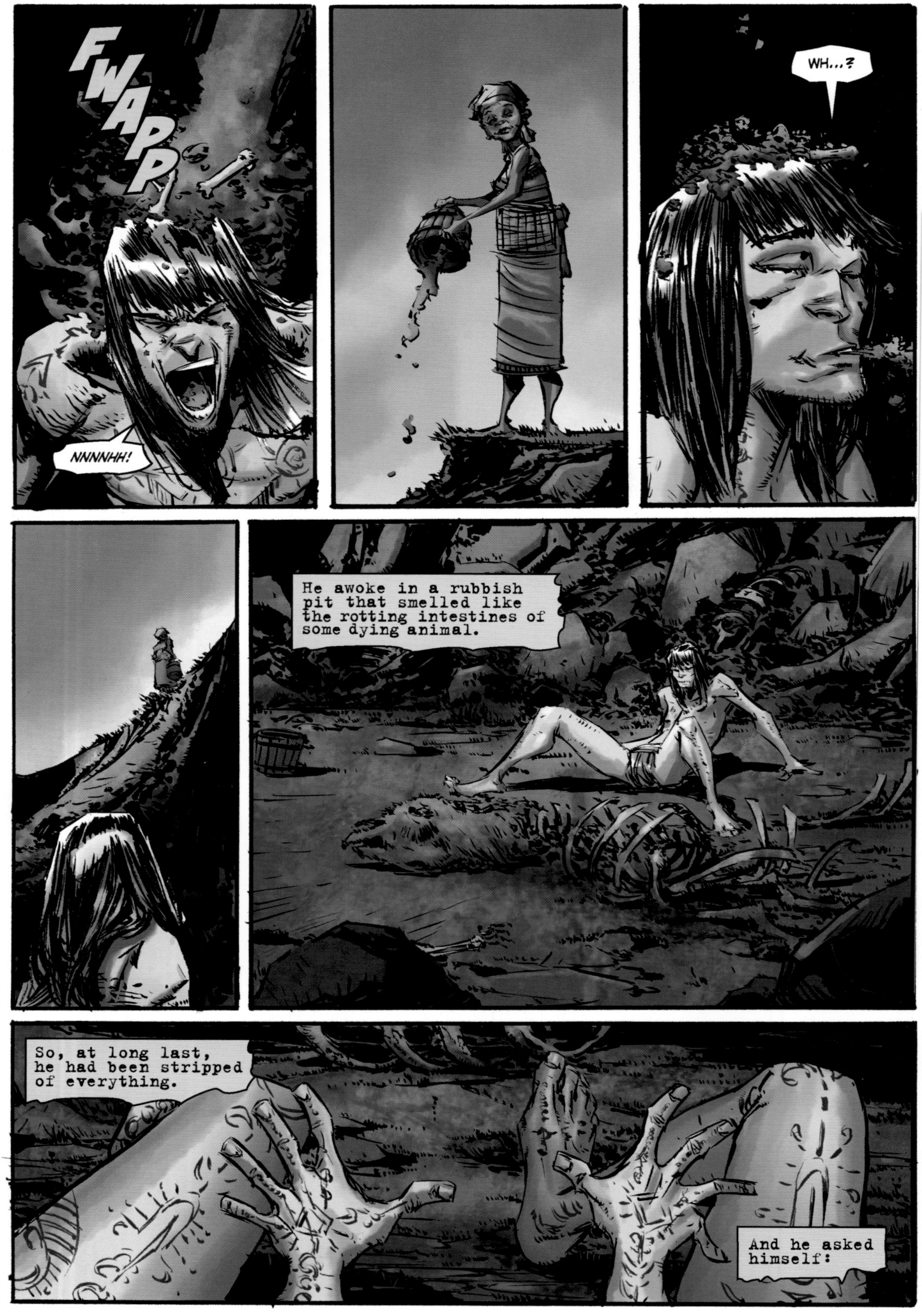
FWAPP
NNNNHH!
WH...?
He awoke in a rubbish pit that smelled like the rotting intestines of some dying animal.
So, at long last, he had been stripped of everything.
And he asked himself:

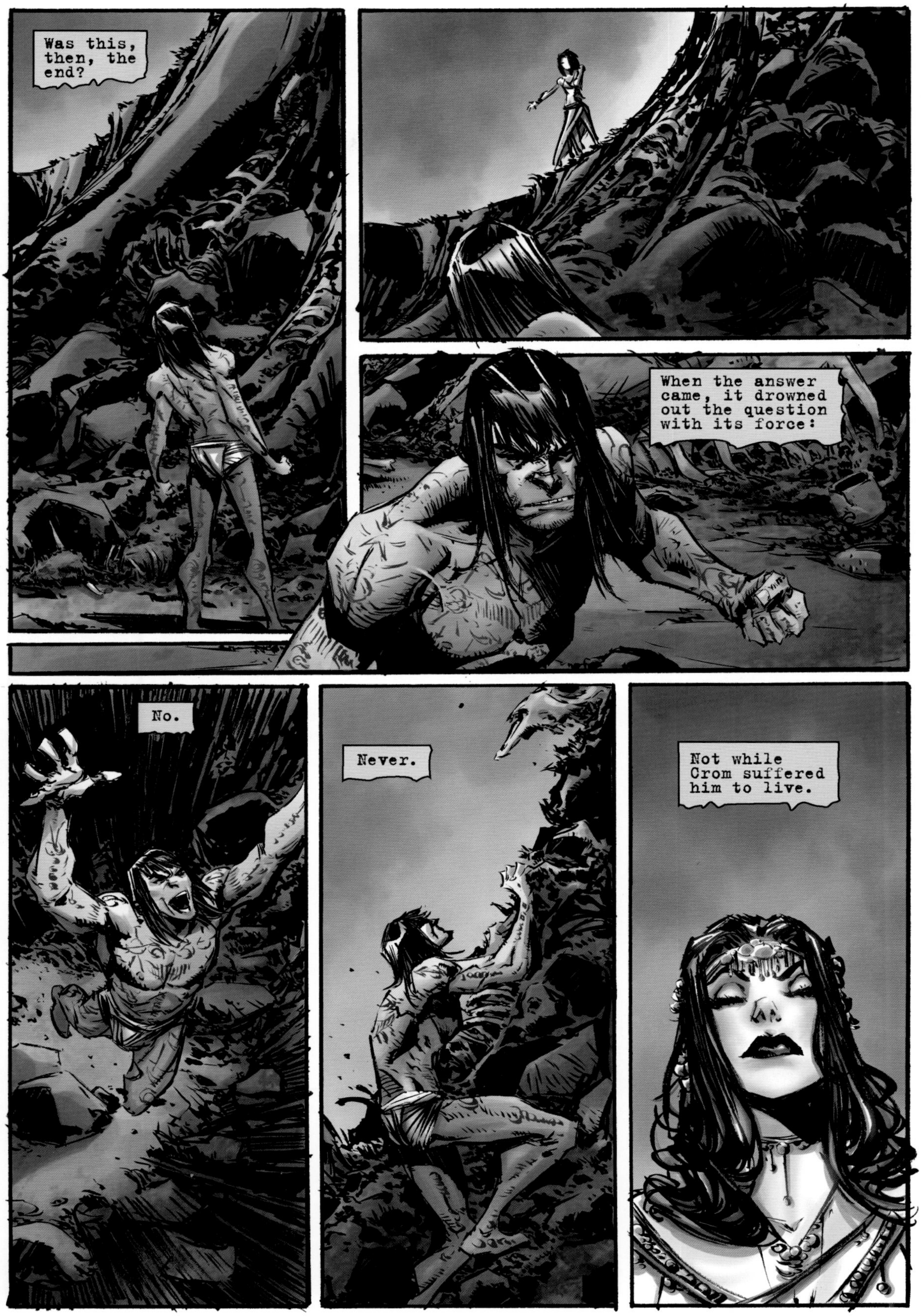
Was this, then, the end?
When the answer came, it drowned out the question with its force:
No.
Never.
Not while Crom suffered him to live.

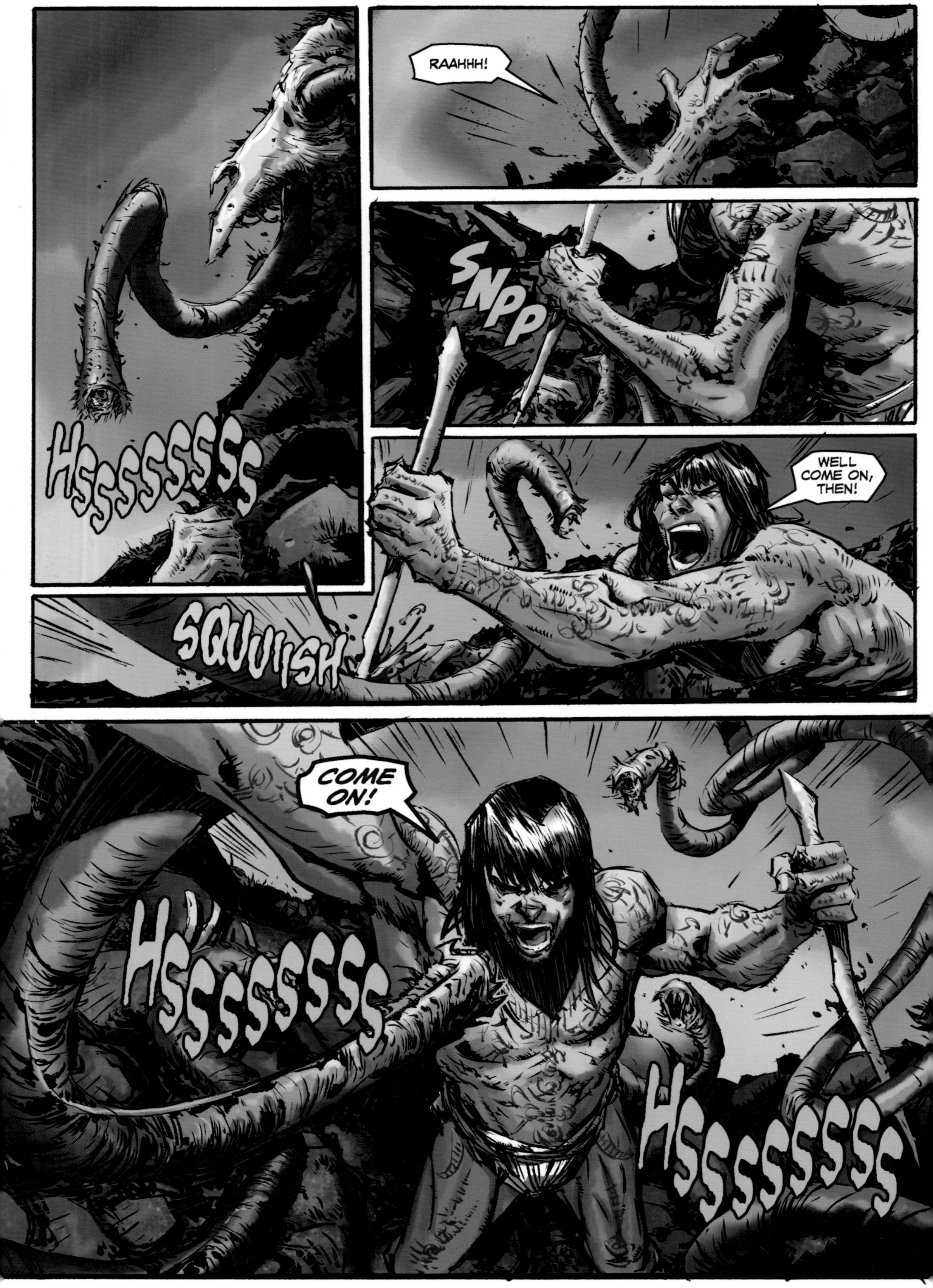
HSSSSSSSS
RAAHHH!
SNPP
WELL COME ON, THEN!
SQUUISH
COME ON!
HSSSSSSSS
HSSSSSSSS

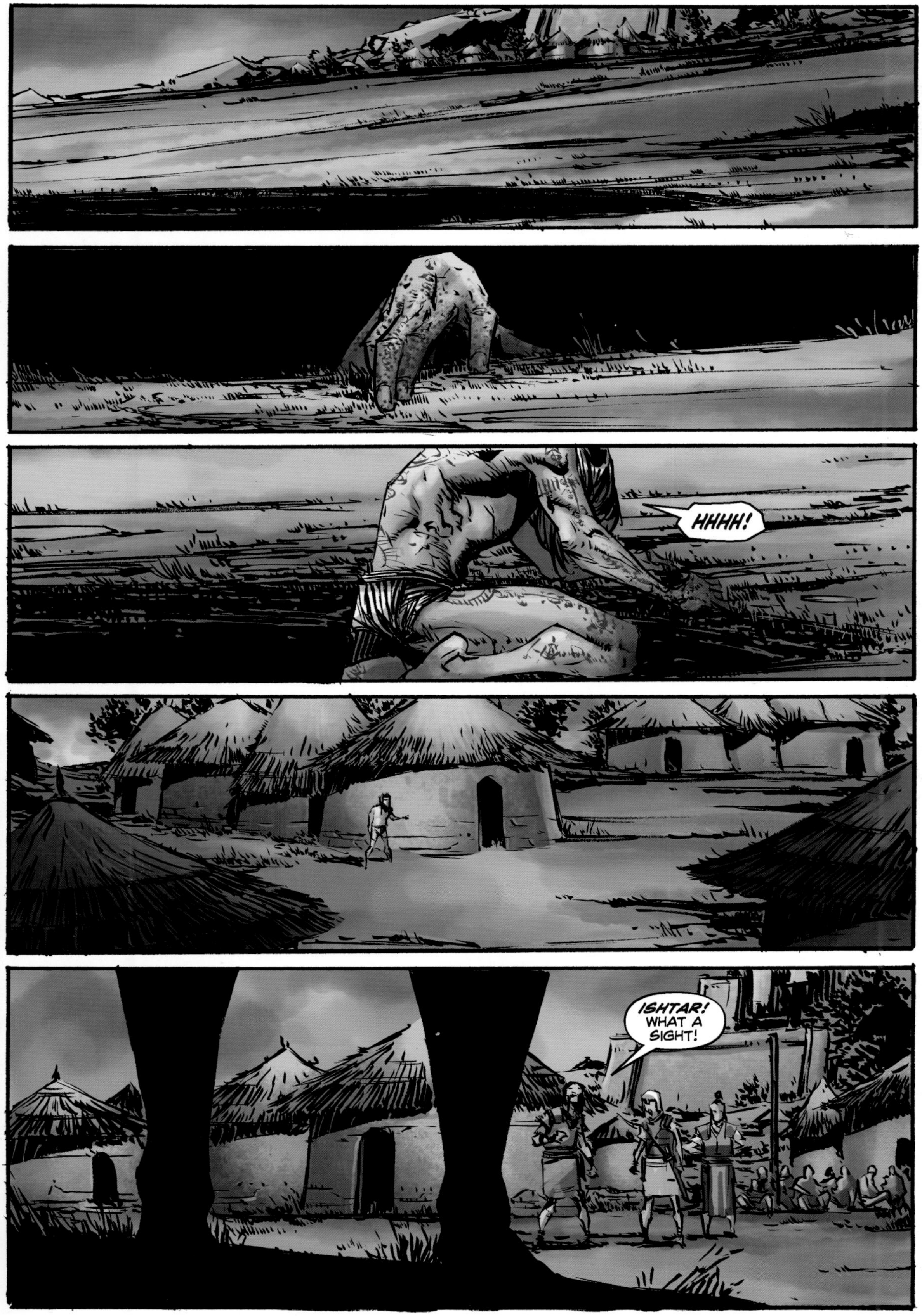
HHHH!
ISHTAR! WHAT A SIGHT!

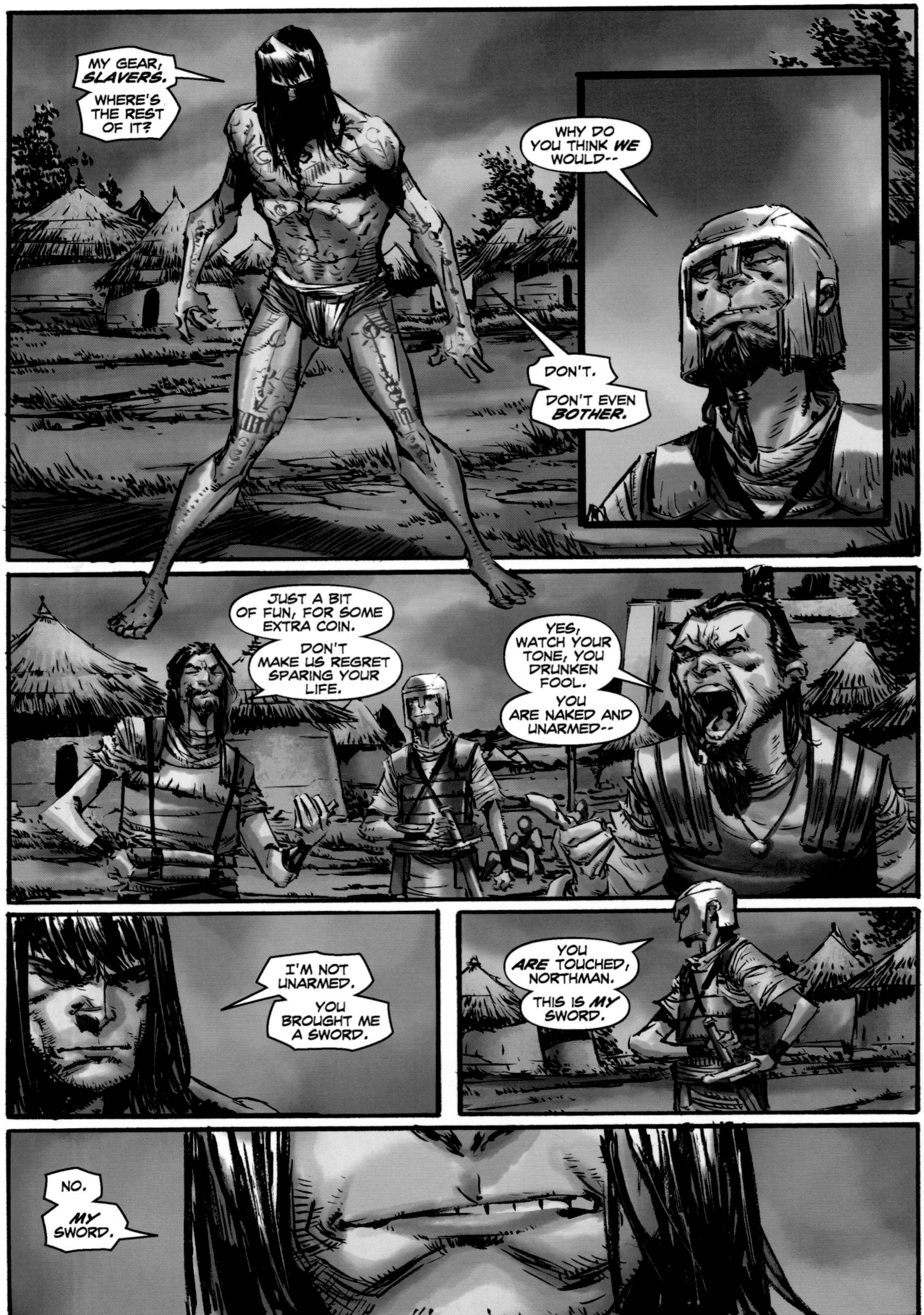
MY GEAR, *SLAVERS.*
WHERE'S THE REST OF IT?
WHY DO YOU THINK *WE* WOULD--
DON'T.
DON'T EVEN *BOTHER.*
JUST A BIT OF FUN, FOR SOME EXTRA COIN.
DON'T MAKE US REGRET SPARING YOUR LIFE.
YES, WATCH YOUR TONE, YOU DRUNKEN FOOL.
YOU ARE NAKED AND UNARMED--
I'M NOT UNARMED.
YOU BROUGHT ME A SWORD.
YOU *ARE* TOUCHED, NORTHMAN.
THIS IS *MY* SWORD.
NO.
MY SWORD.

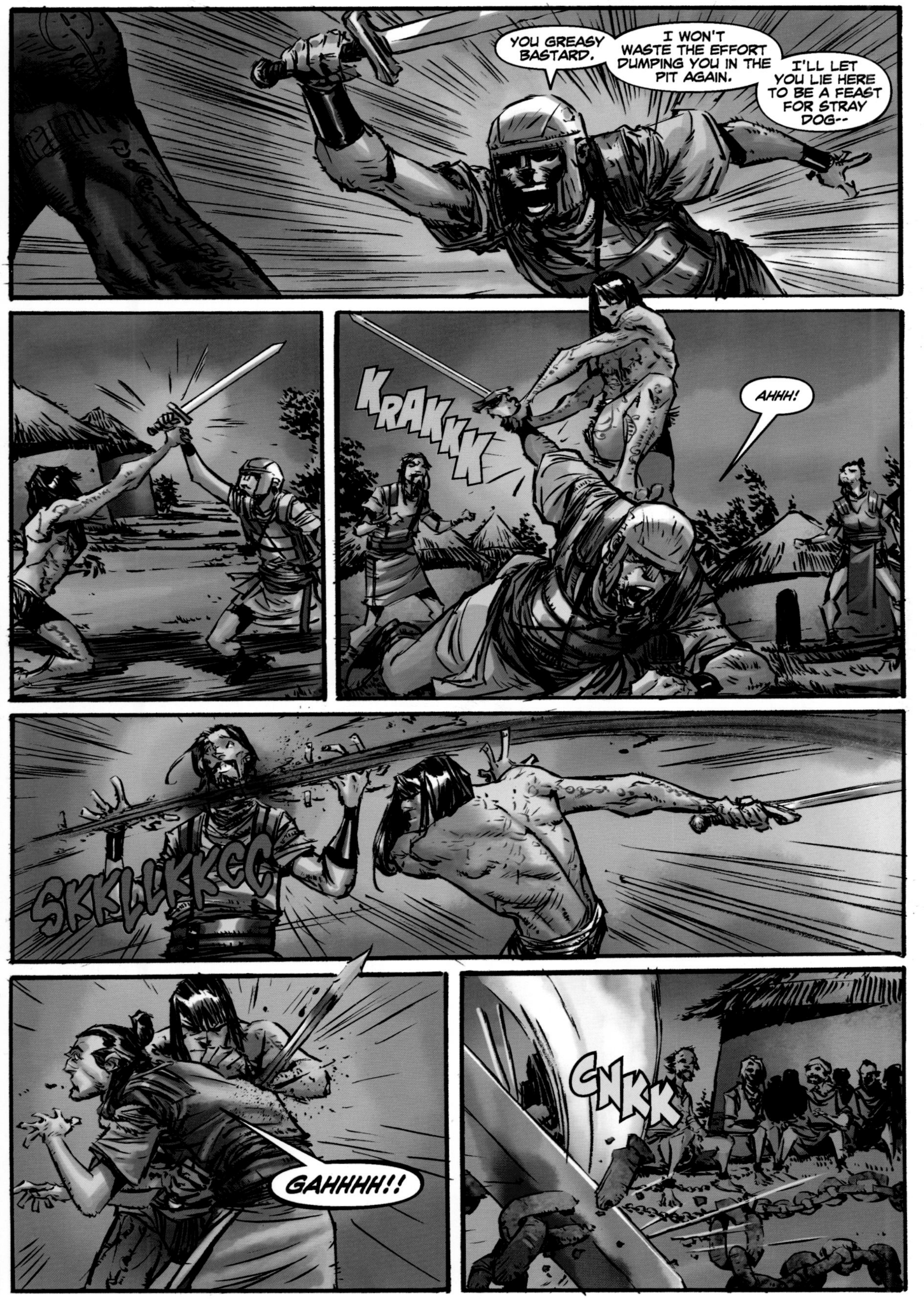
YOU GREASY BASTARD.
I WON'T WASTE THE EFFORT DUMPING YOU IN THE PIT AGAIN.
I'LL LET YOU LIE HERE TO BE A FEAST FOR STRAY DOG--
KRAKKK
AHHH!
SKKLLKKCC
GAHHHH!!
CNKK

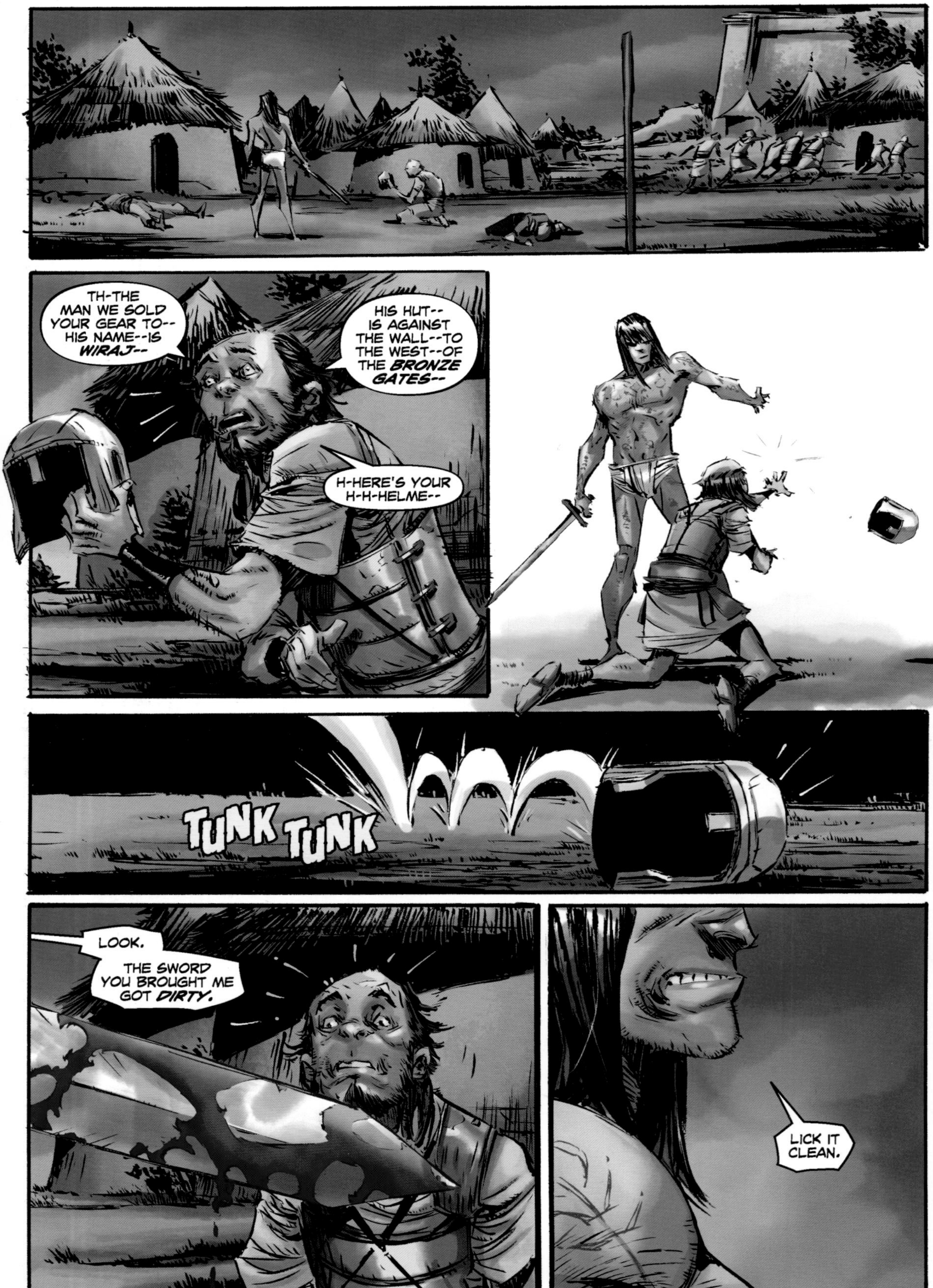
TH-THE MAN WE SOLD YOUR GEAR TO-- HIS NAME--IS *WIRAJ*--
HIS HUT-- IS AGAINST THE WALL--TO THE WEST--OF THE *BRONZE GATES*--
H-HERE'S YOUR H-H-HELME--
TUNK TUNK
LOOK.
THE SWORD YOU BROUGHT ME GOT *DIRTY.*
LICK IT CLEAN.

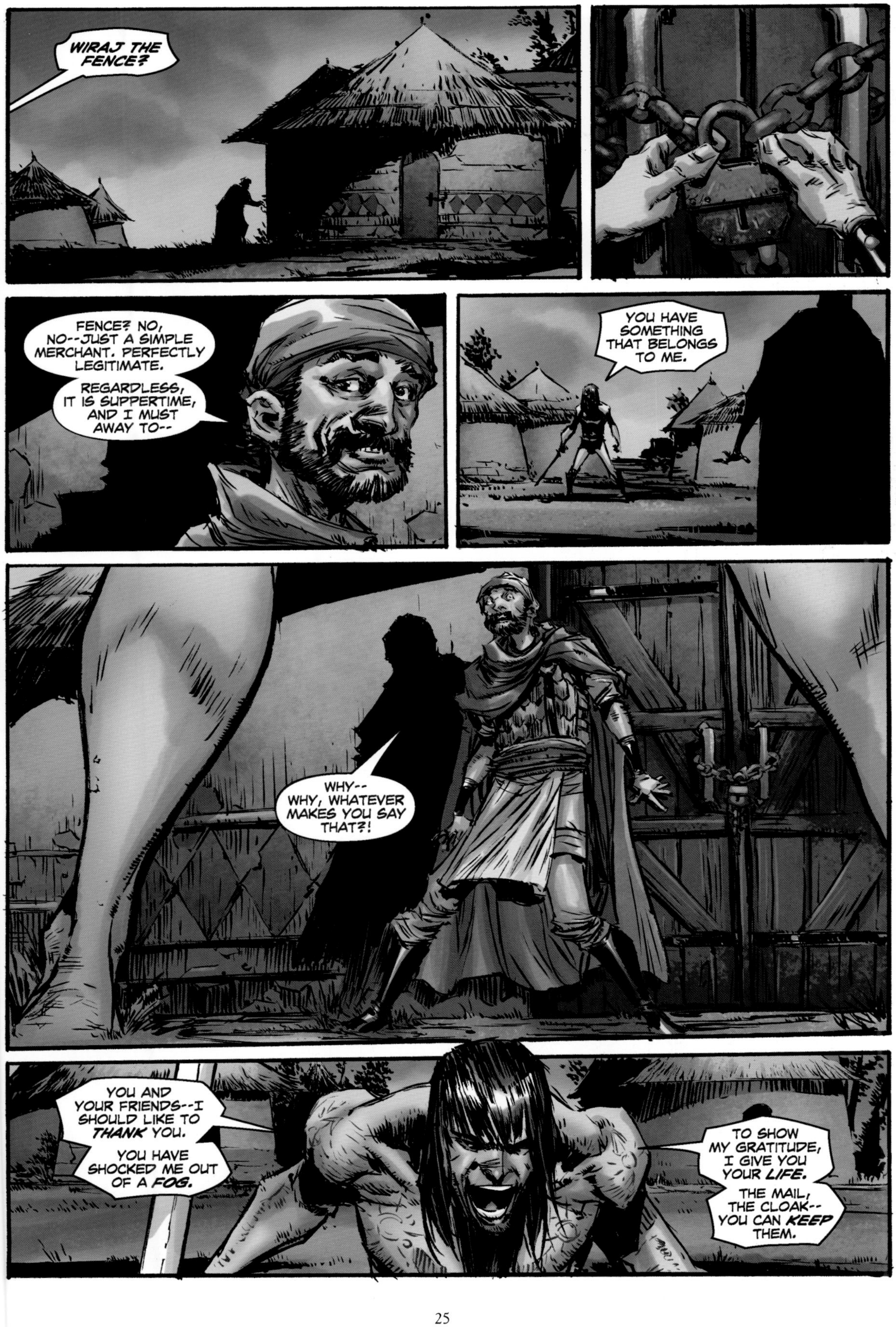
WIRAJ THE FENCE?
FENCE? NO, NO--JUST A SIMPLE MERCHANT. PERFECTLY LEGITIMATE.
REGARDLESS, IT IS SUPPERTIME, AND I MUST AWAY TO--
YOU HAVE SOMETHING THAT BELONGS TO ME.
WHY-- WHY, WHATEVER MAKES YOU SAY THAT?!
YOU AND YOUR FRIENDS--I SHOULD LIKE TO THANK YOU.
YOU HAVE SHOCKED ME OUT OF A FOG.
TO SHOW MY GRATITUDE, I GIVE YOU YOUR LIFE.
THE MAIL, THE CLOAK-- YOU CAN KEEP THEM.

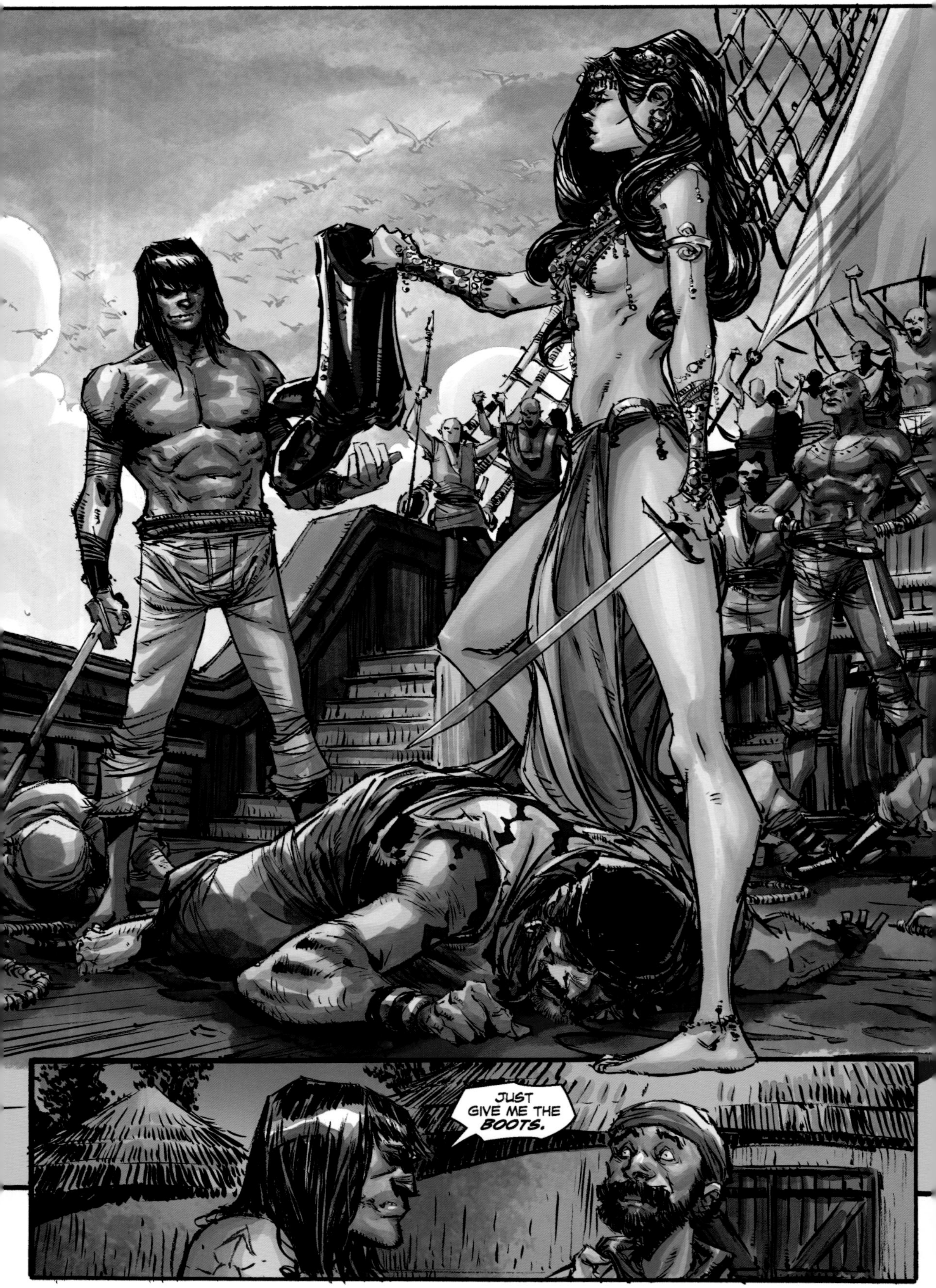
JUST GIVE ME THE BOOTS.

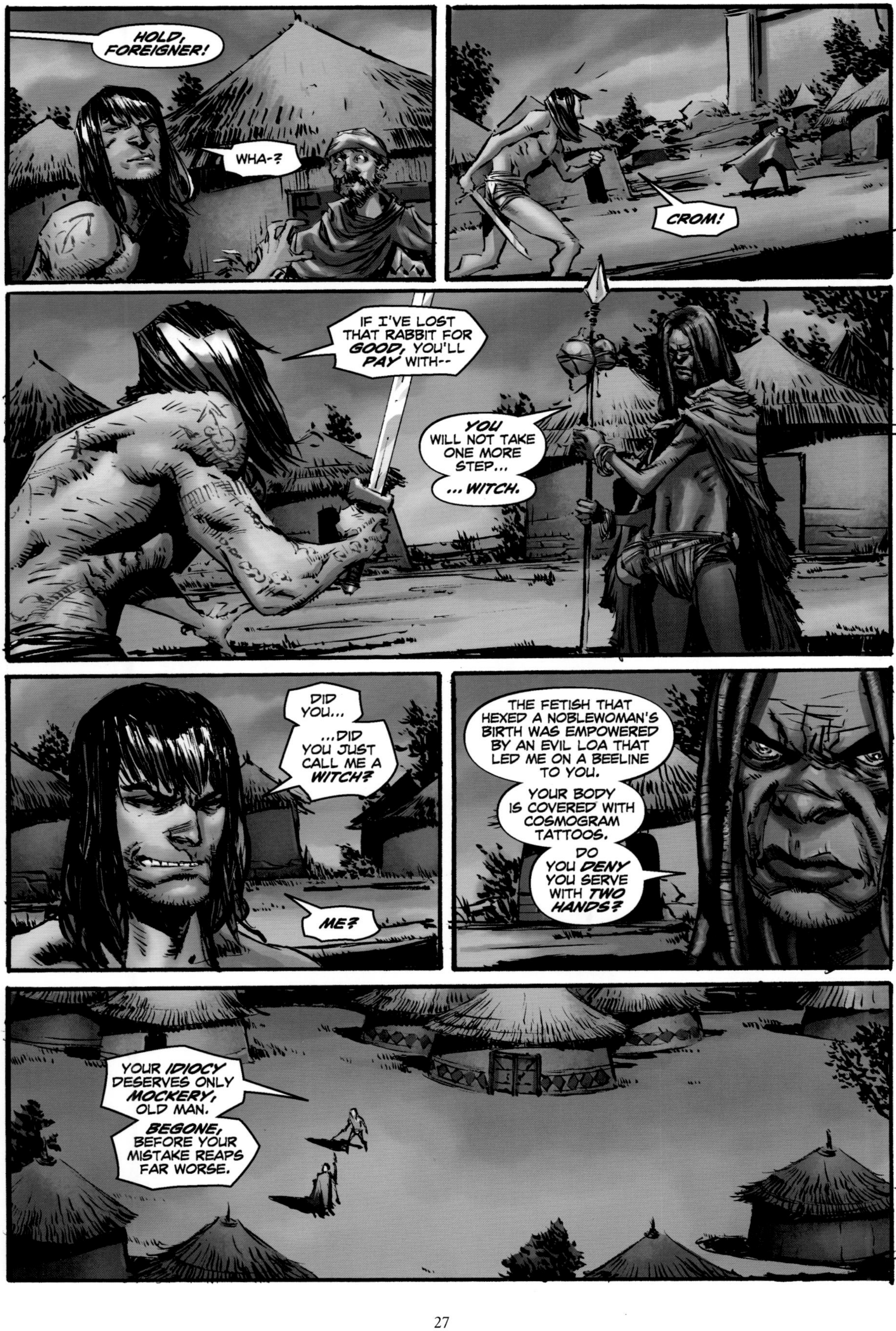
HOLD, FOREIGNER!
WHA-?
CROM!
IF I'VE LOST THAT RABBIT FOR GOOD, YOU'LL PAY WITH--
YOU WILL NOT TAKE ONE MORE STEP...
...WITCH.
DID YOU...
...DID YOU JUST CALL ME A WITCH?
ME?
THE FETISH THAT HEXED A NOBLEWOMAN'S BIRTH WAS EMPOWERED BY AN EVIL LOA THAT LED ME ON A BEELINE TO YOU.
YOUR BODY IS COVERED WITH COSMOGRAM TATTOOS.
DO YOU DENY YOU SERVE WITH TWO HANDS?
YOUR IDIOCY DESERVES ONLY MOCKERY, OLD MAN.
BEGONE, BEFORE YOUR MISTAKE REAPS FAR WORSE.

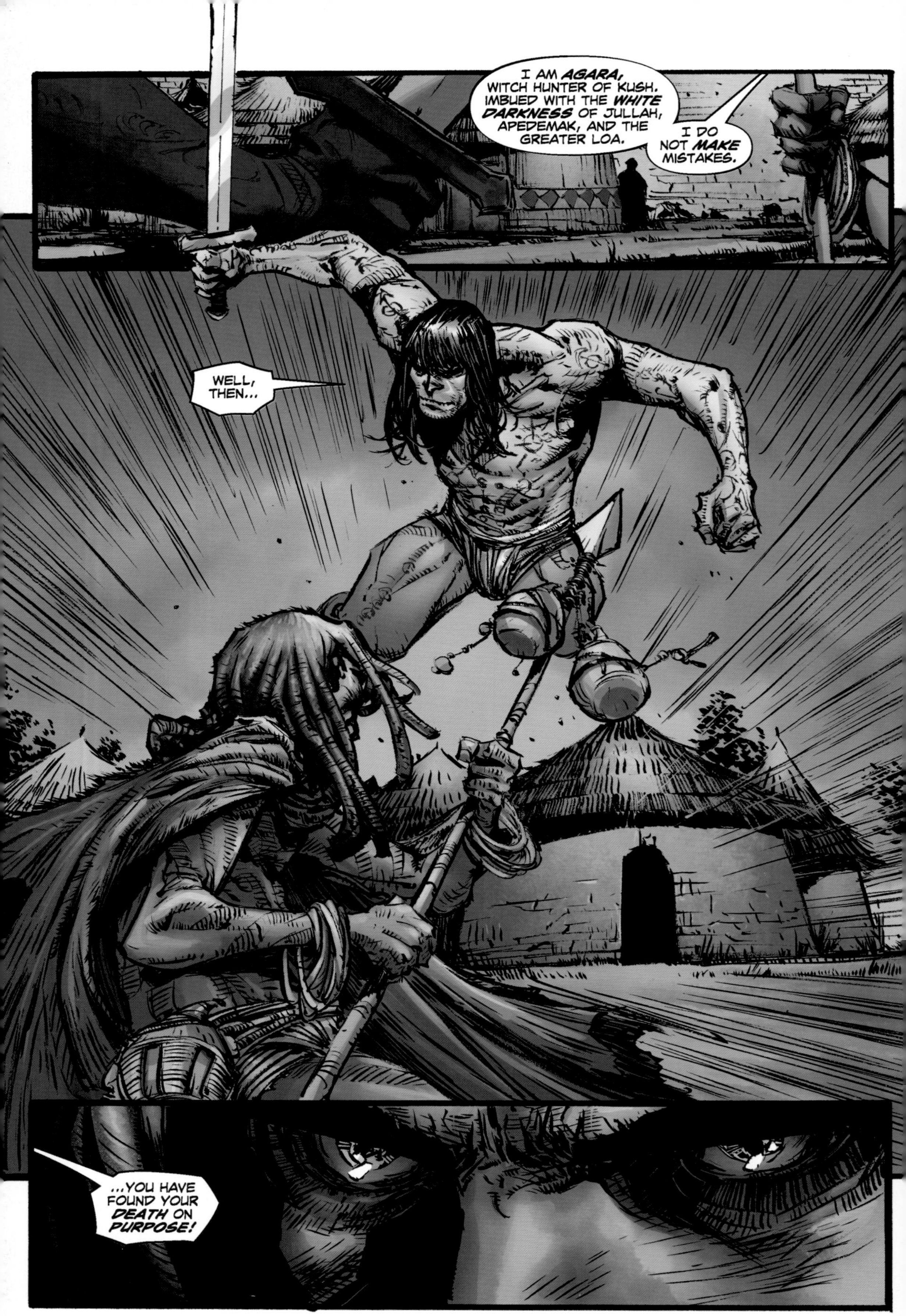
I AM AGARA, WITCH HUNTER OF KUSH. IMBUED WITH THE WHITE DARKNESS OF JULLAH, APEDEMAK, AND THE GREATER LOA.
I DO NOT MAKE MISTAKES.
WELL, THEN...
...YOU HAVE FOUND YOUR DEATH ON PURPOSE!

CHAPTER TWO

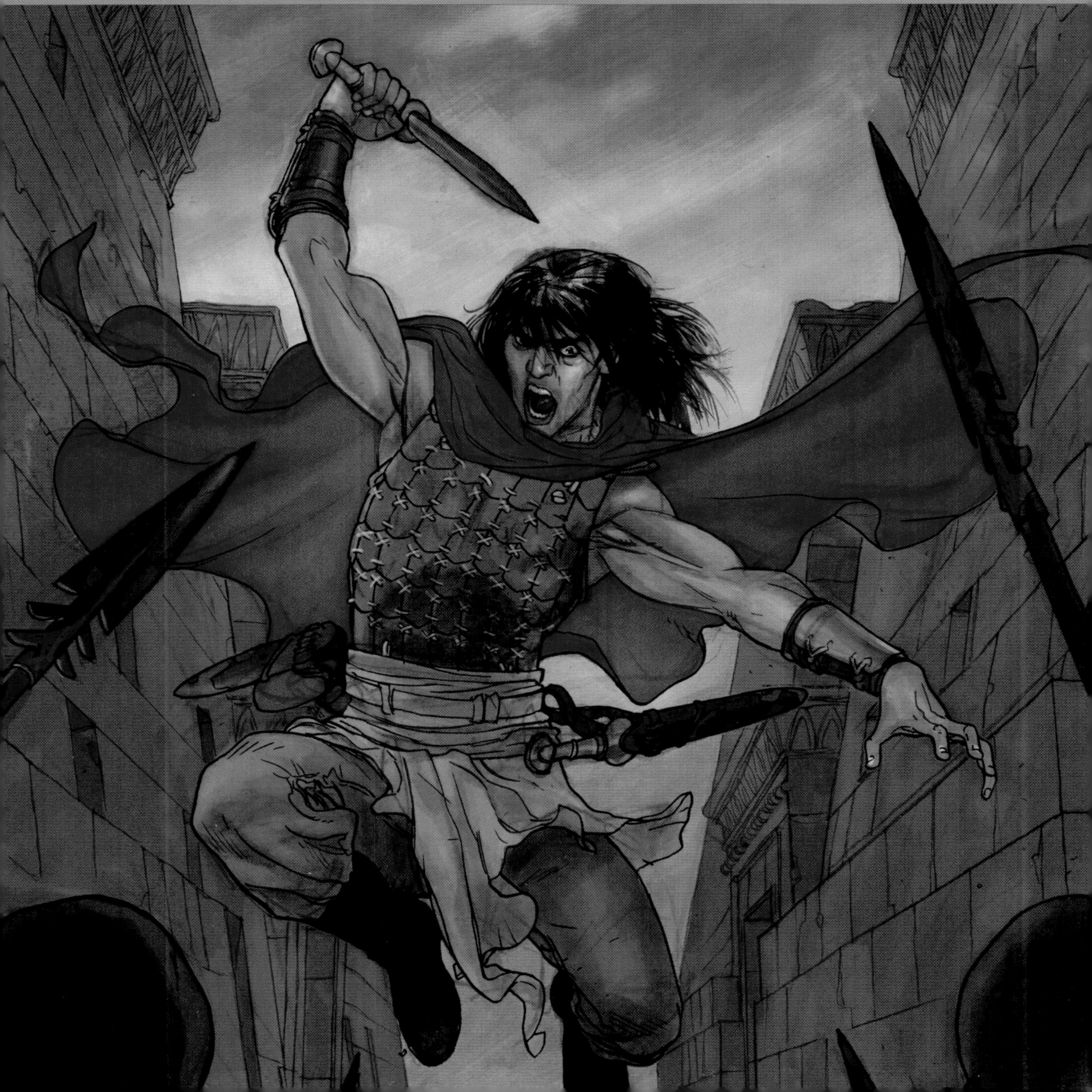

"Wizards! Pfah! Your power waxes and wanes with the moon—while steel is always steel!"

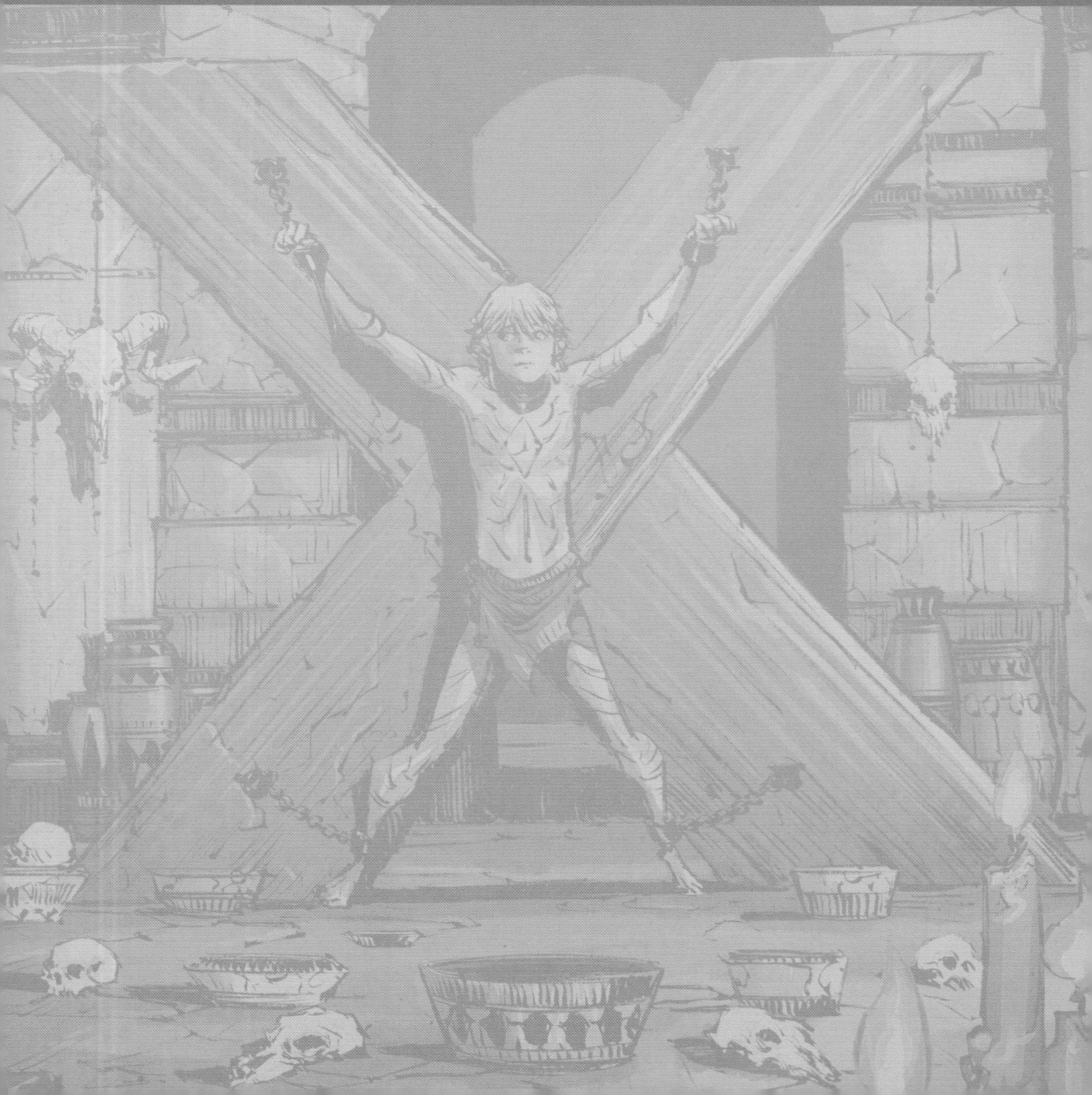

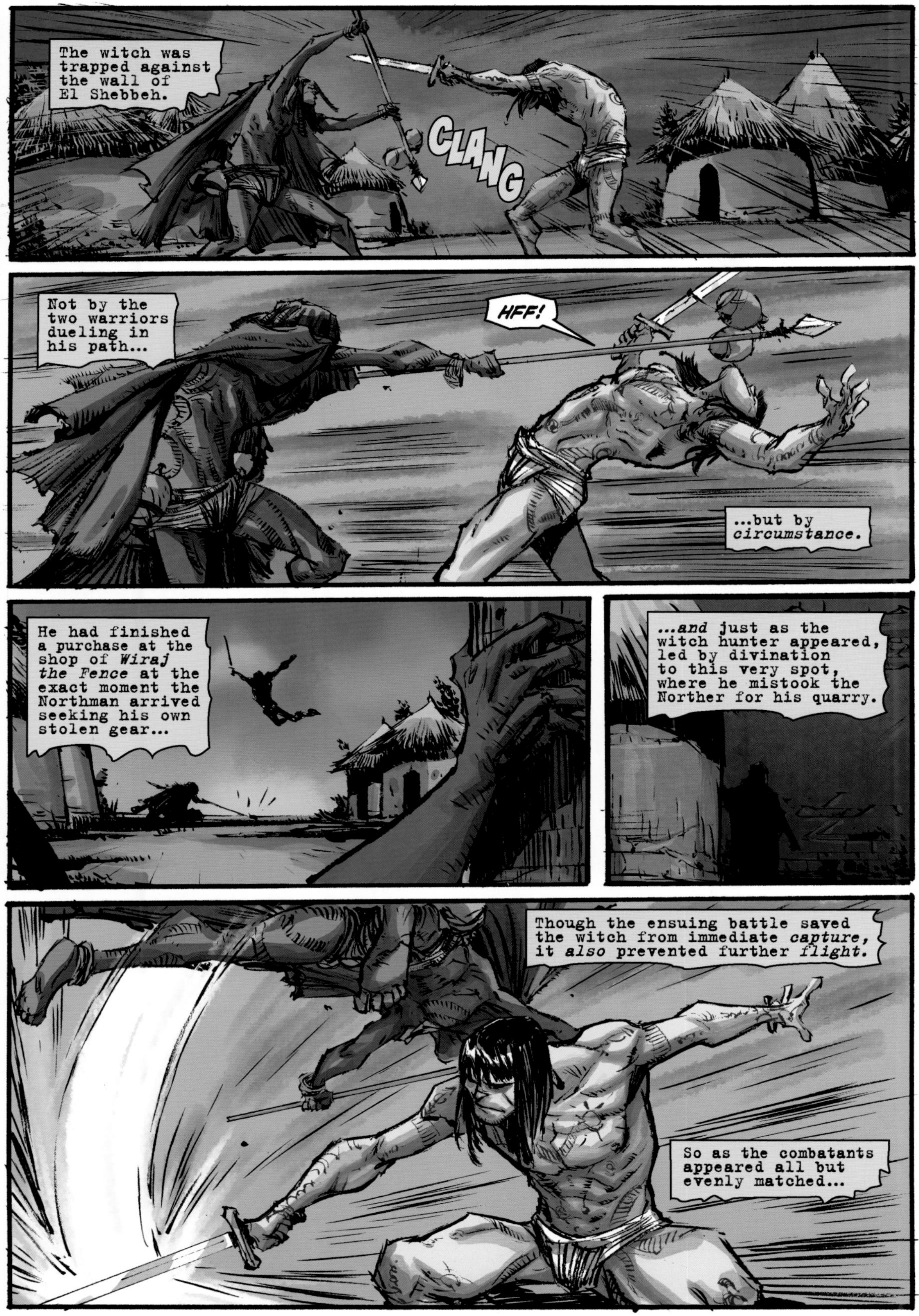
The witch was trapped against the wall of El Shebbeh.
CLANG
Not by the two warriors dueling in his path...
HFF!
...but by *circumstance.*
He had finished a purchase at the shop of *Wiraj the Fence* at the exact moment the Northman arrived seeking his own stolen gear...
...and just as the witch hunter appeared, led by divination to this very spot, where he mistook the Norther for his quarry.
Though the ensuing battle saved the witch from immediate *capture*, it *also* prevented further *flight.*
So as the combatants appeared all but evenly matched...

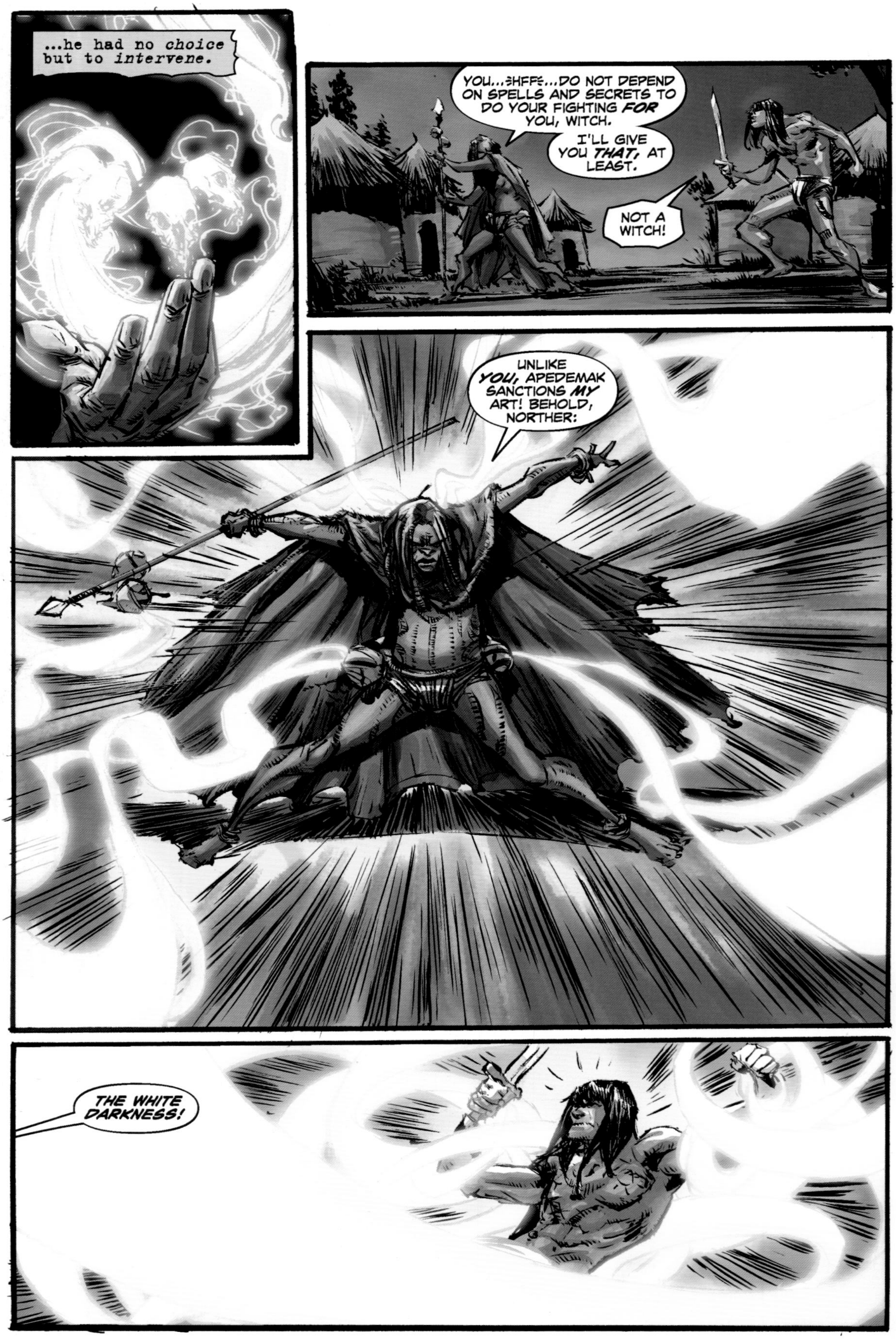

...he had no *choice* but to *intervene.*
YOU...SHFF...DO NOT DEPEND ON SPELLS AND SECRETS TO DO YOUR FIGHTING **FOR** YOU, WITCH.
I'LL GIVE YOU **THAT,** AT LEAST.
NOT A WITCH!
UNLIKE **YOU,** APEDEMAK SANCTIONS **MY** ART! BEHOLD, NORTHER:
THE WHITE DARKNESS!

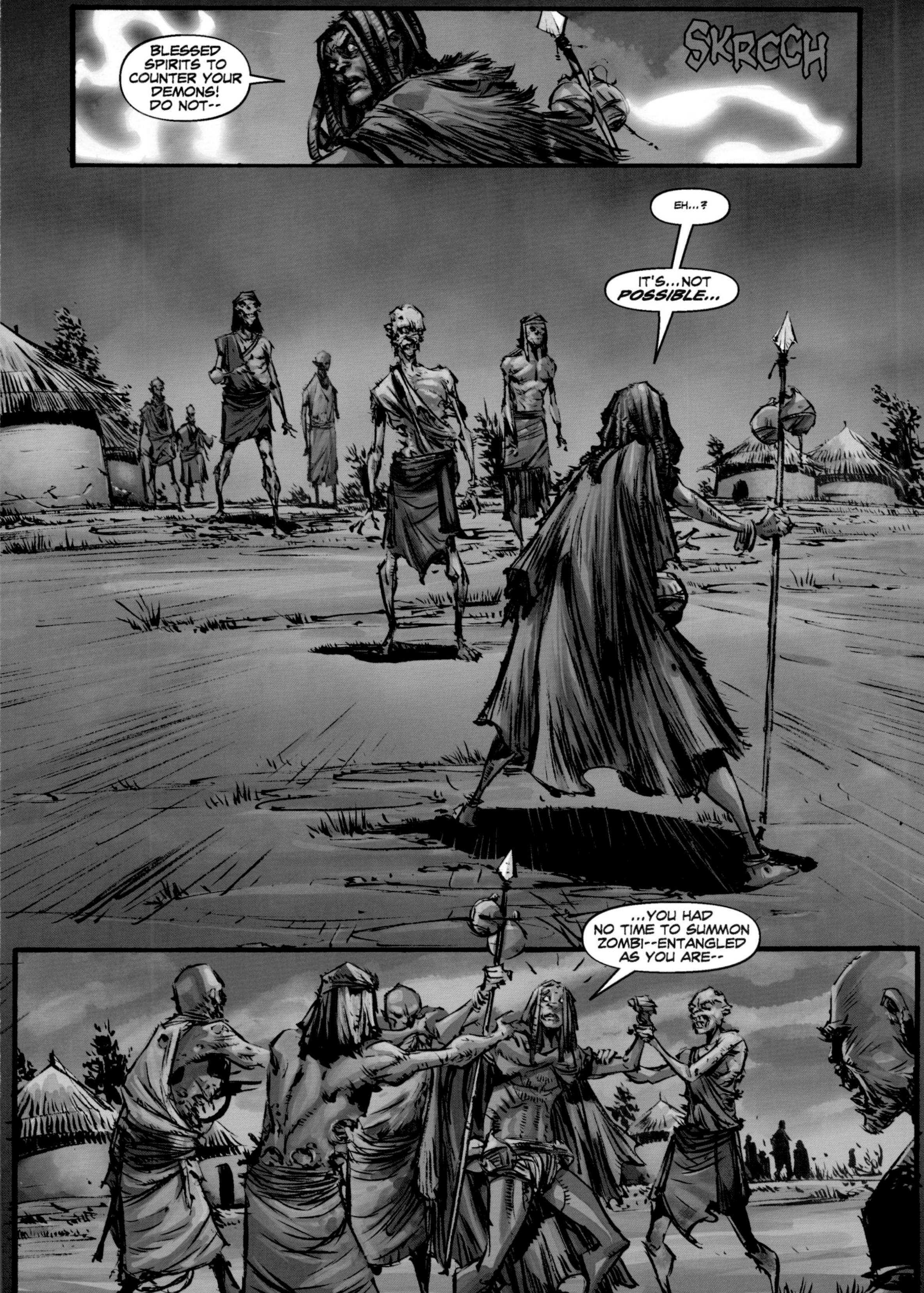
BLESSED SPIRITS TO COUNTER YOUR DEMONS! DO NOT--
SKRCCH
EH...?
IT'S...NOT POSSIBLE...
...YOU HAD NO TIME TO SUMMON ZOMBI--ENTANGLED AS YOU ARE--

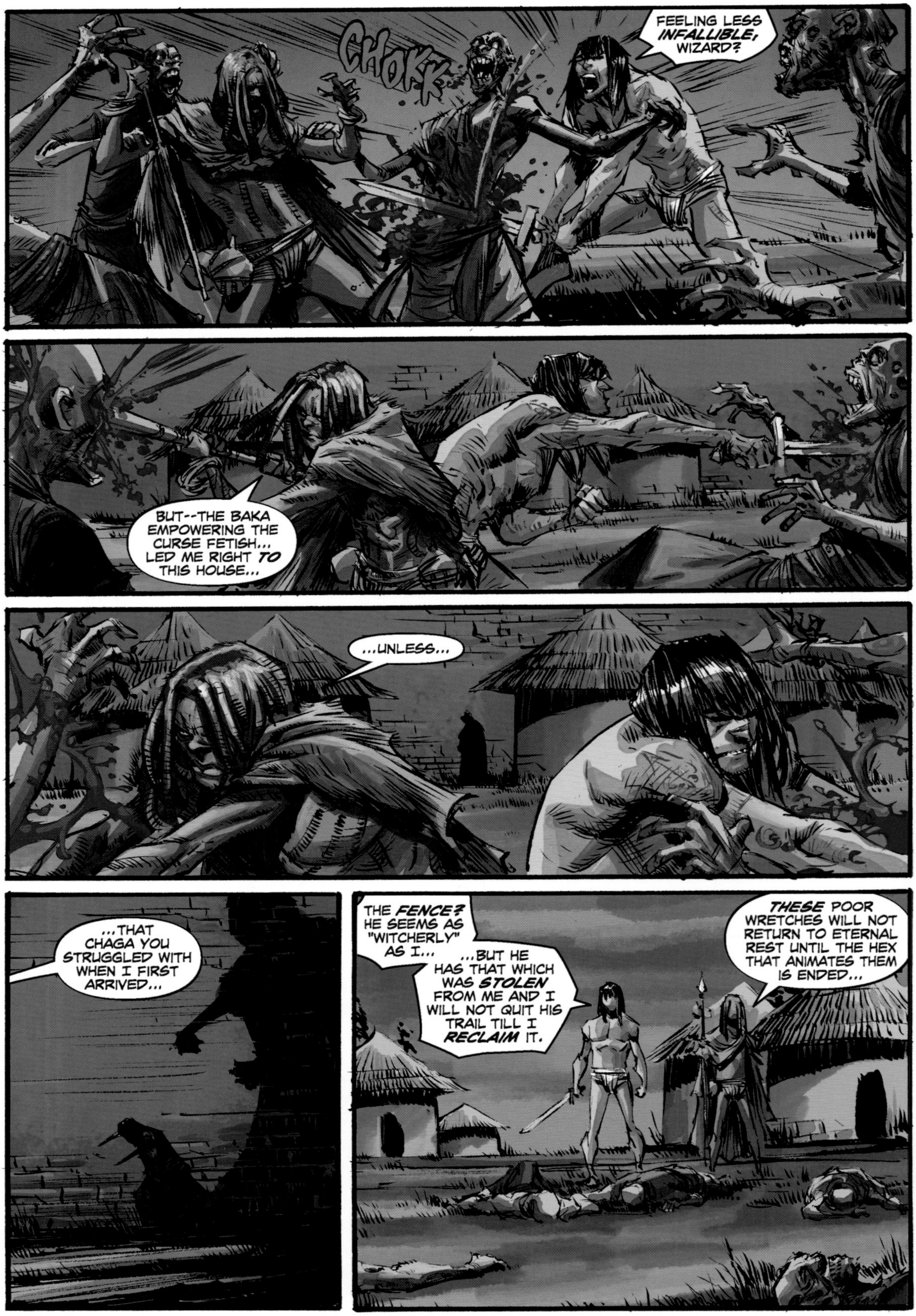
CHOKK
FEELING LESS INFALLIBLE, WIZARD?
BUT--THE BAKA EMPOWERING THE CURSE FETISH... LED ME RIGHT TO THIS HOUSE...
...UNLESS...
...THAT CHAGA YOU STRUGGLED WITH WHEN I FIRST ARRIVED...
THE FENCE? HE SEEMS AS "WITCHERLY" AS I...
...BUT HE HAS THAT WHICH WAS STOLEN FROM ME AND I WILL NOT QUIT HIS TRAIL TILL I RECLAIM IT.
THESE POOR WRETCHES WILL NOT RETURN TO ETERNAL REST UNTIL THE HEX THAT ANIMATES THEM IS ENDED...

...SO NOW HE IS *MY* QUARRY TOO. WHERE COULD HE HAVE GOTTEN TO?

WELL, IF YOU HADN'T INTERRUPTED MY *SKEWERING* HIM, *BOTH* OUR PROBLEMS WOULD HAVE BEEN SOLV...

THIS WAY.

SO YOU *STILL* CLAIM TO HAVE NO MYSTIC SIGHT, NORTHMAN?

THE NAME IS *CONAN.*

COME *WITH,* OR *DON'T.* IT MAKES NO DIFFERENCE TO ME.

YOUR *OLD BONES* WILL PROBABLY JUST *SLOW ME DOWN,* ANYWAY.

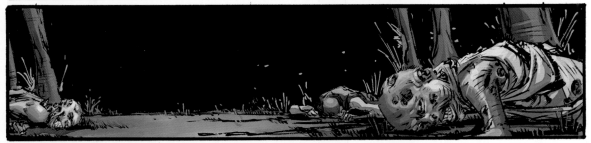

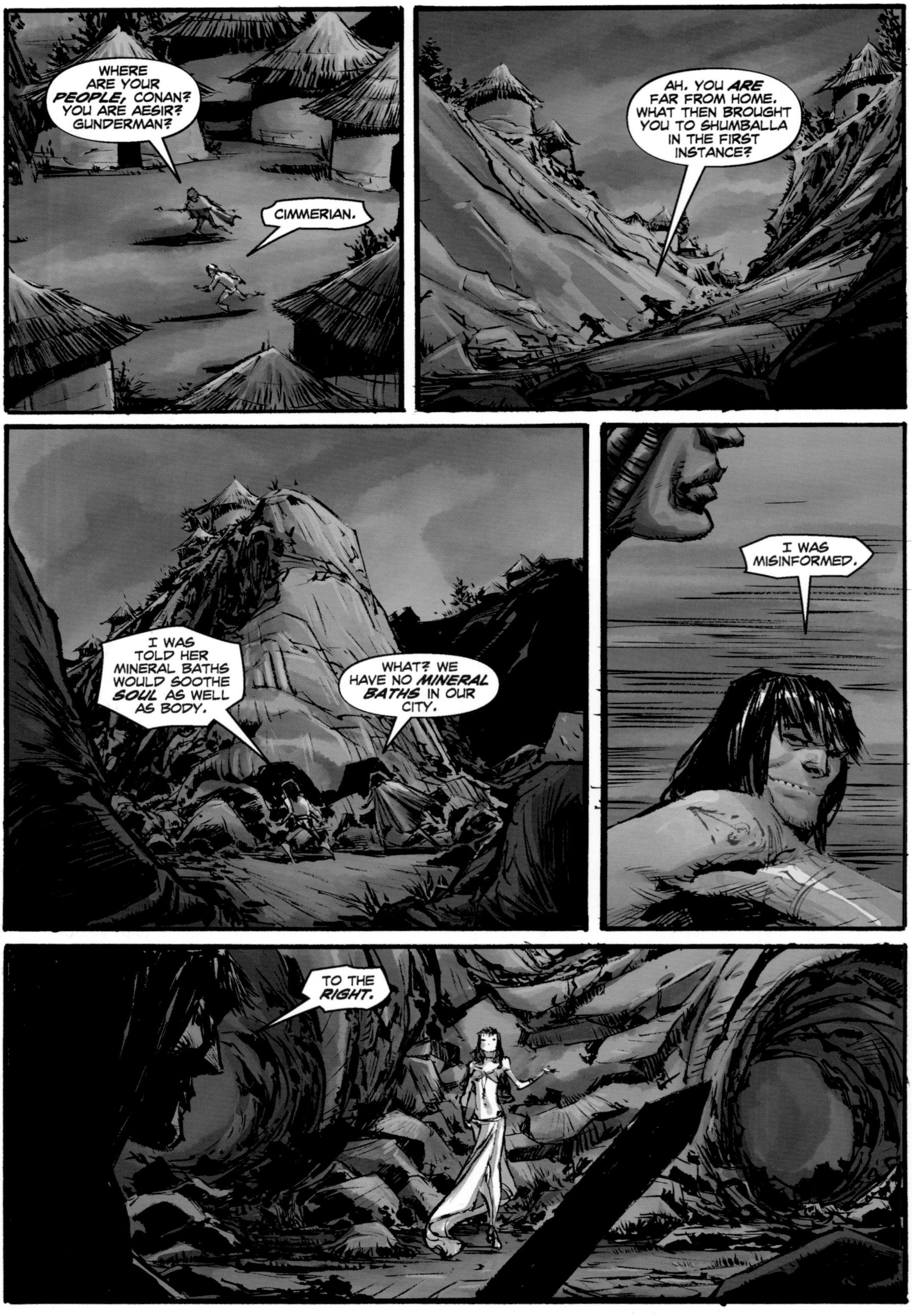
WHERE ARE YOUR PEOPLE, CONAN? YOU ARE AESIR? GUNDERMAN?
CIMMERIAN.
AH. YOU ARE FAR FROM HOME. WHAT THEN BROUGHT YOU TO SHUMBALLA IN THE FIRST INSTANCE?
I WAS TOLD HER MINERAL BATHS WOULD SOOTHE SOUL AS WELL AS BODY.
WHAT? WE HAVE NO MINERAL BATHS IN OUR CITY.
I WAS MISINFORMED.
TO THE RIGHT.

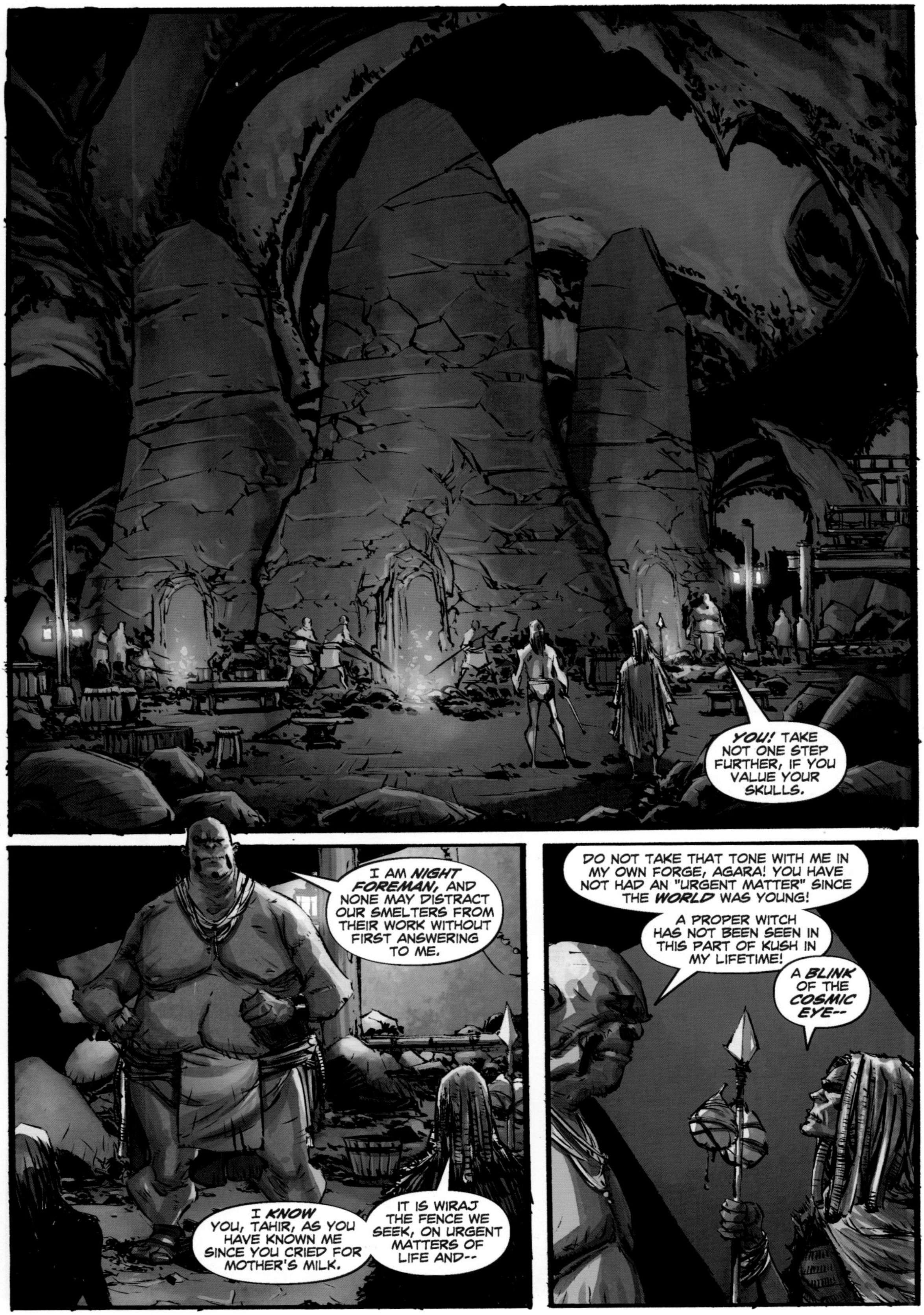
YOU! TAKE NOT ONE STEP FURTHER, IF YOU VALUE YOUR SKULLS.
I AM NIGHT FOREMAN, AND NONE MAY DISTRACT OUR SMELTERS FROM THEIR WORK WITHOUT FIRST ANSWERING TO ME.
I KNOW YOU, TAHIR, AS YOU HAVE KNOWN ME SINCE YOU CRIED FOR MOTHER'S MILK.
IT IS WIRAJ THE FENCE WE SEEK, ON URGENT MATTERS OF LIFE AND--
DO NOT TAKE THAT TONE WITH ME IN MY OWN FORGE, AGARA! YOU HAVE NOT HAD AN "URGENT MATTER" SINCE THE WORLD WAS YOUNG!
A PROPER WITCH HAS NOT BEEN SEEN IN THIS PART OF KUSH IN MY LIFETIME!
A BLINK OF THE COSMIC EYE--

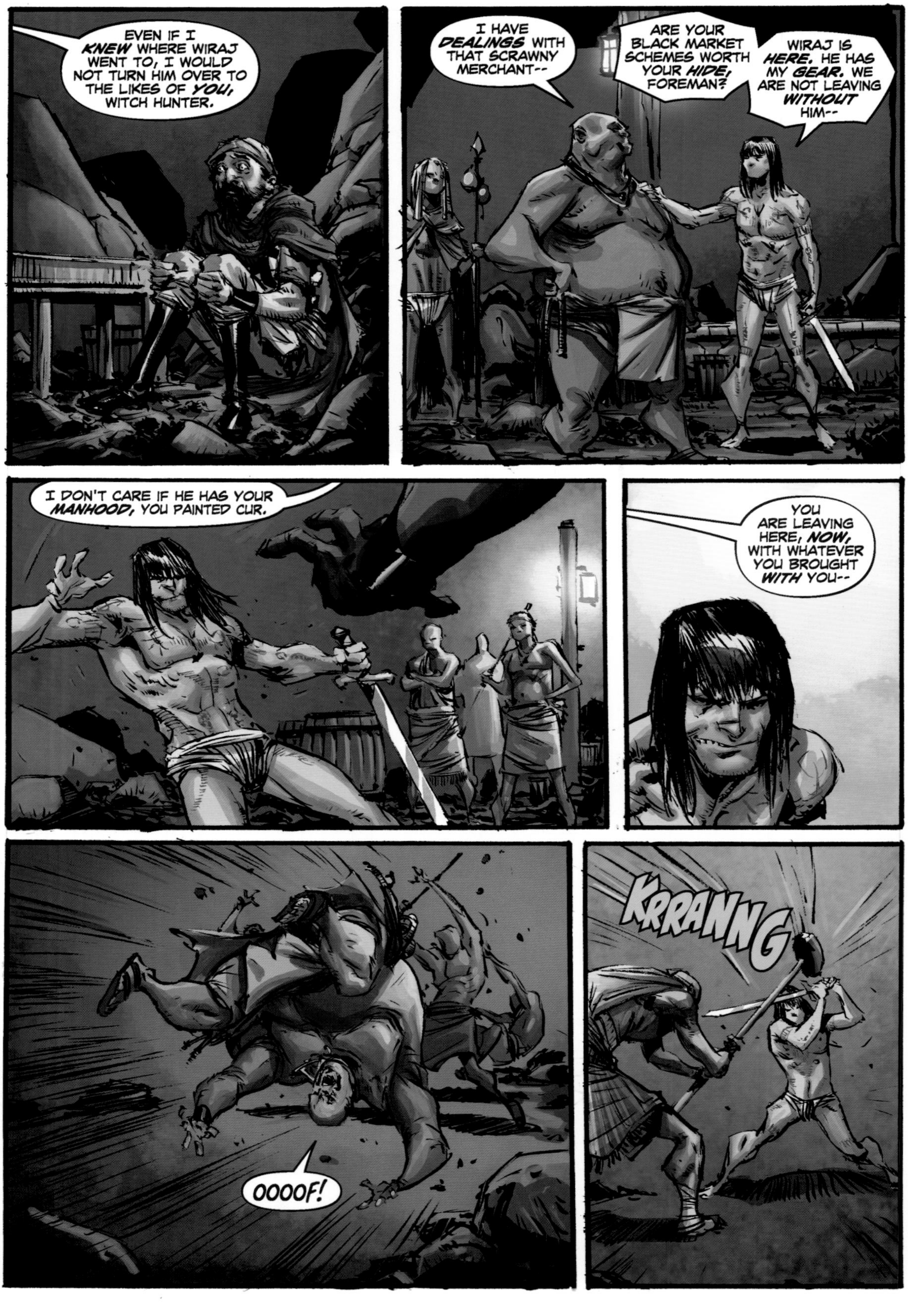
EVEN IF I KNEW WHERE WIRAJ WENT TO, I WOULD NOT TURN HIM OVER TO THE LIKES OF YOU, WITCH HUNTER.
I HAVE DEALINGS WITH THAT SCRAWNY MERCHANT--
ARE YOUR BLACK MARKET SCHEMES WORTH YOUR HIDE, FOREMAN?
WIRAJ IS HERE. HE HAS MY GEAR. WE ARE NOT LEAVING WITHOUT HIM--
I DON'T CARE IF HE HAS YOUR MANHOOD, YOU PAINTED CUR.
YOU ARE LEAVING HERE, NOW, WITH WHATEVER YOU BROUGHT WITH YOU--
OOOOF!
KRRANNG

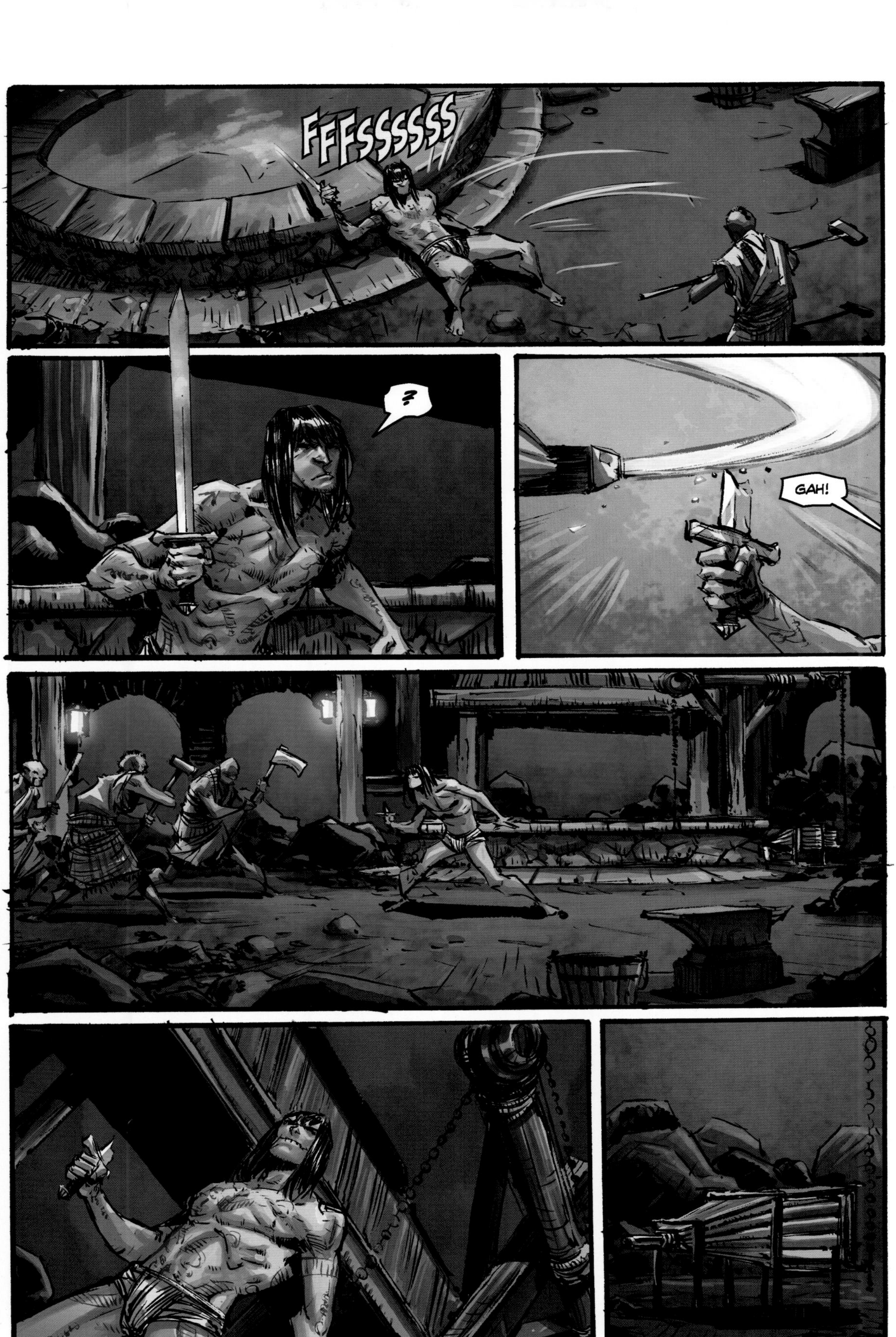
FFFSSSSSS
?
GAH!

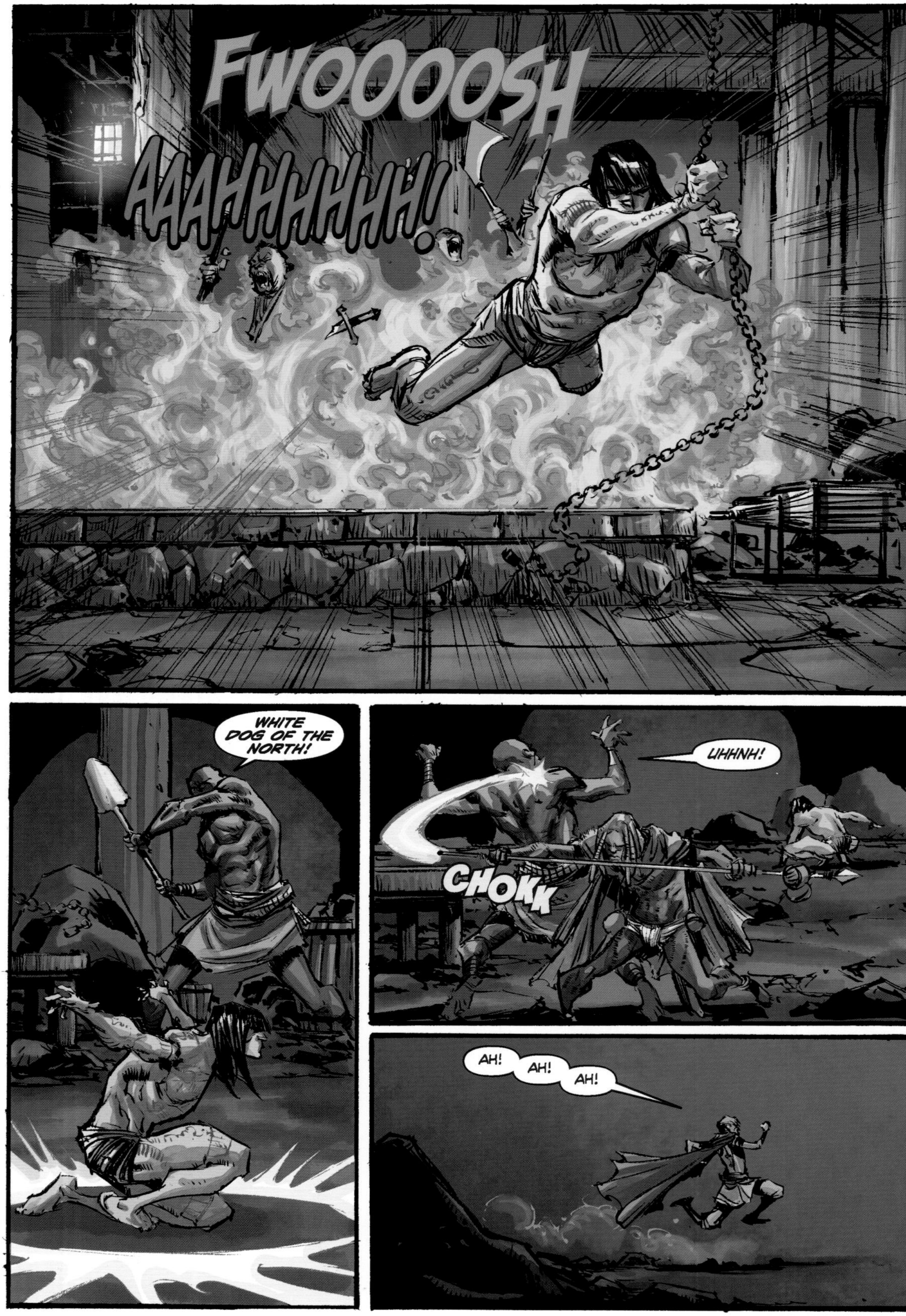
FWOOOOSH
AAAHHHHHH!
WHITE DOG OF THE NORTH!
UHHNH!
CHOKK
AH!
AH!
AH!

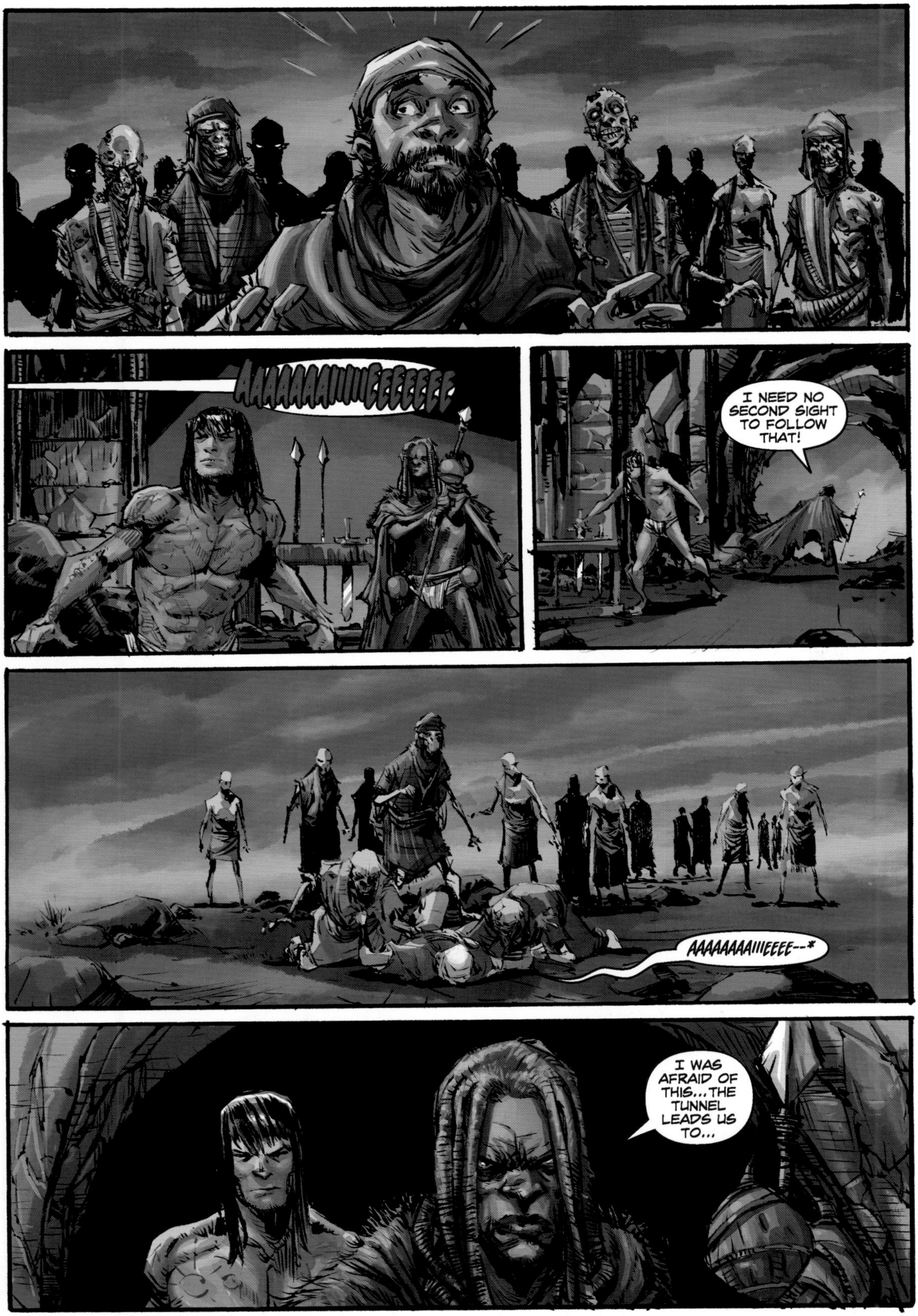
AAAAAAAIIIIIEEEEEEE
I NEED NO SECOND SIGHT TO FOLLOW THAT!
AAAAAAAIIIEEEE--*
I WAS AFRAID OF THIS...THE TUNNEL LEADS US TO...

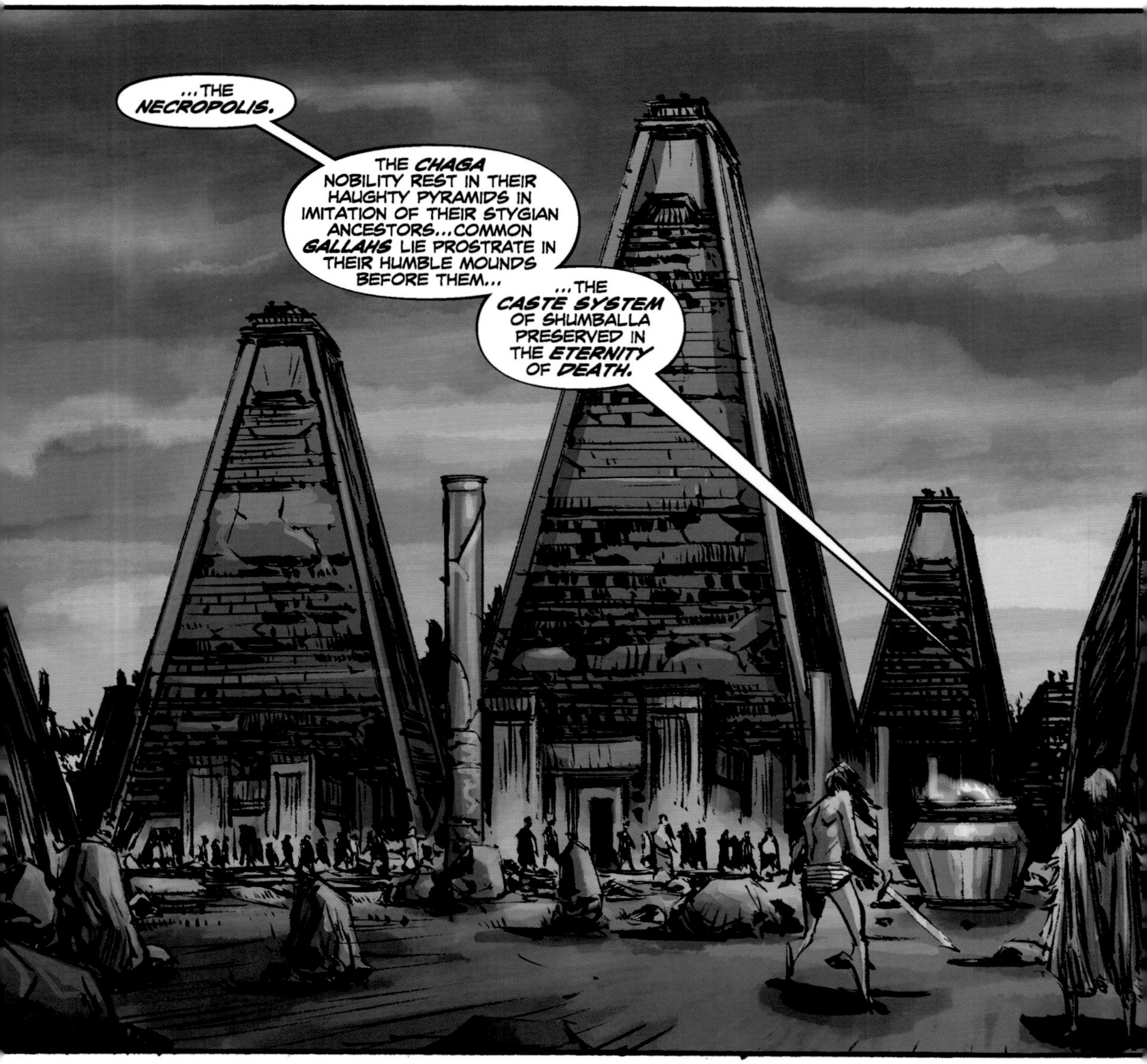
...THE NECROPOLIS.
THE CHAGA NOBILITY REST IN THEIR HAUGHTY PYRAMIDS IN IMITATION OF THEIR STYGIAN ANCESTORS...COMMON GALLAHS LIE PROSTRATE IN THEIR HUMBLE MOUNDS BEFORE THEM...
...THE CASTE SYSTEM OF SHUMBALLA PRESERVED IN THE ETERNITY OF DEATH.
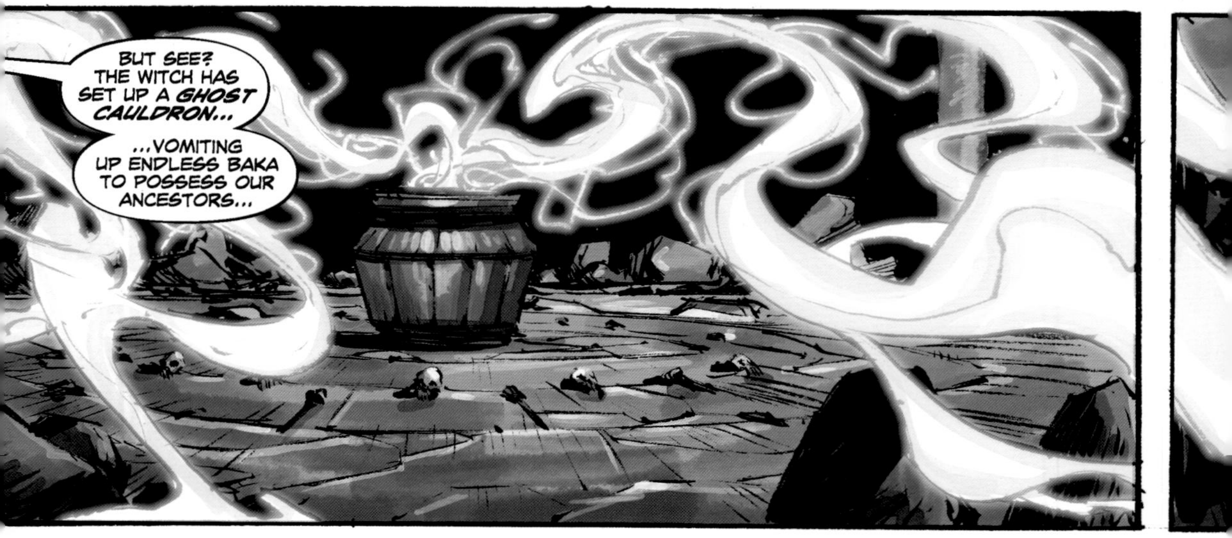
BUT SEE? THE WITCH HAS SET UP A GHOST CAULDRON...
...VOMITING UP ENDLESS BAKA TO POSSESS OUR ANCESTORS...

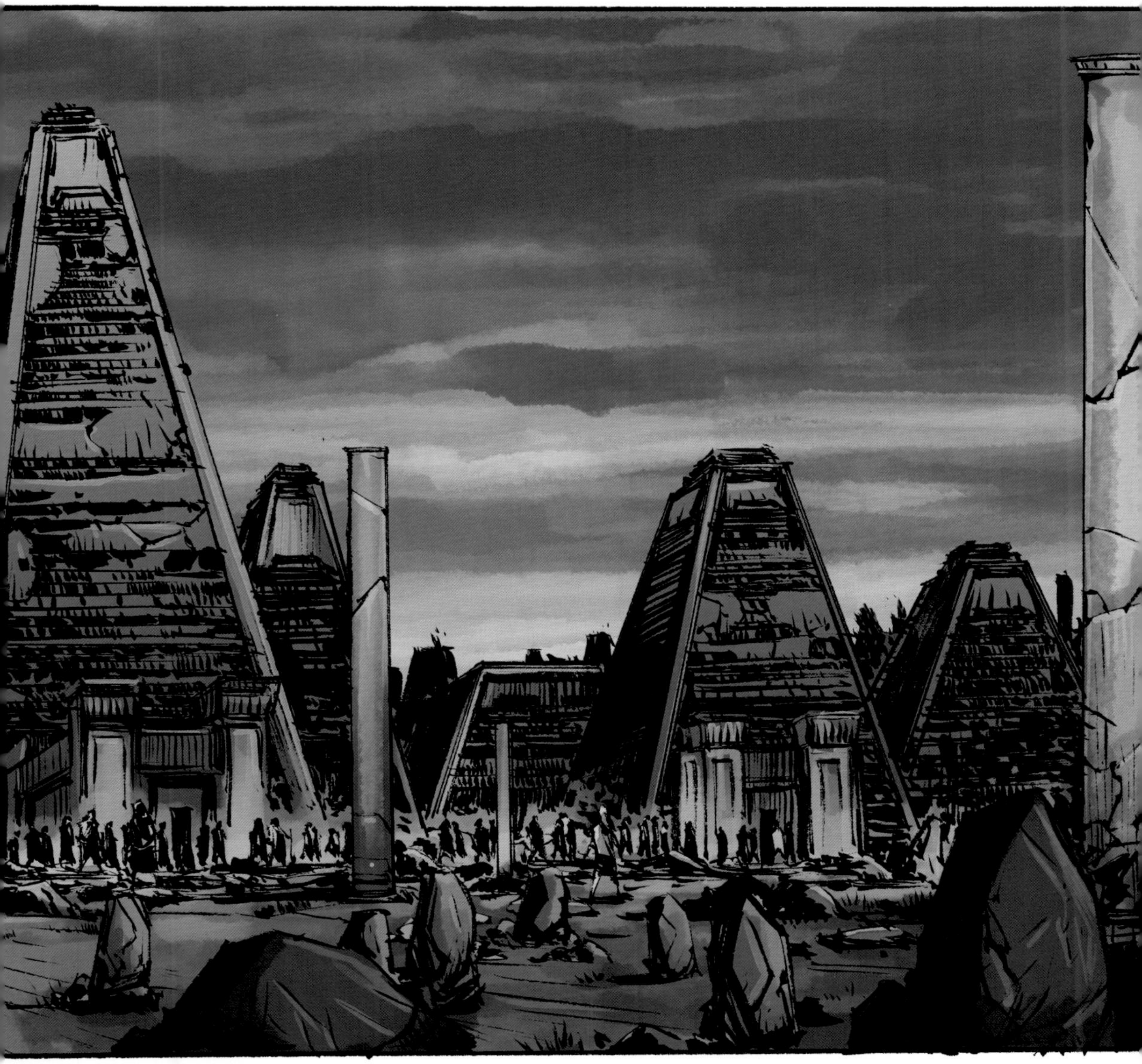

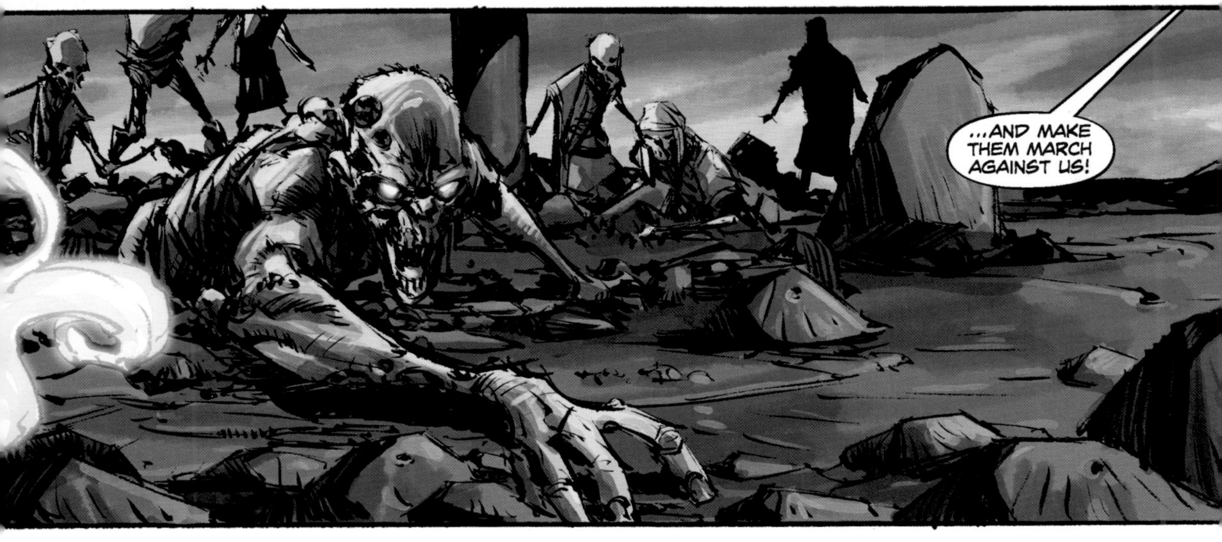
...AND MAKE THEM MARCH AGAINST US!

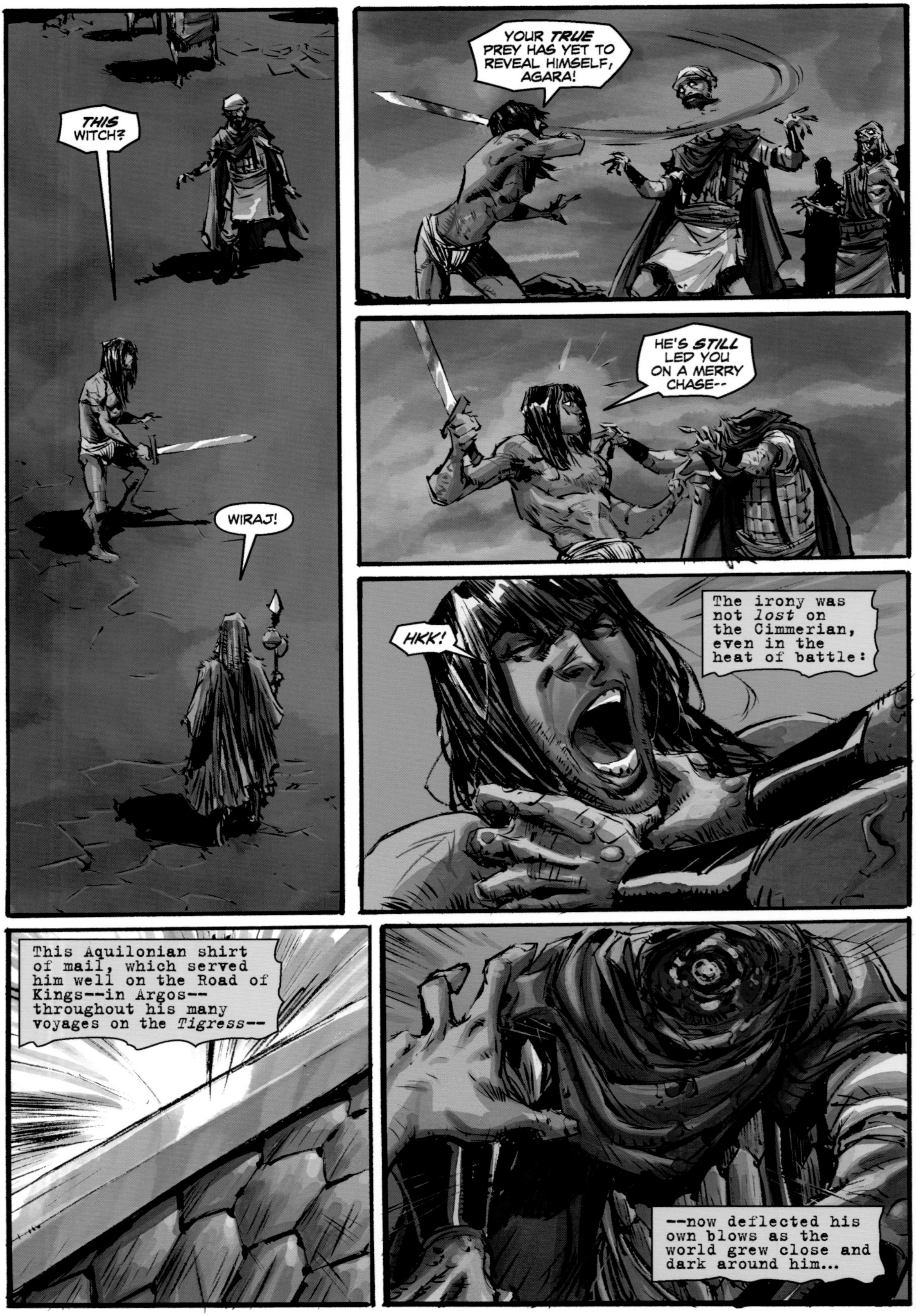
THIS WITCH?
WIRAJ!
YOUR TRUE PREY HAS YET TO REVEAL HIMSELF, AGARA!
HE'S STILL LED YOU ON A MERRY CHASE--
HKK!
The irony was not lost on the Cimmerian, even in the heat of battle:
This Aquilonian shirt of mail, which served him well on the Road of Kings--in Argos--throughout his many voyages on the Tigress--
--now deflected his own blows as the world grew close and dark around him...

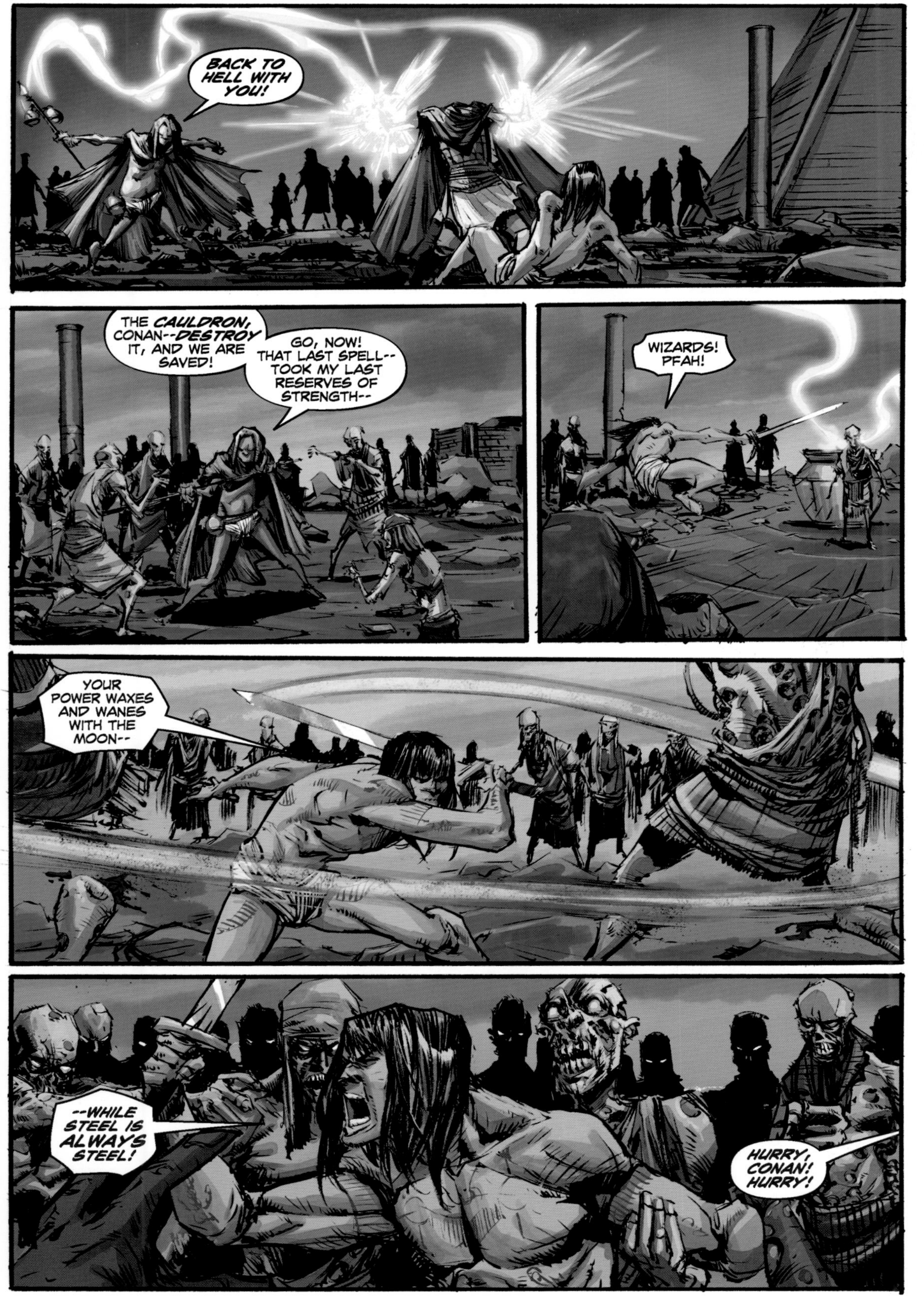
BACK TO HELL WITH YOU!
THE CAULDRON, CONAN--DESTROY IT, AND WE ARE SAVED!
GO, NOW! THAT LAST SPELL--TOOK MY LAST RESERVES OF STRENGTH--
WIZARDS! PFAH!
YOUR POWER WAXES AND WANES WITH THE MOON--
--WHILE STEEL IS ALWAYS STEEL!
HURRY, CONAN! HURRY!

...

CHOOOMMM

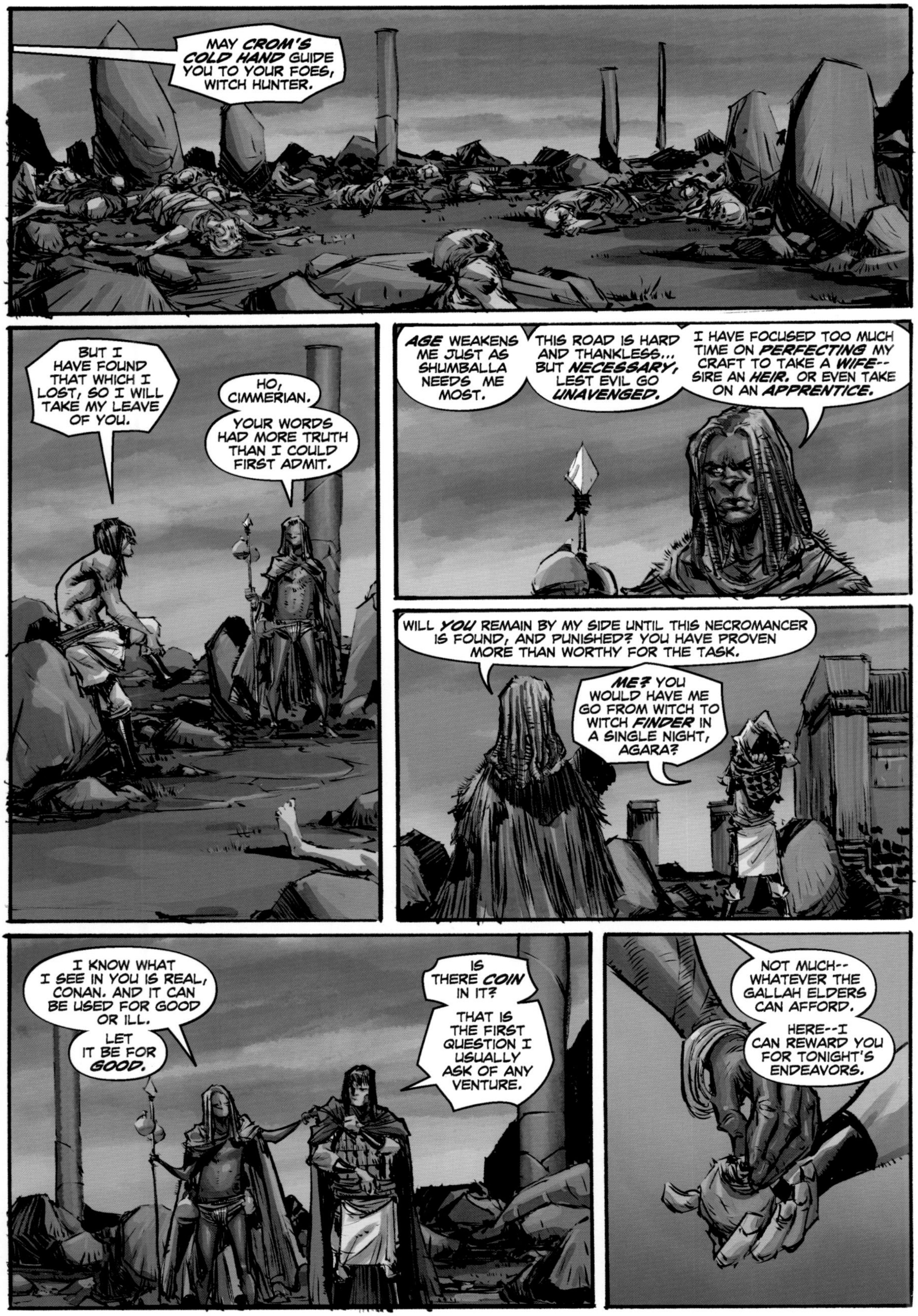
MAY CROM'S COLD HAND GUIDE YOU TO YOUR FOES, WITCH HUNTER.
BUT I HAVE FOUND THAT WHICH I LOST, SO I WILL TAKE MY LEAVE OF YOU.
HO, CIMMERIAN.
YOUR WORDS HAD MORE TRUTH THAN I COULD FIRST ADMIT.
AGE WEAKENS ME JUST AS SHUMBALLA NEEDS ME MOST.
THIS ROAD IS HARD AND THANKLESS... BUT NECESSARY, LEST EVIL GO UNAVENGED.
I HAVE FOCUSED TOO MUCH TIME ON PERFECTING MY CRAFT TO TAKE A WIFE--SIRE AN HEIR. OR EVEN TAKE ON AN APPRENTICE.
WILL YOU REMAIN BY MY SIDE UNTIL THIS NECROMANCER IS FOUND, AND PUNISHED? YOU HAVE PROVEN MORE THAN WORTHY FOR THE TASK.
ME? YOU WOULD HAVE ME GO FROM WITCH TO WITCH FINDER IN A SINGLE NIGHT, AGARA?
I KNOW WHAT I SEE IN YOU IS REAL, CONAN. AND IT CAN BE USED FOR GOOD OR ILL.
LET IT BE FOR GOOD.
IS THERE COIN IN IT?
THAT IS THE FIRST QUESTION I USUALLY ASK OF ANY VENTURE.
NOT MUCH--WHATEVER THE GALLAH ELDERS CAN AFFORD.
HERE--I CAN REWARD YOU FOR TONIGHT'S ENDEAVORS.

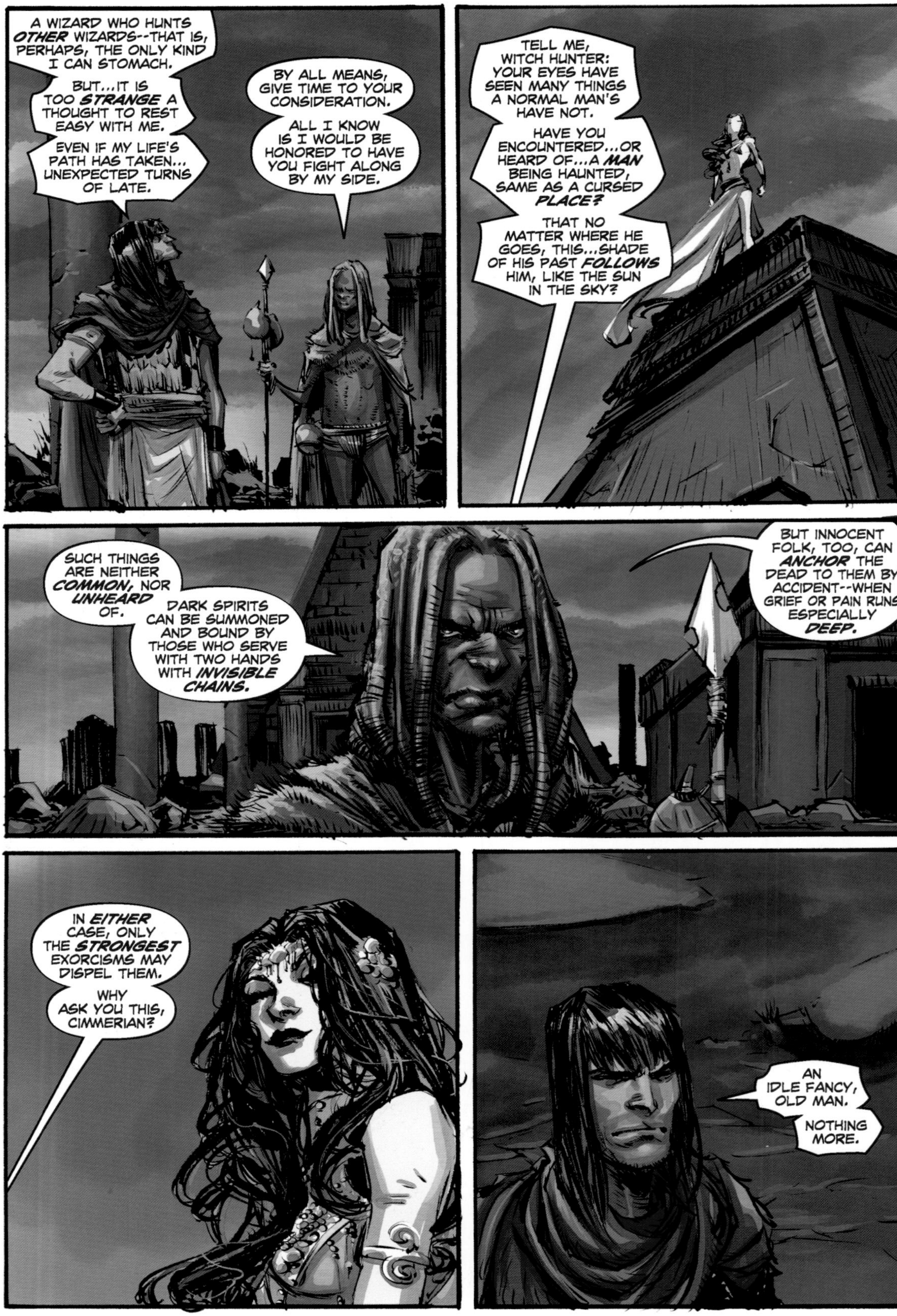

A WIZARD WHO HUNTS OTHER WIZARDS--THAT IS, PERHAPS, THE ONLY KIND I CAN STOMACH.
BUT...IT IS TOO STRANGE A THOUGHT TO REST EASY WITH ME.
EVEN IF MY LIFE'S PATH HAS TAKEN... UNEXPECTED TURNS OF LATE.
BY ALL MEANS, GIVE TIME TO YOUR CONSIDERATION.
ALL I KNOW IS I WOULD BE HONORED TO HAVE YOU FIGHT ALONG BY MY SIDE.
TELL ME, WITCH HUNTER: YOUR EYES HAVE SEEN MANY THINGS A NORMAL MAN'S HAVE NOT.
HAVE YOU ENCOUNTERED...OR HEARD OF...A MAN BEING HAUNTED, SAME AS A CURSED PLACE?
THAT NO MATTER WHERE HE GOES, THIS...SHADE OF HIS PAST FOLLOWS HIM, LIKE THE SUN IN THE SKY?
SUCH THINGS ARE NEITHER COMMON, NOR UNHEARD OF.
DARK SPIRITS CAN BE SUMMONED AND BOUND BY THOSE WHO SERVE WITH TWO HANDS WITH INVISIBLE CHAINS.
BUT INNOCENT FOLK, TOO, CAN ANCHOR THE DEAD TO THEM BY ACCIDENT--WHEN GRIEF OR PAIN RUNS ESPECIALLY DEEP.
IN EITHER CASE, ONLY THE STRONGEST EXORCISMS MAY DISPEL THEM.
WHY ASK YOU THIS, CIMMERIAN?
AN IDLE FANCY, OLD MAN.
NOTHING MORE.

The witch remained free, unidentified...

...but not happy.

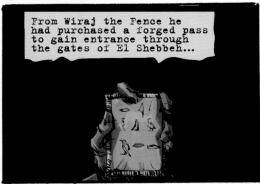

From Wiraj the Fence he had purchased a forged pass to gain entrance through the gates of El Shebbeh...

...without the *master* learning *his* pass had been stolen from him.

The ghost cauldron he had mounted in the necropolis was meant to be the *climax* of his reign of terror, though. Not its *inauguration*.

The witch hunter and the barbarian interloper had forced his hand.

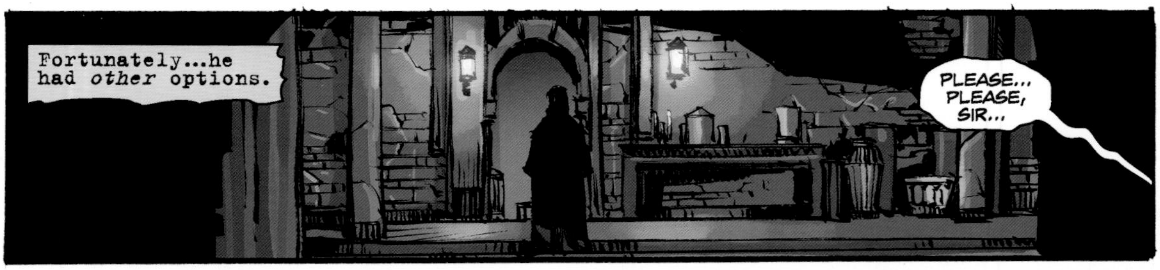
Fortunately...he had *other* options.
PLEASE... PLEASE, SIR...

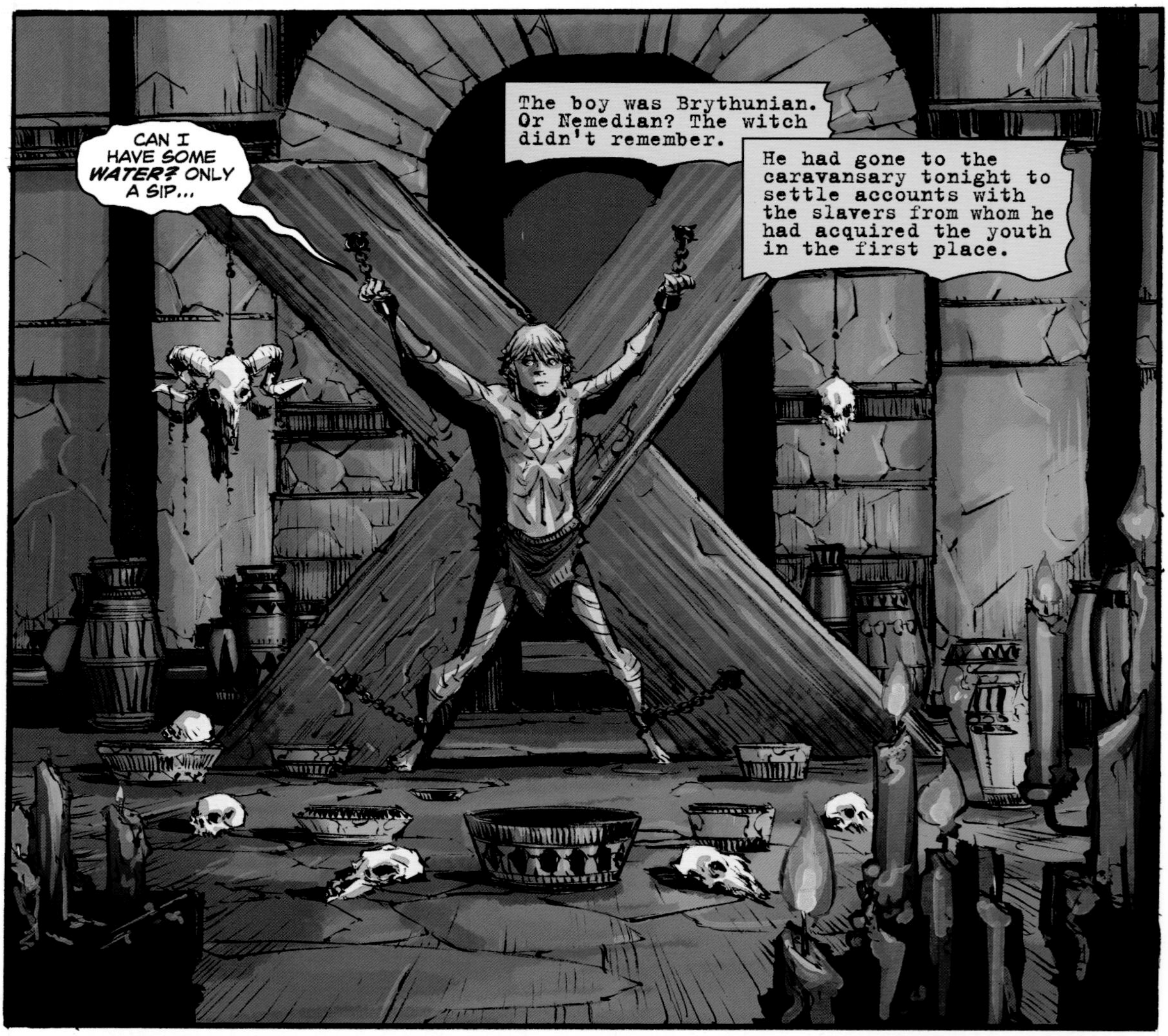
CAN I HAVE SOME *WATER?* ONLY A SIP...
The boy was Brythunian. Or Nemedian? The witch didn't remember.
He had gone to the caravansary tonight to settle accounts with the slavers from whom he had acquired the youth in the first place.

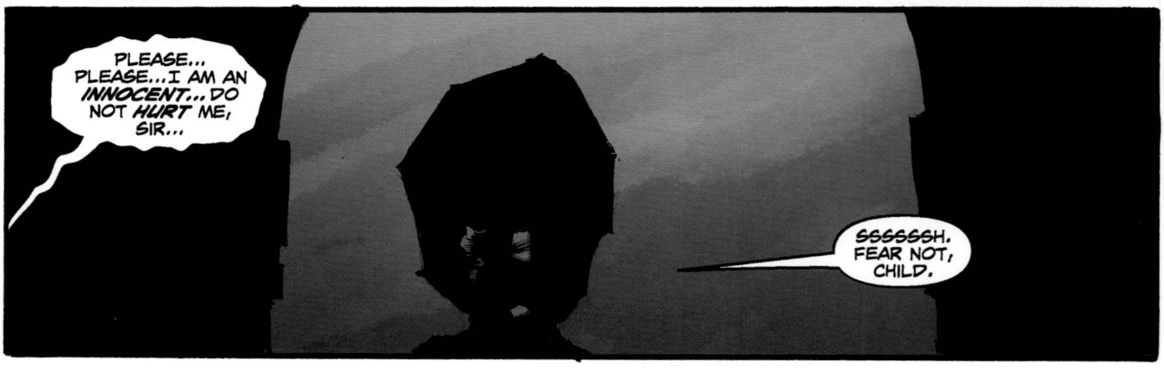
PLEASE... PLEASE...I AM AN *INNOCENT*... DO NOT *HURT* ME, SIR...
SSSSSSH. FEAR NOT, CHILD.

I WON'T.

For twelve hours between two moons' zeniths the signs of gating had dried on the boy's skin.

NGGK-- WHA--

GGG RGGGGRKKLLL

JAMANKH, L'UVRI BAYÈ PU MWÈ, AGOÉ!

PAPA-JAMANKH, L'UVRI BAYÈ PU MWÈ...

He had not had anything to eat or drink in that time.

IT BURNS, SIR, IT...

OH... OH, SIR-- HELP...

He was a *purified vessel.*

AAAAAGGHHH!! NO! *NOOOO!*

SKKRRSSHHHQQQQSSHHHHHH

GGYYYAAAAAAAA!

51

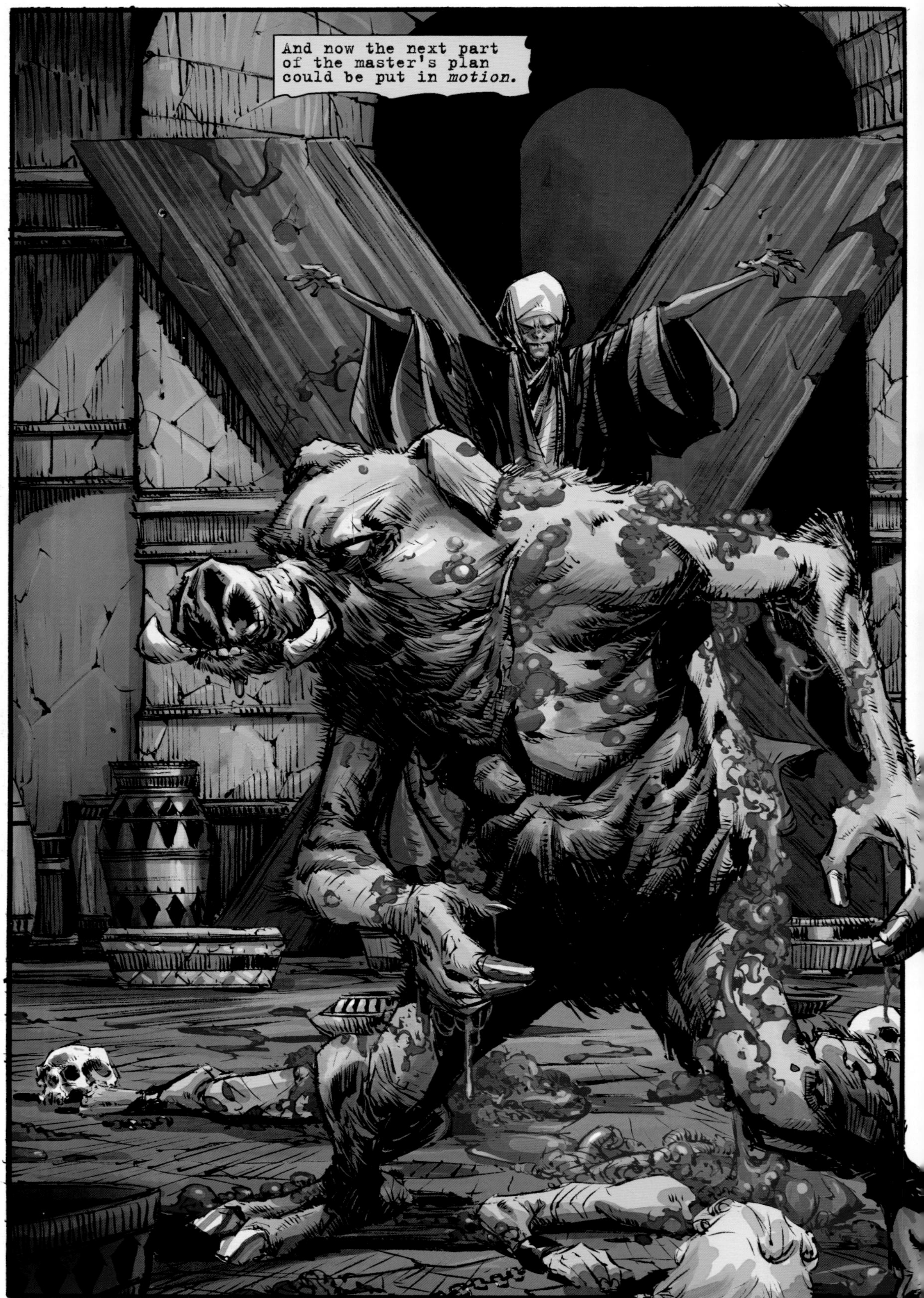
And now the next part of the master's plan could be put in *motion.*

CHAPTER THREE

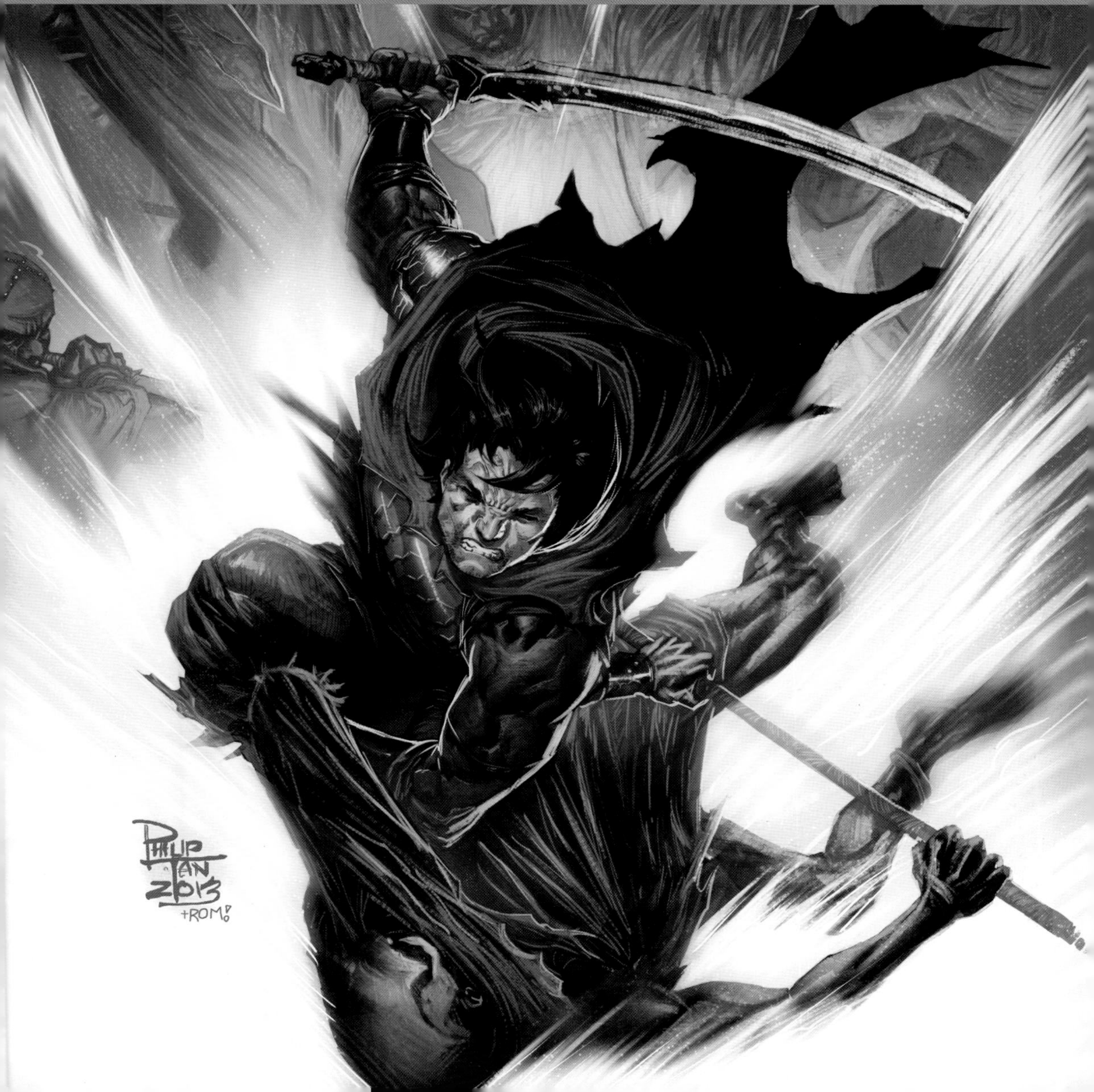

"Crom gave you breath and Crom gave you blood.
That is all you need to get what you want in this world.
Anyone who tells you different is a liar."

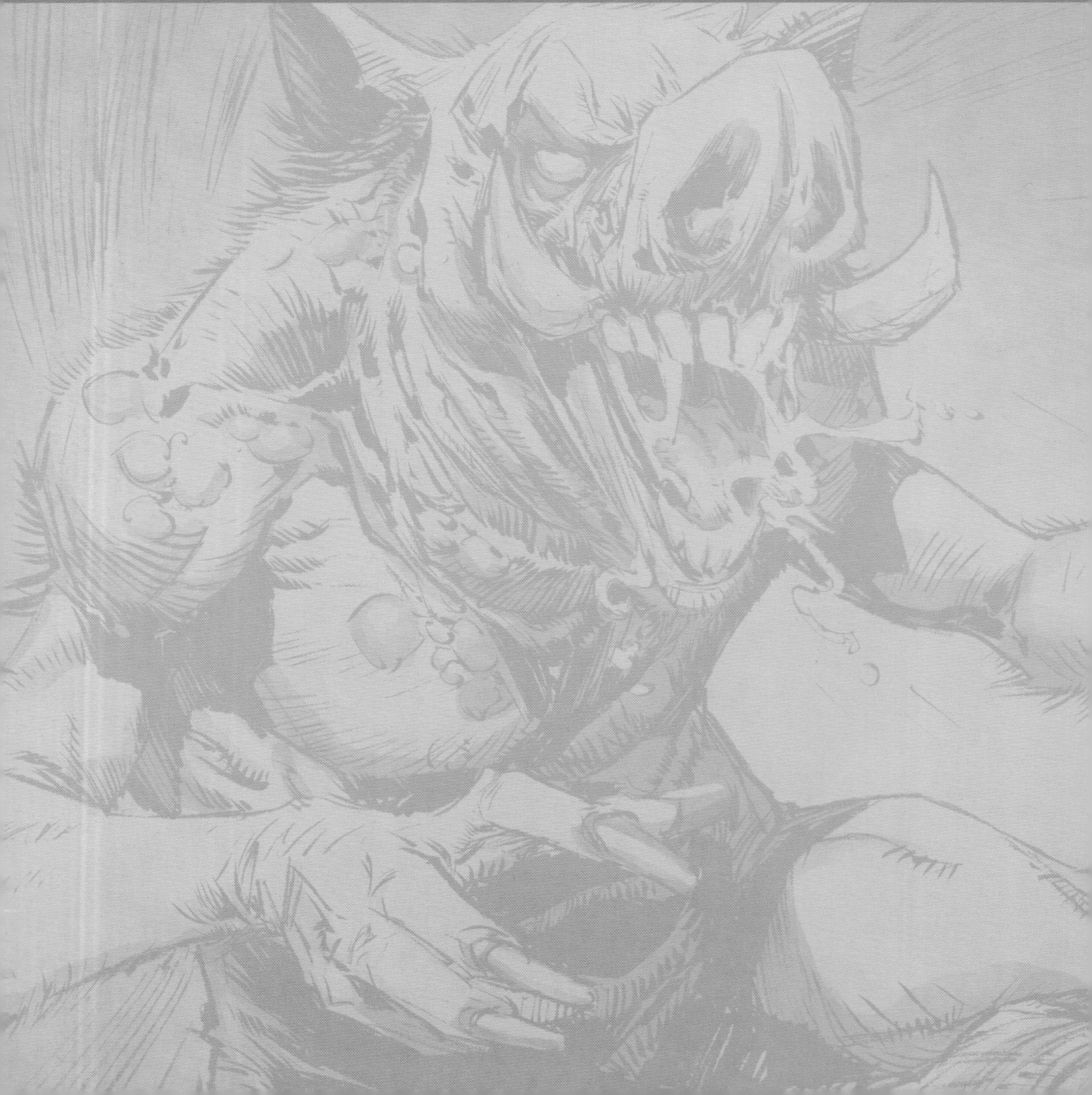

Amboola awakened slowly, his senses still sluggish from the wine he had guzzled the night before.

For a muddled moment he could not remember where he was; the moonlight, streaming through the barred window, shone on unfamiliar surroundings.

Then he remembered:

He was lying in the upper cell of the prison tower where the anger of Tanada, sister to the king of Kush, had consigned him.

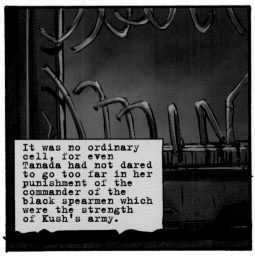

It was no ordinary cell, for even Tanada had not dared to go too far in her punishment of the commander of the black spearmen which were the strength of Kush's army.

He remembered that he had been awakened...

...and wondered *why.*

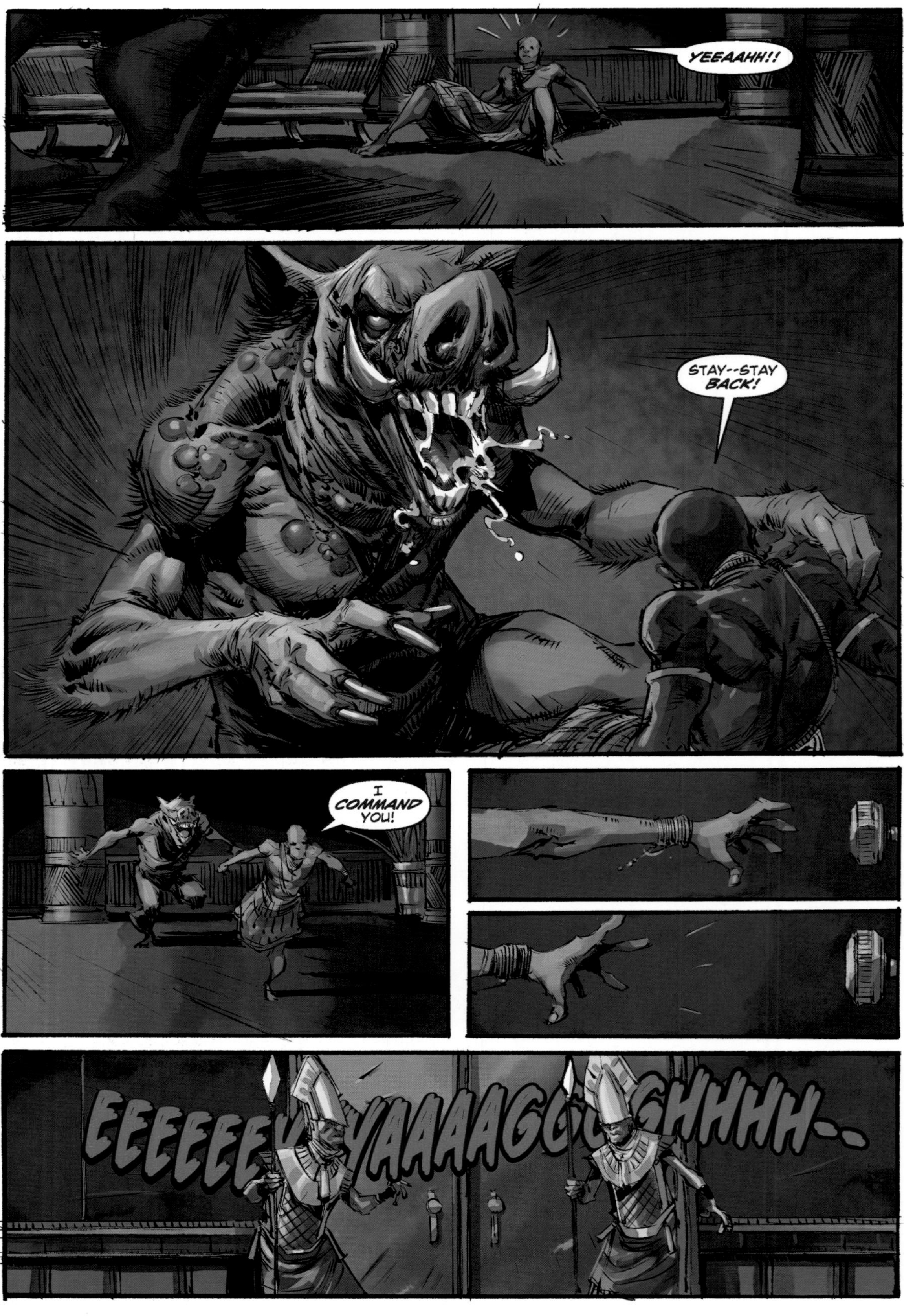
YEEAAHH!!
STAY--STAY BACK!
I COMMAND YOU!
EEEEEEYYAAAAGGGGHHHH--

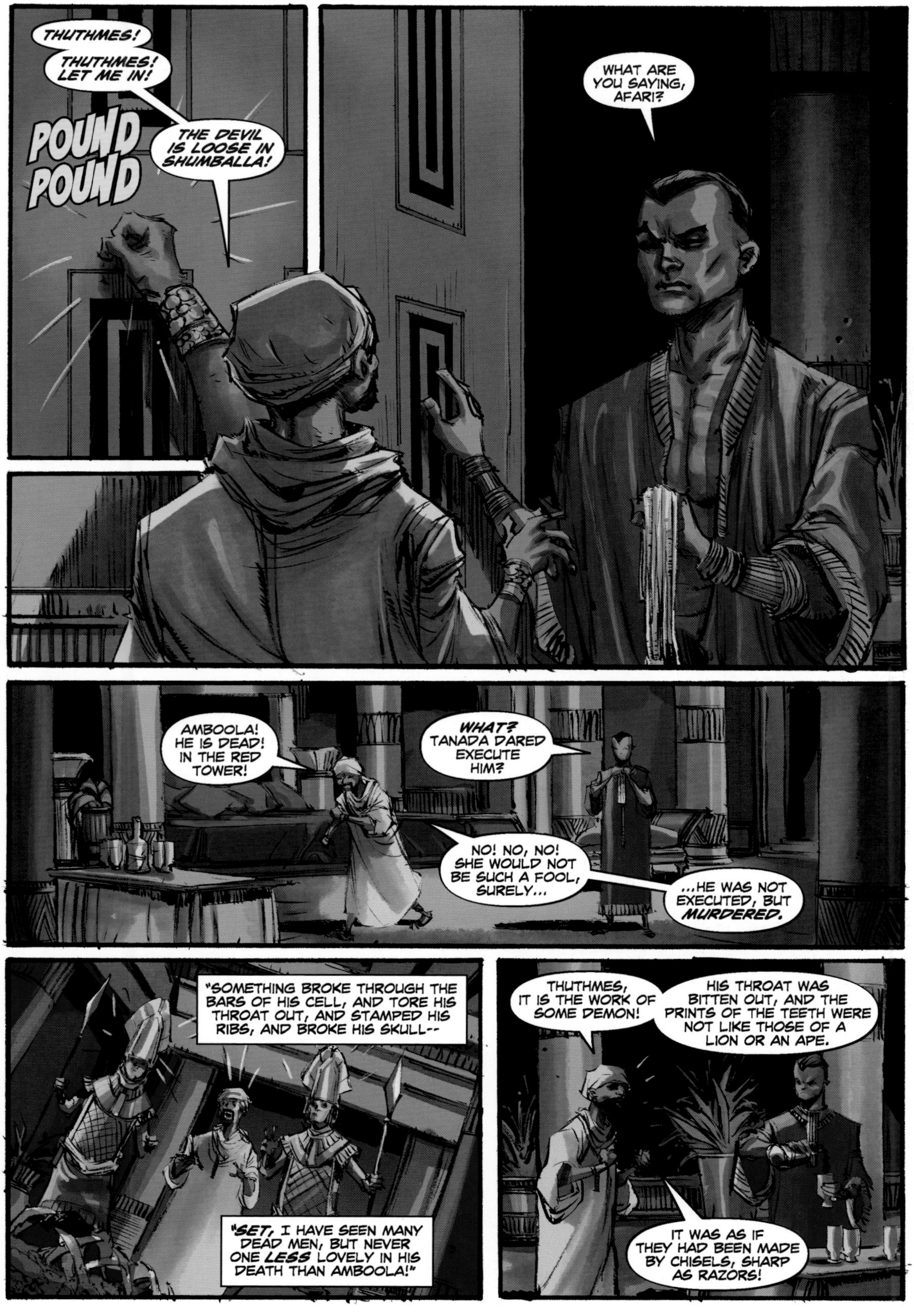
THUTHMES!
THUTHMES! LET ME IN!
POUND POUND
THE DEVIL IS LOOSE IN SHUMBALLA!
WHAT ARE YOU SAYING, AFARI?
AMBOOLA! HE IS DEAD! IN THE RED TOWER!
WHAT? TANADA DARED EXECUTE HIM?
NO! NO, NO! SHE WOULD NOT BE SUCH A FOOL, SURELY...
...HE WAS NOT EXECUTED, BUT MURDERED.
"SOMETHING BROKE THROUGH THE BARS OF HIS CELL, AND TORE HIS THROAT OUT, AND STAMPED HIS RIBS, AND BROKE HIS SKULL--
"SET, I HAVE SEEN MANY DEAD MEN, BUT NEVER ONE LESS LOVELY IN HIS DEATH THAN AMBOOLA!"
THUTHMES, IT IS THE WORK OF SOME DEMON!
HIS THROAT WAS BITTEN OUT, AND THE PRINTS OF THE TEETH WERE NOT LIKE THOSE OF A LION OR AN APE.
IT WAS AS IF THEY HAD BEEN MADE BY CHISELS, SHARP AS RAZORS!

GODS AND DEMONS WORK FOR A BOLD MAN. I DO NOT THINK TANADA WAS FOOL ENOUGH TO HAVE AMBOOLA MURDERED, HOWEVER MUCH SHE DESIRED IT.

THE BLACKS HAVE BEEN SULLEN, EVER SINCE SHE CAST HIM INTO PRISON. SHE COULD NOT HAVE KEPT HIM IMPRISONED MUCH LONGER.

BUT THIS PUTS A WEAPON INTO OUR HANDS. IF THE GALLAHS *THINK* SHE DID IT, SO MUCH THE BETTER. EACH RESENTMENT AGAINST THE DYNASTY IS A WEAPON FOR US.

GO, NOW, AND STRIKE BEFORE THE KING CAN LEARN OF IT.

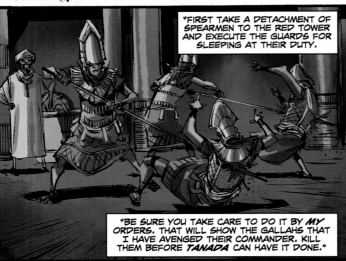

"FIRST TAKE A DETACHMENT OF SPEARMEN TO THE RED TOWER AND EXECUTE THE GUARDS FOR SLEEPING AT THEIR DUTY.

"BE SURE YOU TAKE CARE TO DO IT BY *MY* ORDERS. THAT WILL SHOW THE GALLAHS THAT I HAVE AVENGED THEIR COMMANDER. KILL THEM BEFORE *TANADA* CAN HAVE IT DONE."

THEN GO INTO PUNT--FIND OLD *AGARA*, THE WITCH FINDER. DO NOT TELL HIM FLATLY THAT TANADA HAD THIS DEED DONE, BUT HINT AT IT.

HOW CAN A COMMON MAN LIE TO THAT BLACK DEVIL? HIS EYES ARE LIKE COALS OF RED FIRE THAT LOOK INTO DEPTHS UNNAMEABLE!

I HAVE SEEN HIM MAKE CORPSES RISE AND WALK, AND SKULLS CLAMP AND GRIND THEIR NAKED JAWS!

DON'T *LIE*. SIMPLY HINT TO HIM YOUR OWN... *SUSPICIONS*.

AFTER ALL, EVEN IF A DEMON *DID* SLAY AMBOOLA, SOME HUMAN SUMMONED IT OUT OF THE NIGHT.

PERHAPS TANADA *IS* BEHIND THIS!

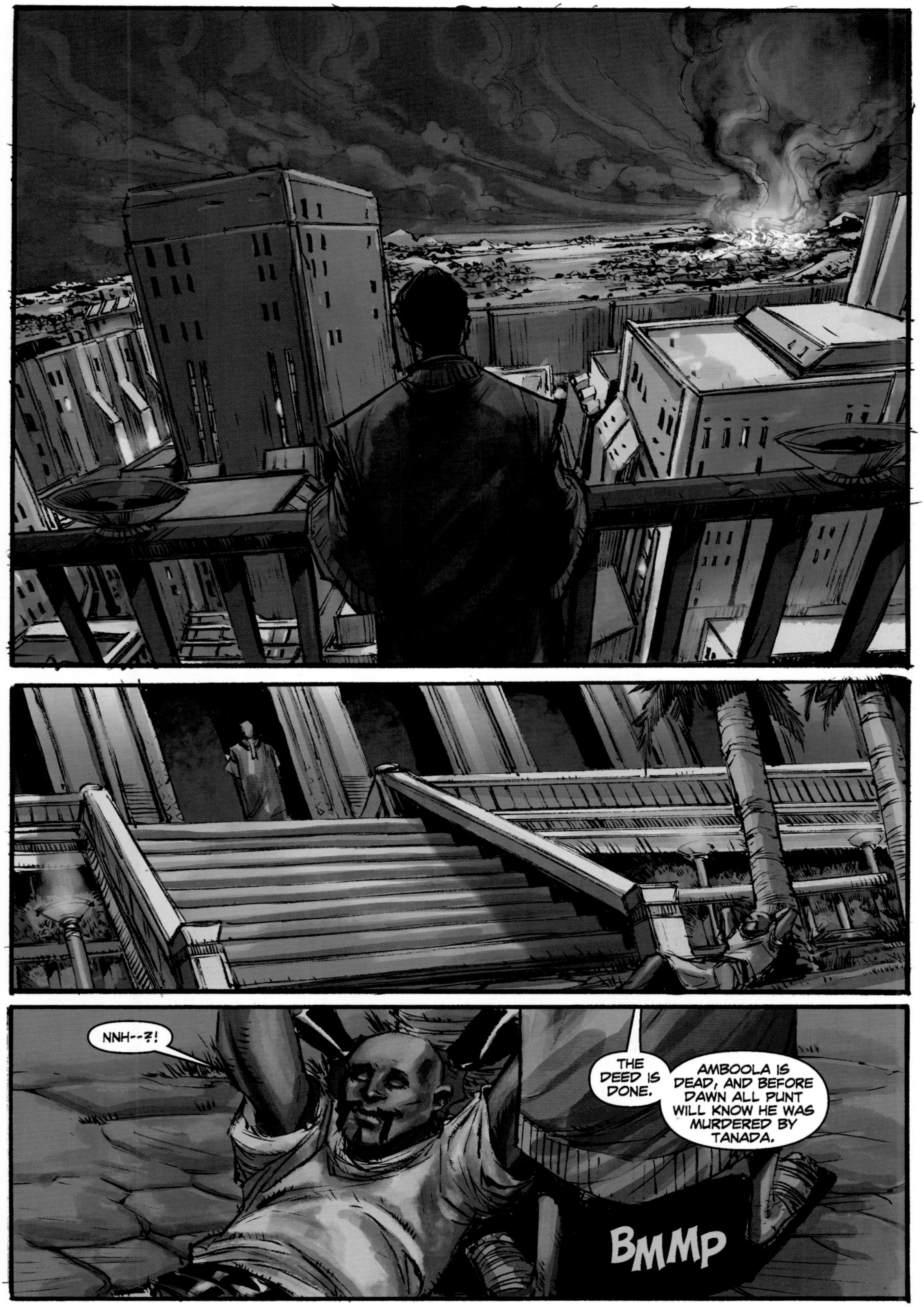

NNH--?!
THE DEED IS DONE.
AMBOOLA IS DEAD, AND BEFORE DAWN ALL PUNT WILL KNOW HE WAS MURDERED BY TANADA.
BMMP

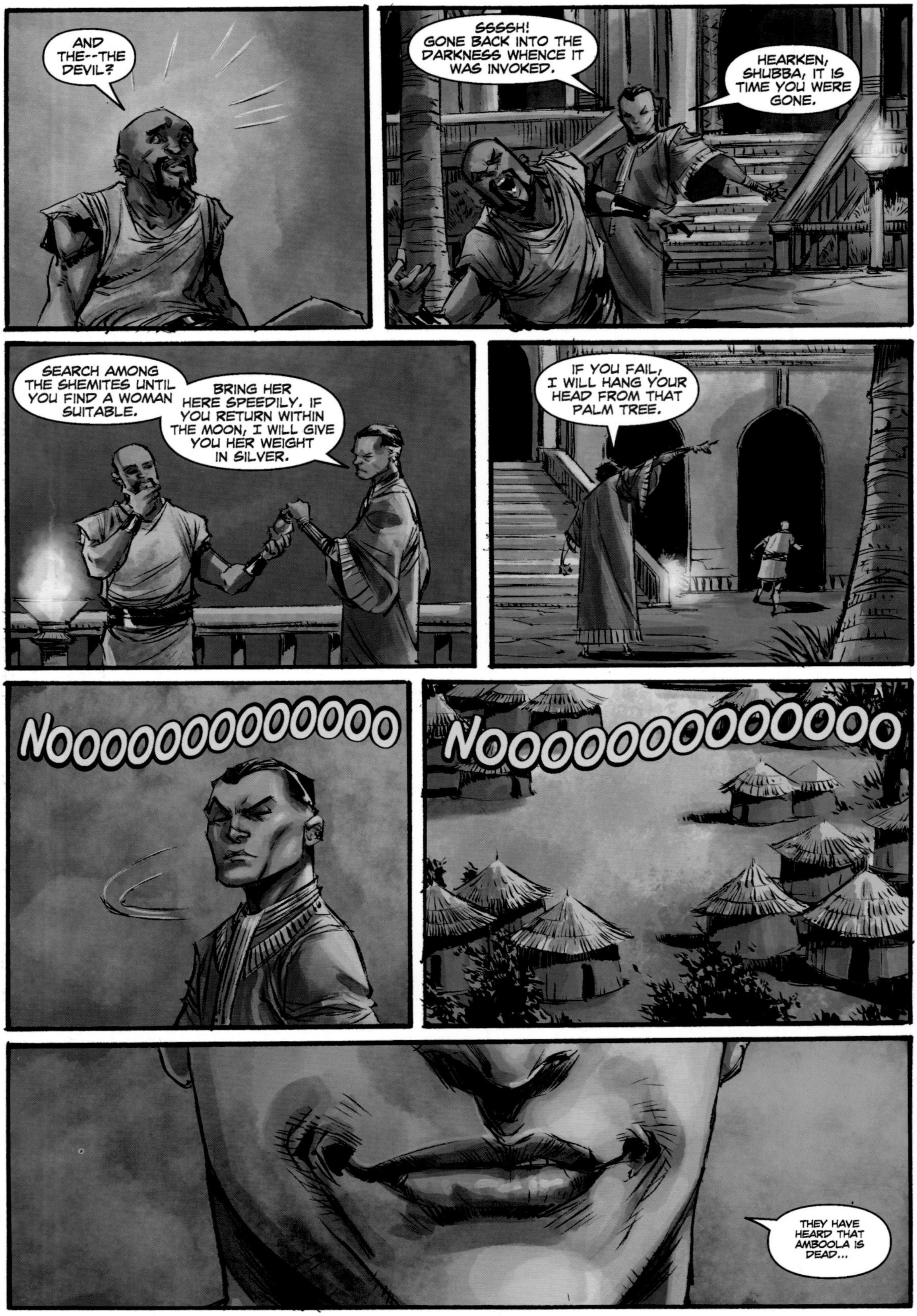
AND THE--THE DEVIL?
SSSSH! GONE BACK INTO THE DARKNESS WHENCE IT WAS INVOKED.
HEARKEN, SHUBBA, IT IS TIME YOU WERE GONE.
SEARCH AMONG THE SHEMITES UNTIL YOU FIND A WOMAN SUITABLE.
BRING HER HERE SPEEDILY. IF YOU RETURN WITHIN THE MOON, I WILL GIVE YOU HER WEIGHT IN SILVER.
IF YOU FAIL, I WILL HANG YOUR HEAD FROM THAT PALM TREE.
NOOOOOOOOOOOOO
NOOOOOOOOOOOOO
THEY HAVE HEARD THAT AMBOOLA IS DEAD...

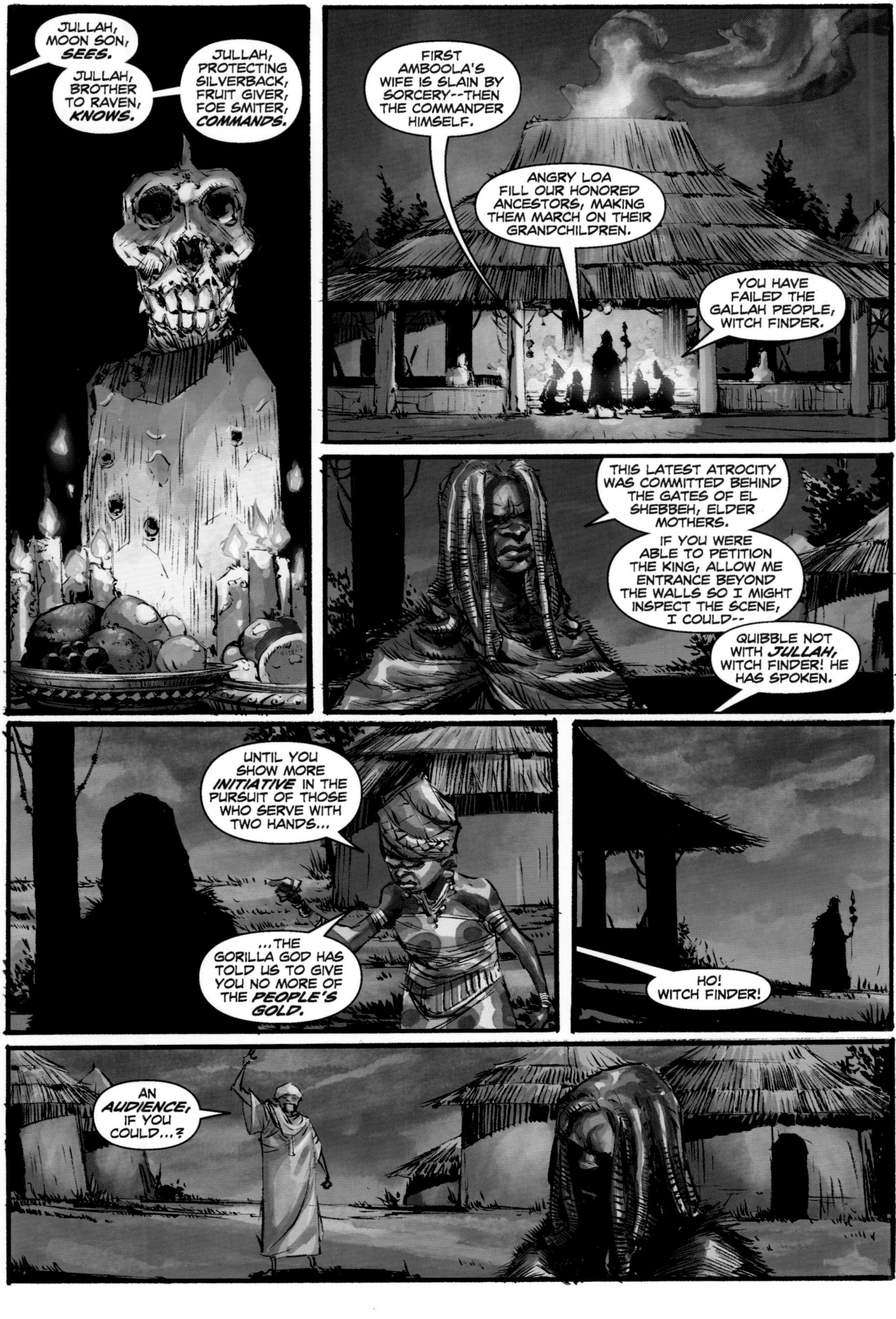
JULLAH, MOON SON, SEES.
JULLAH, BROTHER TO RAVEN, KNOWS.
JULLAH, PROTECTING SILVERBACK, FRUIT GIVER, FOE SMITER, COMMANDS.
FIRST AMBOOLA'S WIFE IS SLAIN BY SORCERY--THEN THE COMMANDER HIMSELF.
ANGRY LOA FILL OUR HONORED ANCESTORS, MAKING THEM MARCH ON THEIR GRANDCHILDREN.
YOU HAVE FAILED THE GALLAH PEOPLE, WITCH FINDER.
THIS LATEST ATROCITY WAS COMMITTED BEHIND THE GATES OF EL SHEBBEH, ELDER MOTHERS.
IF YOU WERE ABLE TO PETITION THE KING, ALLOW ME ENTRANCE BEYOND THE WALLS SO I MIGHT INSPECT THE SCENE, I COULD--
QUIBBLE NOT WITH JULLAH, WITCH FINDER! HE HAS SPOKEN.
UNTIL YOU SHOW MORE INITIATIVE IN THE PURSUIT OF THOSE WHO SERVE WITH TWO HANDS...
...THE GORILLA GOD HAS TOLD US TO GIVE YOU NO MORE OF THE PEOPLE'S GOLD.
HO! WITCH FINDER!
AN AUDIENCE, IF YOU COULD...?

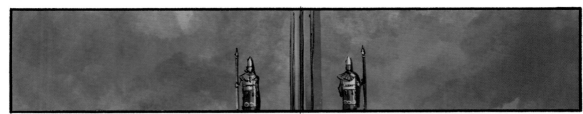

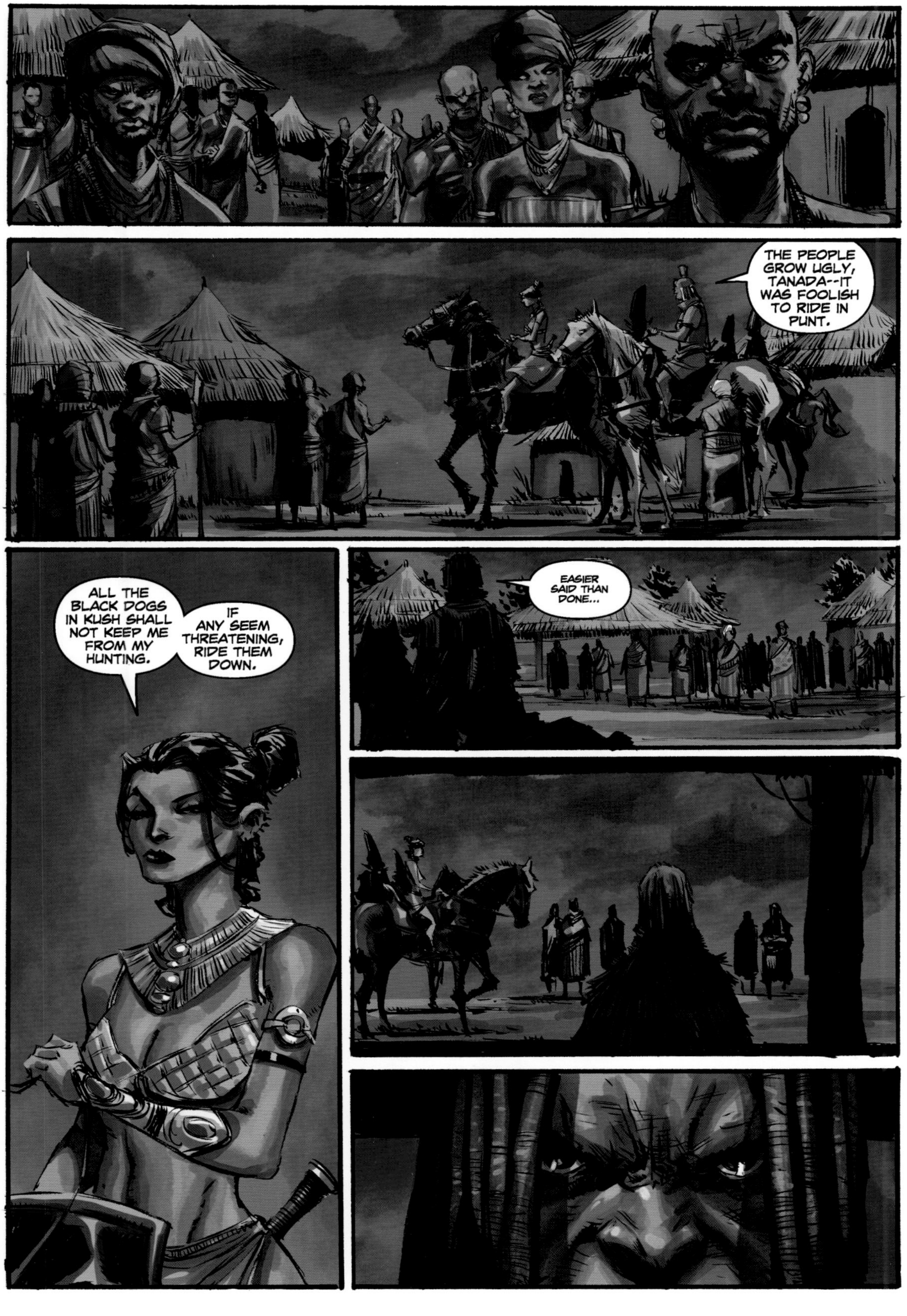
THE PEOPLE GROW UGLY, TANADA--IT WAS FOOLISH TO RIDE IN PUNT.
ALL THE BLACK DOGS IN KUSH SHALL NOT KEEP ME FROM MY HUNTING.
IF ANY SEEM THREATENING, RIDE THEM DOWN.
EASIER SAID THAN DONE...

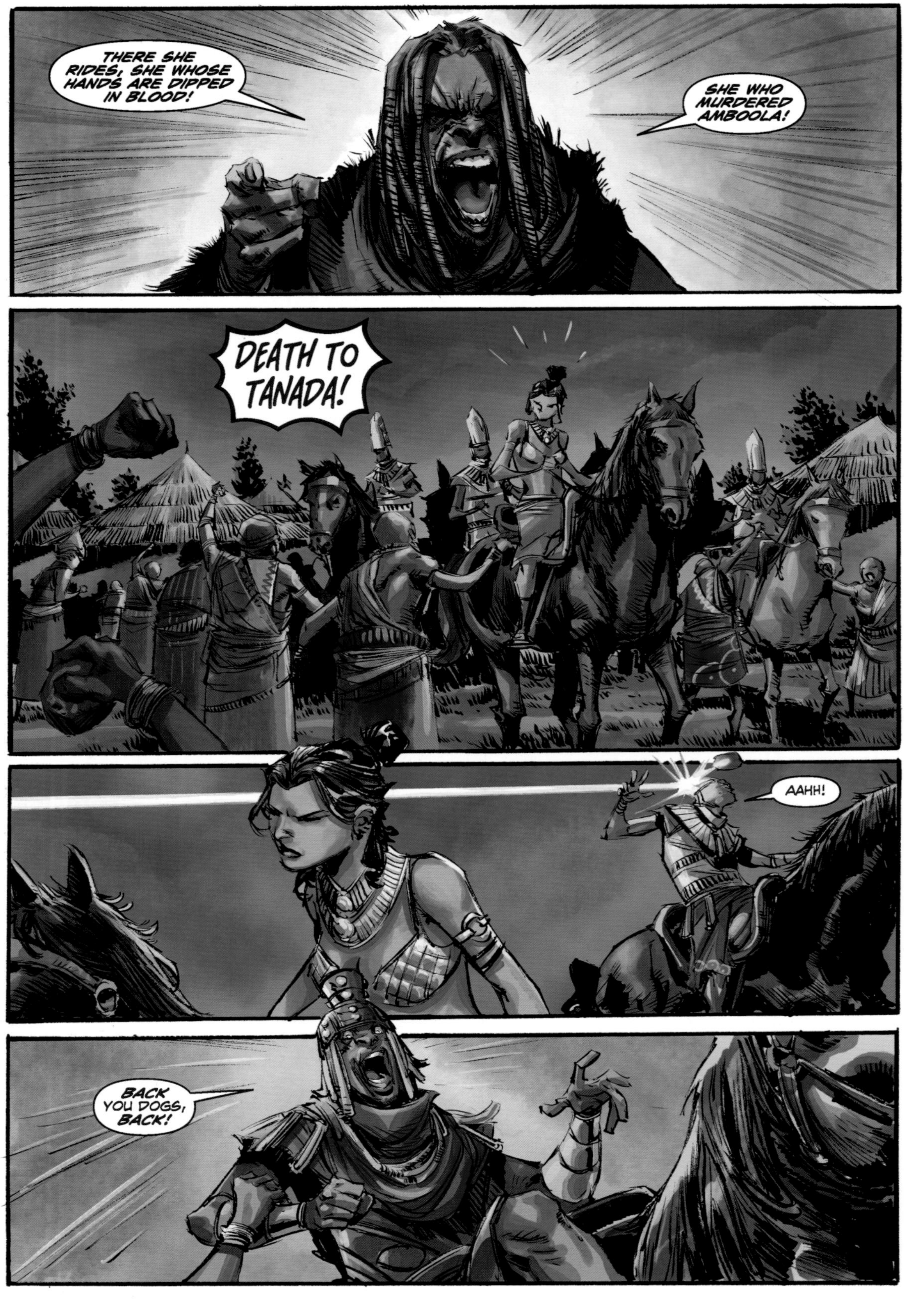
THERE SHE RIDES, SHE WHOSE HANDS ARE DIPPED IN BLOOD!
SHE WHO MURDERED AMBOOLA!
DEATH TO TANADA!
AAHH!
BACK YOU DOGS, BACK!

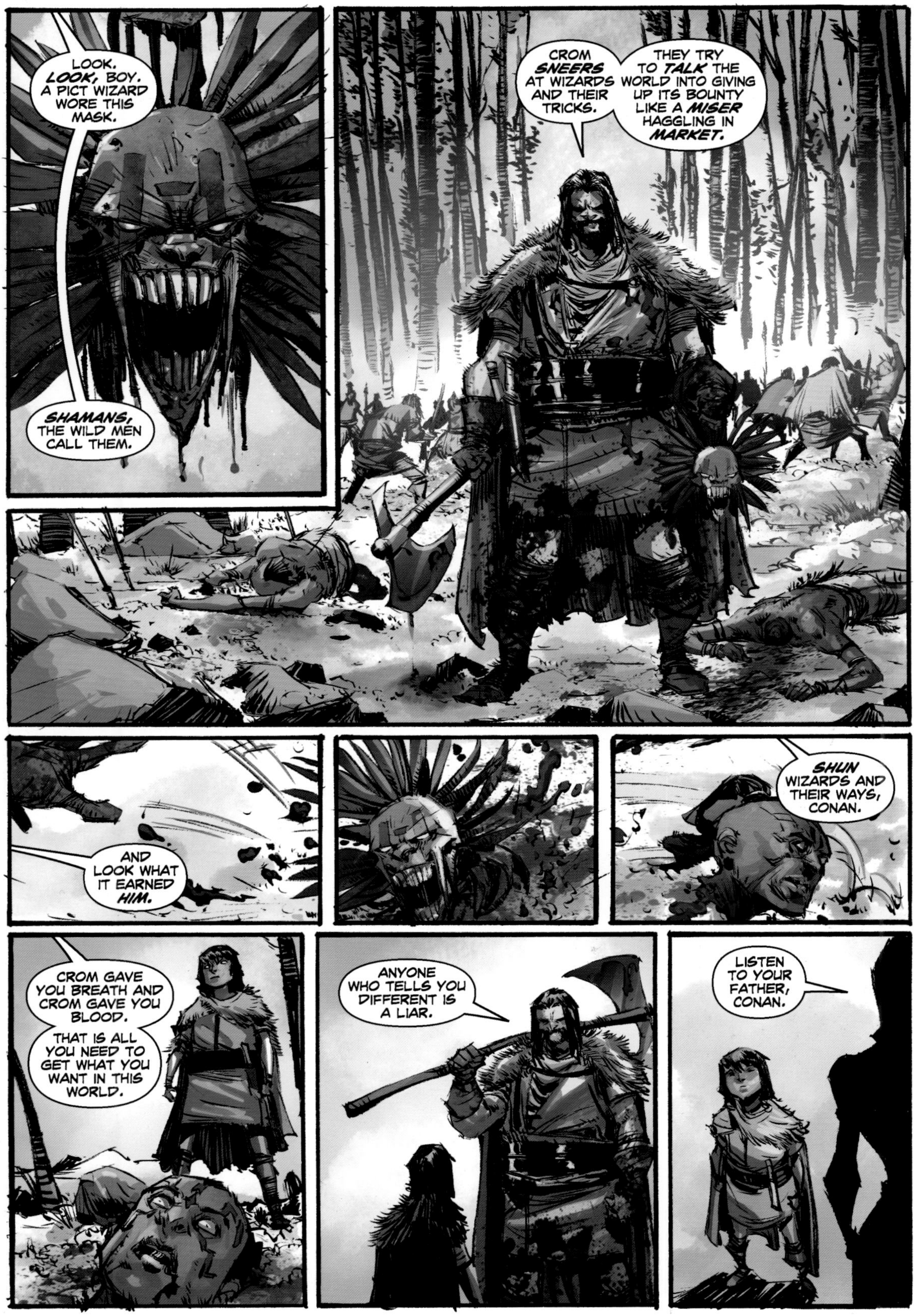
LOOK. LOOK, BOY. A PICT WIZARD WORE THIS MASK.
SHAMANS, THE WILD MEN CALL THEM.
CROM SNEERS AT WIZARDS AND THEIR TRICKS.
THEY TRY TO TALK THE WORLD INTO GIVING UP ITS BOUNTY LIKE A MISER HAGGLING IN MARKET.
AND LOOK WHAT IT EARNED HIM.
SHUN WIZARDS AND THEIR WAYS, CONAN.
CROM GAVE YOU BREATH AND CROM GAVE YOU BLOOD.
THAT IS ALL YOU NEED TO GET WHAT YOU WANT IN THIS WORLD.
ANYONE WHO TELLS YOU DIFFERENT IS A LIAR.
LISTEN TO YOUR FATHER, CONAN.

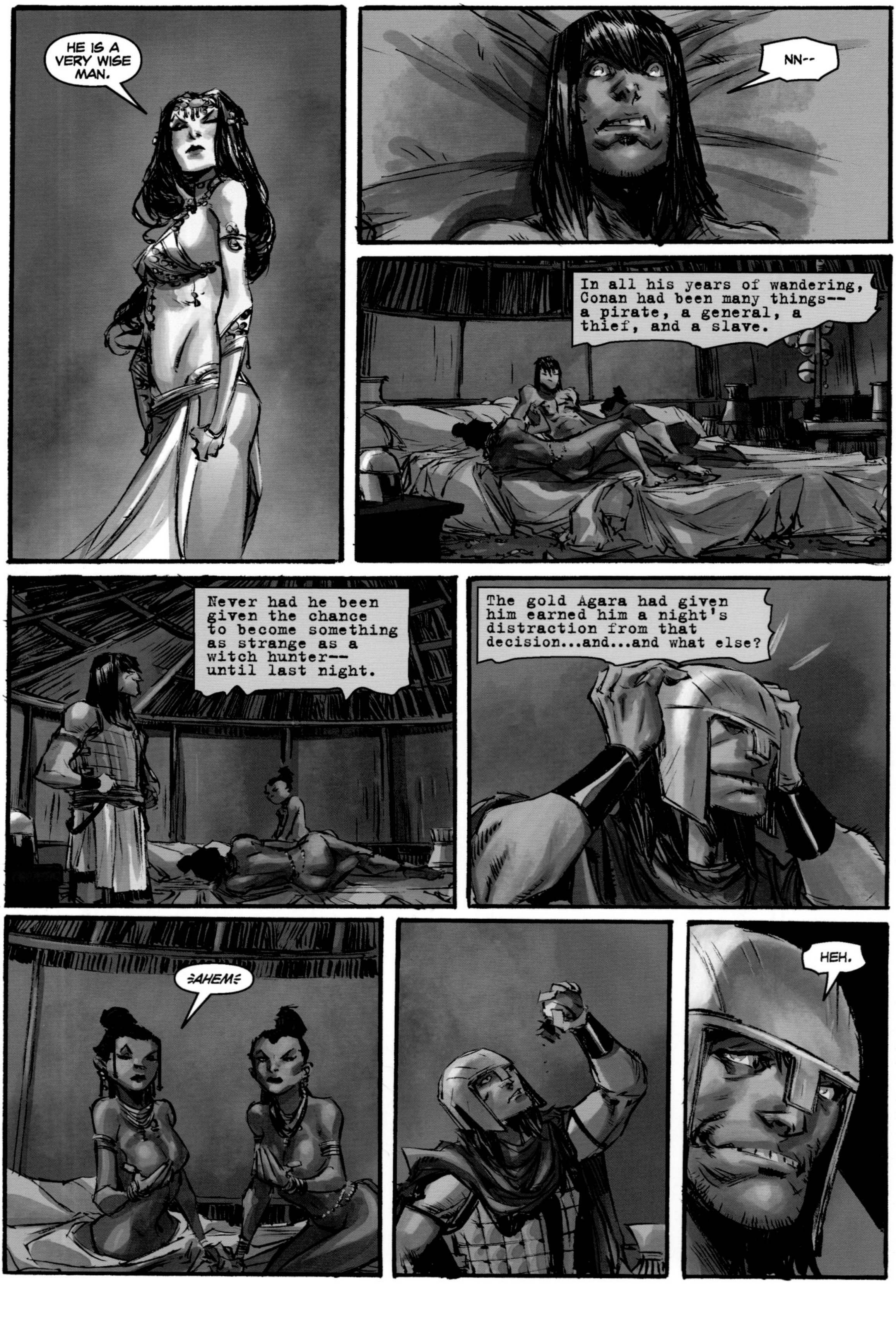
HE IS A VERY WISE MAN.
NN--
In all his years of wandering, Conan had been many things--a pirate, a general, a thief, and a slave.
Never had he been given the chance to become something as strange as a witch hunter--until last night.
The gold Agara had given him earned him a night's distraction from that decision...and...and what else?
AHEM
HEH.

Ah, yes.

A horse.

LONG-HAIRED BASTARD!

But in which direction should the mare take him? *Toward* Agara--or as far away from the old man as he could ride?

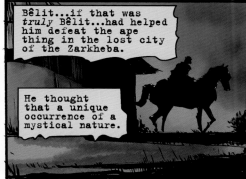

Bêlit...if that was *truly* Bêlit...had helped him defeat the ape thing in the lost city of the Zarkheba.

He thought that a unique occurrence of a mystical nature.

But she did not appear inclined to quit his side.

And so he may have finally found a situation in which his father's dictum proved wrong.

One in which only an exorcism by *wizardry* could free him from the ghost--

EEYAAAAAWWWW!

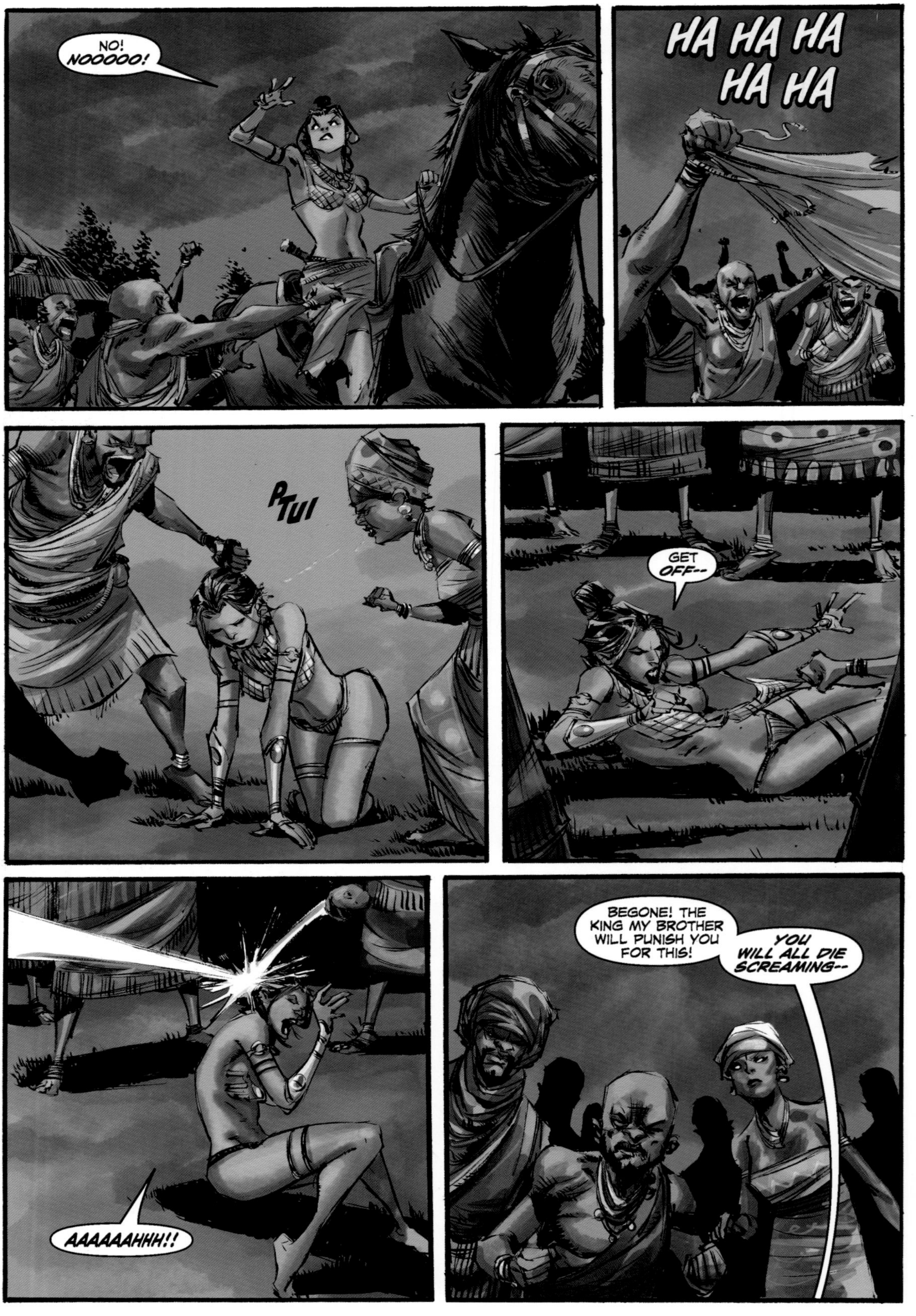
NO! NOOOOO!
HA HA HA HA HA
PTUI
GET OFF--
AAAAAAHHH!!
BEGONE! THE KING MY BROTHER WILL PUNISH YOU FOR THIS!
YOU WILL ALL DIE SCREAMING--

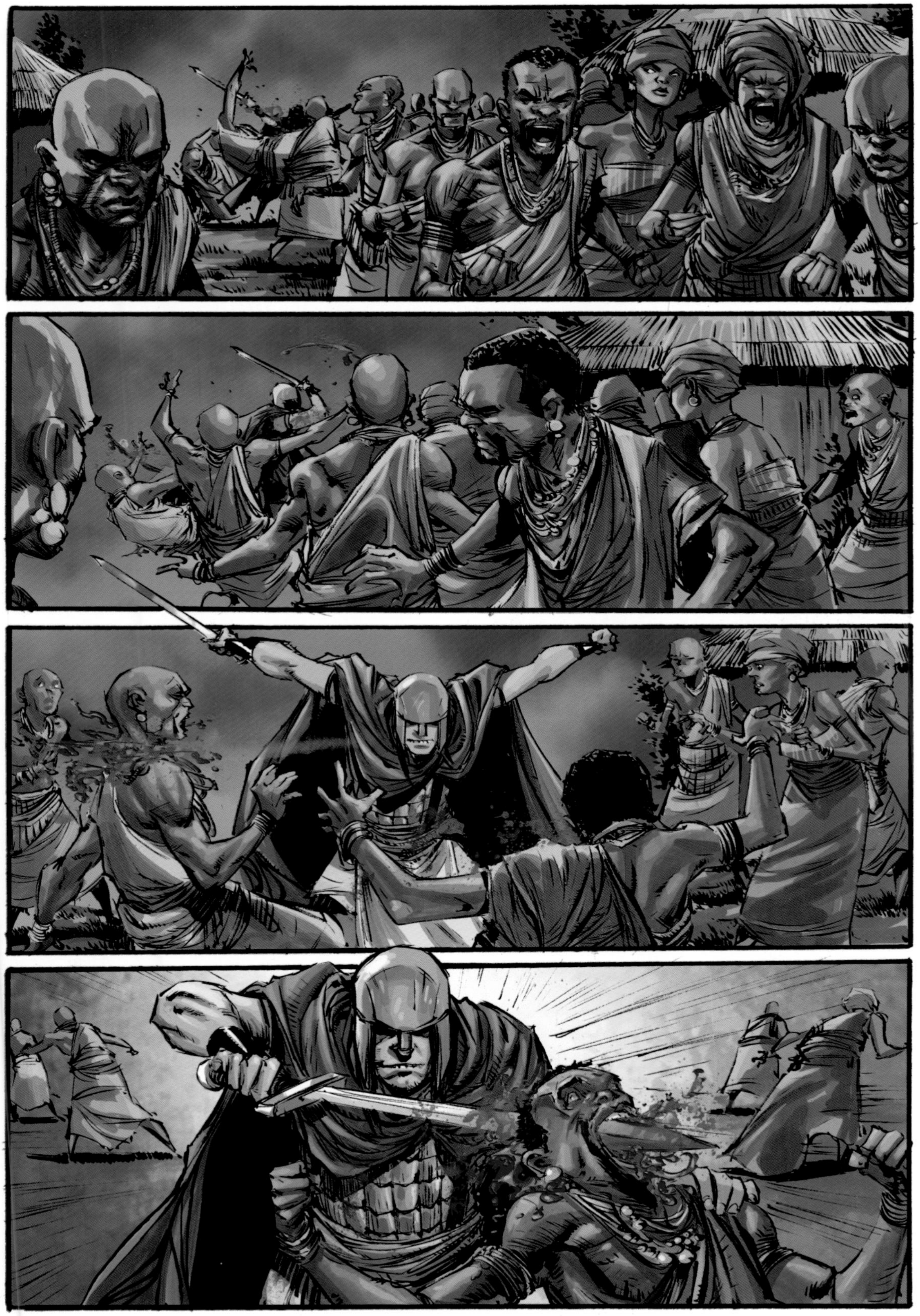

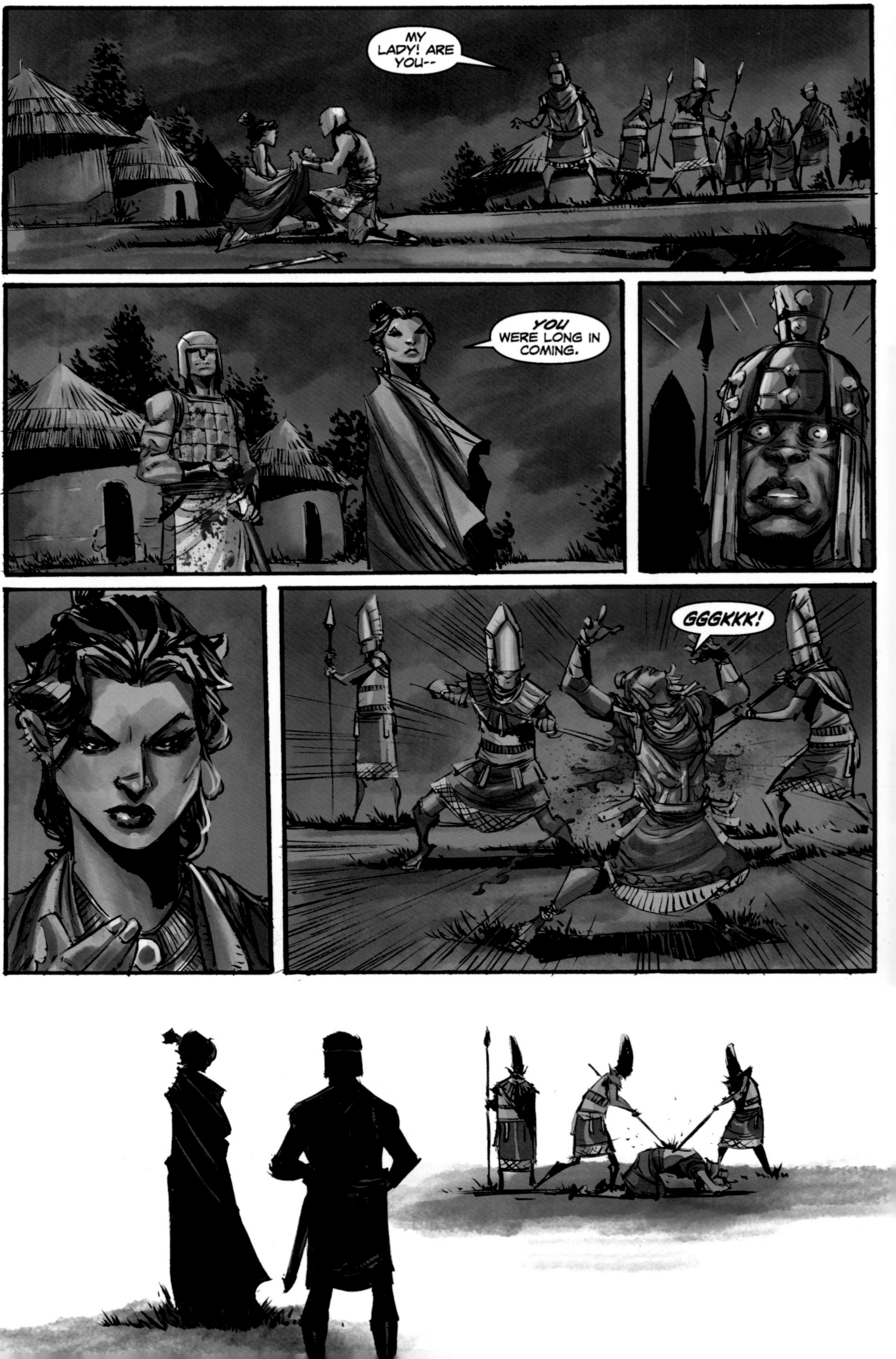
MY LADY! ARE YOU--
YOU WERE LONG IN COMING.
GGGKKK!

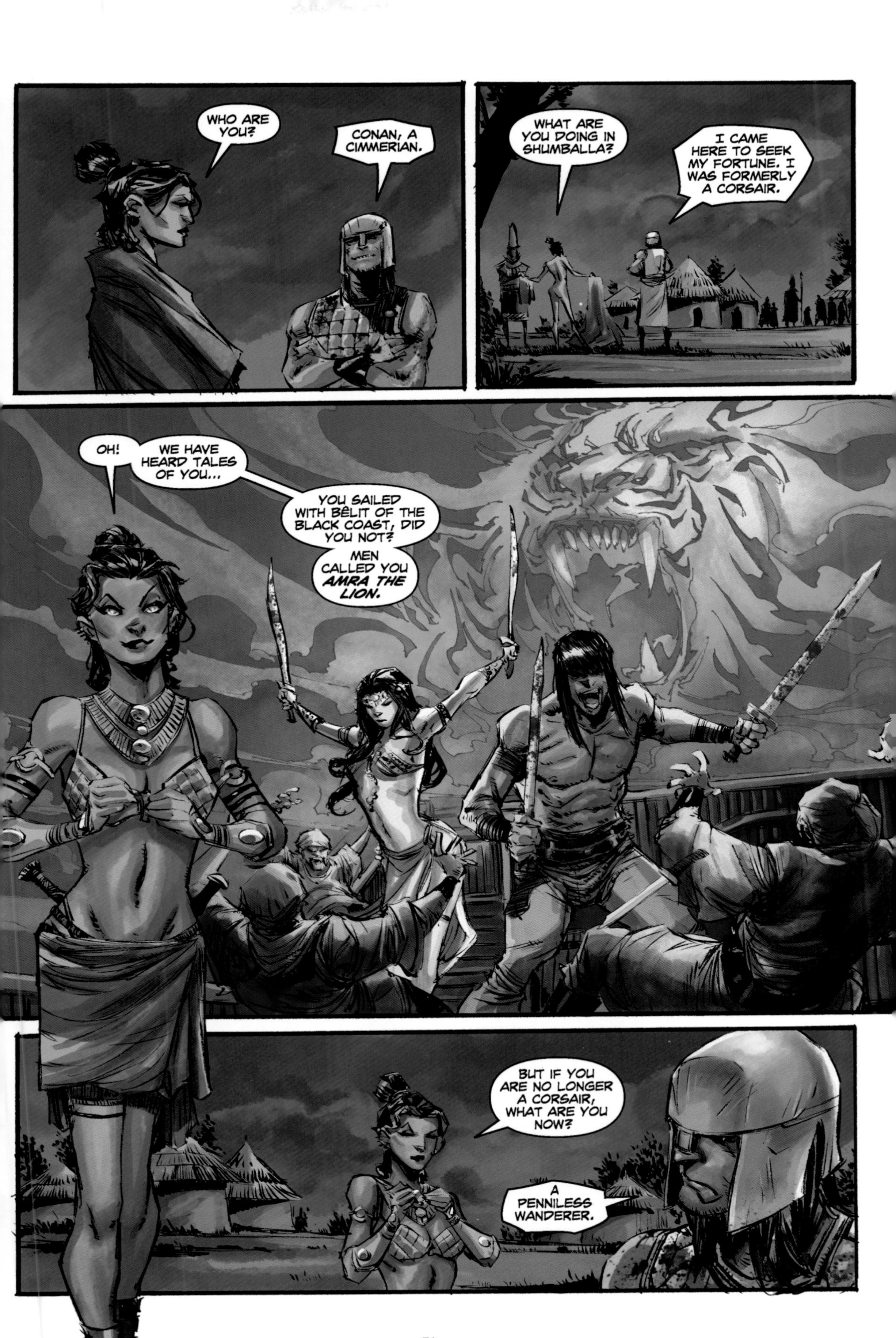
WHO ARE YOU?
CONAN, A CIMMERIAN.
WHAT ARE YOU DOING IN SHUMBALLA?
I CAME HERE TO SEEK MY FORTUNE. I WAS FORMERLY A CORSAIR.
OH!
WE HAVE HEARD TALES OF YOU...
YOU SAILED WITH BÊLIT OF THE BLACK COAST, DID YOU NOT?
MEN CALLED YOU *AMRA THE LION.*
BUT IF YOU ARE NO LONGER A CORSAIR, WHAT ARE YOU NOW?
A PENNILESS WANDERER.

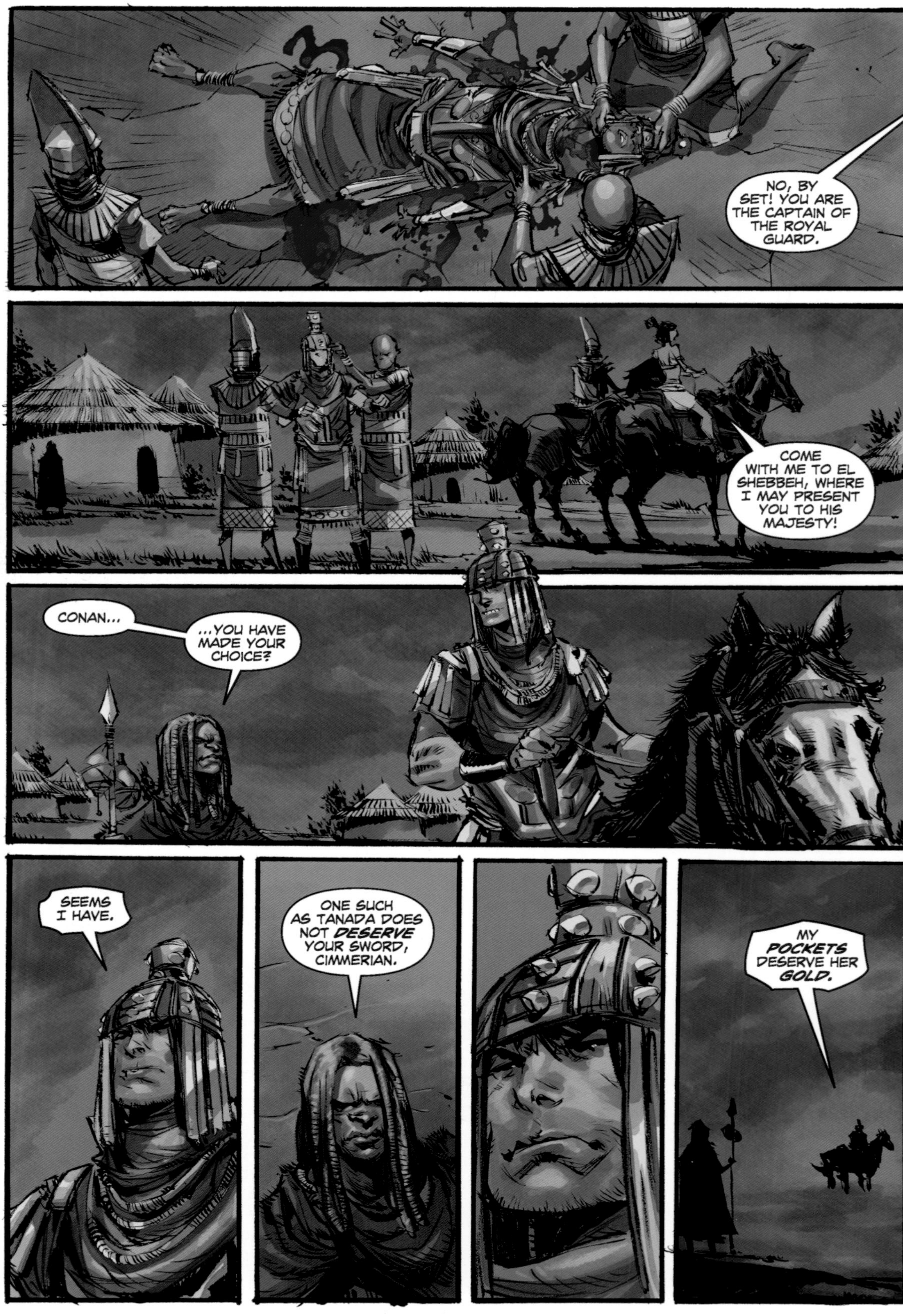
NO, BY SET! YOU ARE THE CAPTAIN OF THE ROYAL GUARD.
COME WITH ME TO EL SHEBBEH, WHERE I MAY PRESENT YOU TO HIS MAJESTY!
CONAN...
...YOU HAVE MADE YOUR CHOICE?
SEEMS I HAVE.
ONE SUCH AS TANADA DOES NOT *DESERVE* YOUR SWORD, CIMMERIAN.
MY *POCKETS* DESERVE HER *GOLD*.

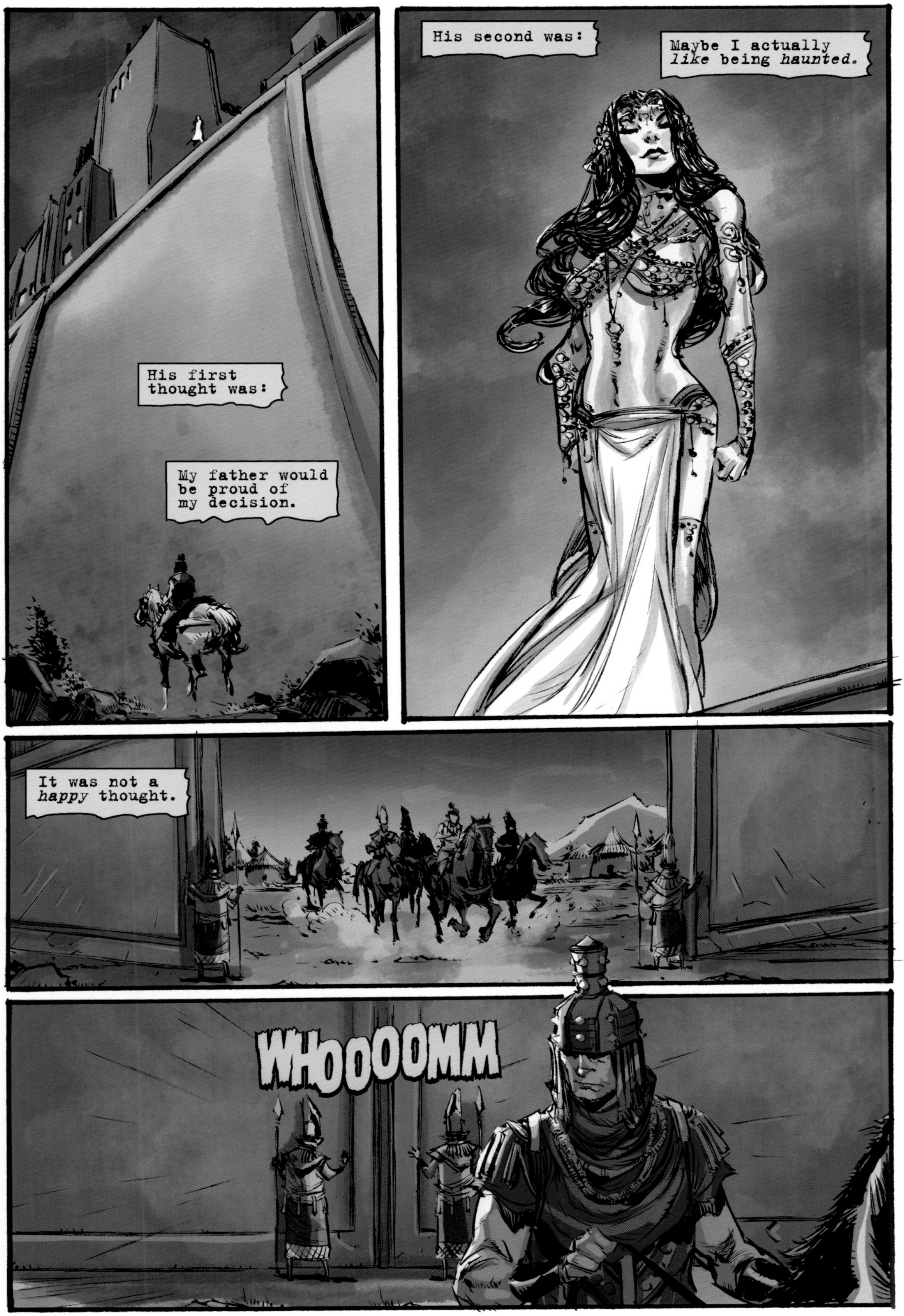
His first thought was:
My father would be proud of my decision.
His second was:
Maybe I actually *like* being *haunted.*
It was not a *happy* thought.
WHOOOOMM

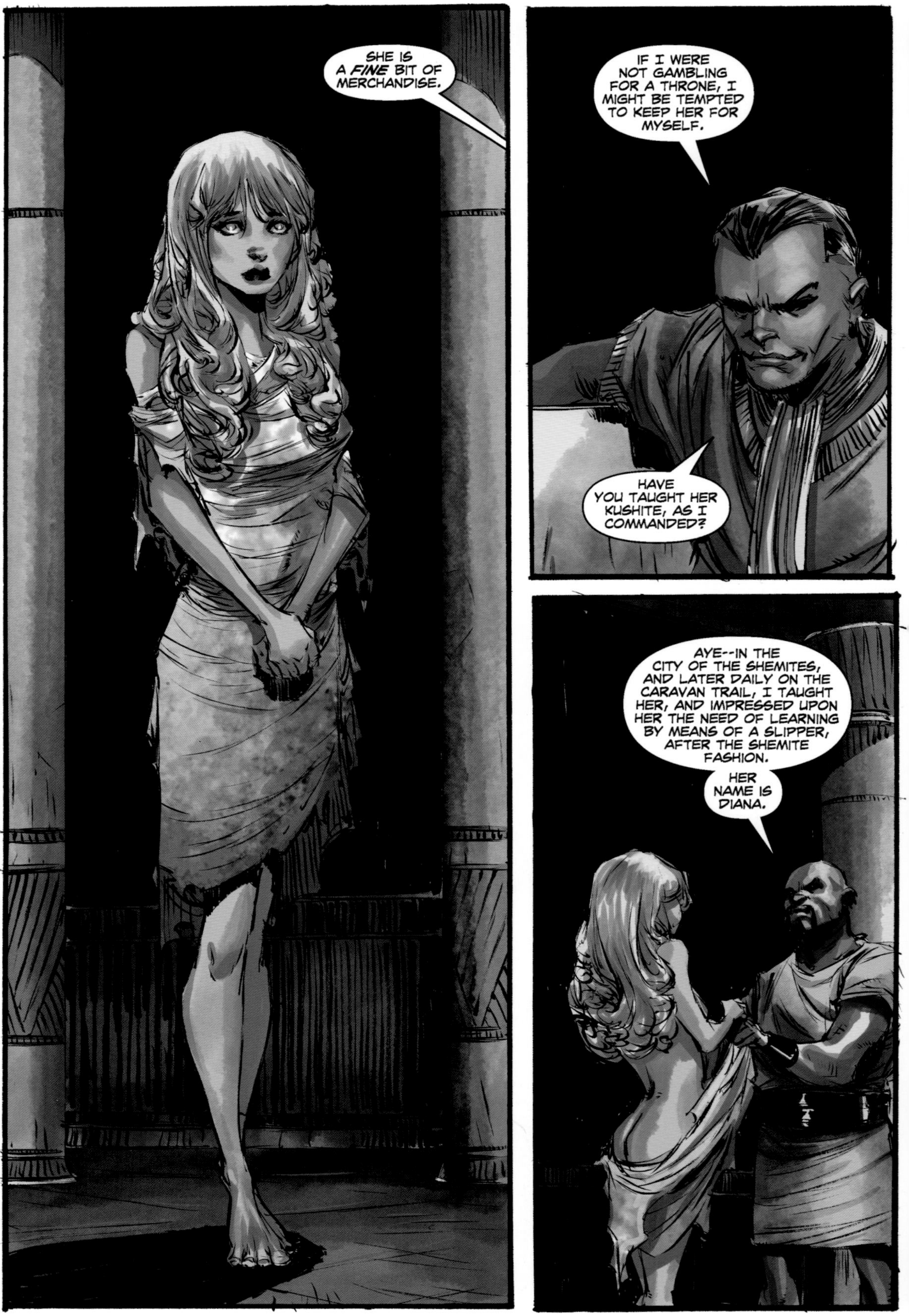
SHE IS A *FINE* BIT OF MERCHANDISE.
IF I WERE NOT GAMBLING FOR A THRONE, I MIGHT BE TEMPTED TO KEEP HER FOR MYSELF.
HAVE YOU TAUGHT HER KUSHITE, AS I COMMANDED?
AYE--IN THE CITY OF THE SHEMITES, AND LATER DAILY ON THE CARAVAN TRAIL, I TAUGHT HER, AND IMPRESSED UPON HER THE NEED OF LEARNING BY MEANS OF A SLIPPER, AFTER THE SHEMITE FASHION.
HER NAME IS DIANA.

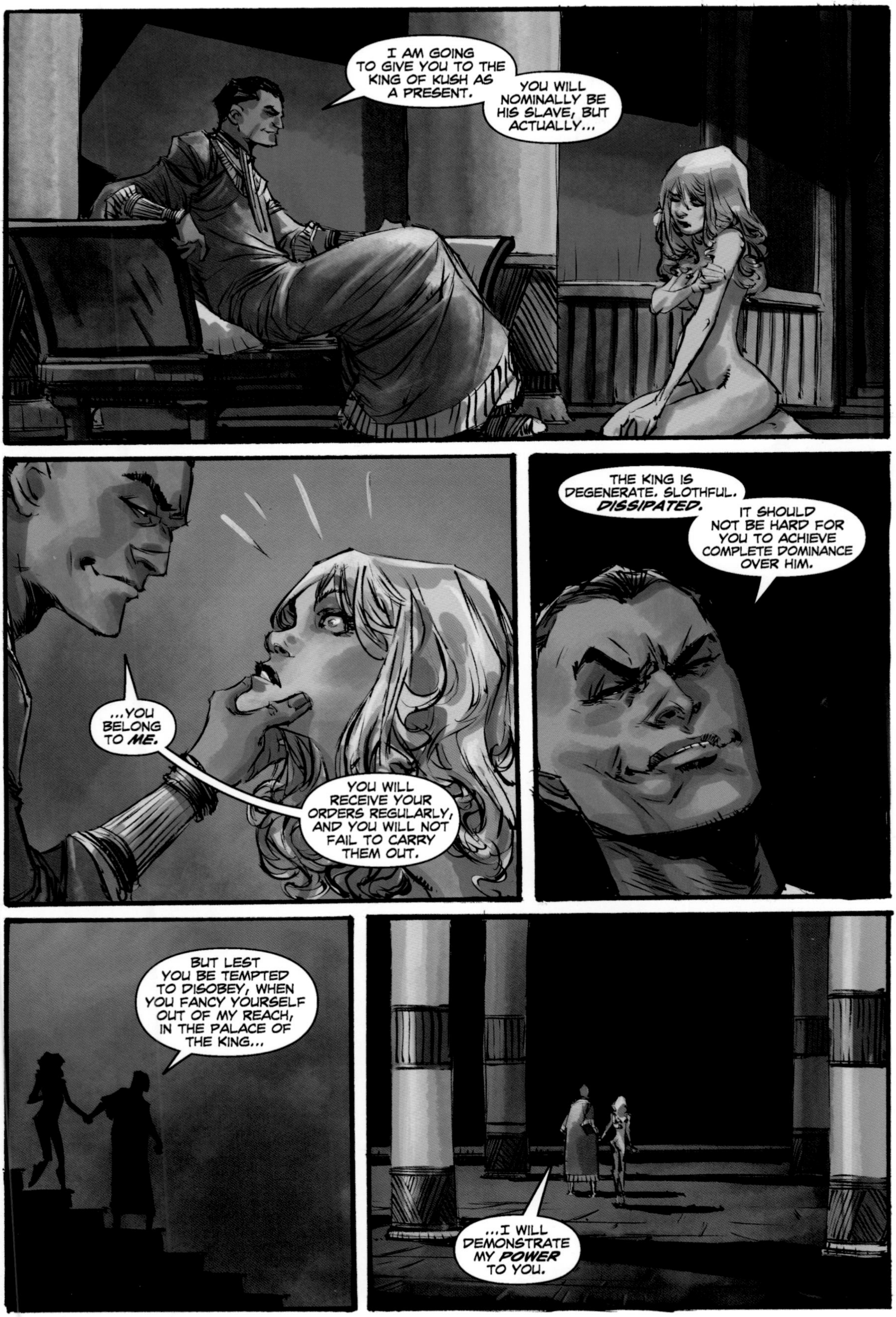
I AM GOING TO GIVE YOU TO THE KING OF KUSH AS A PRESENT.
YOU WILL NOMINALLY BE HIS SLAVE, BUT ACTUALLY...
...YOU BELONG TO *ME.*
YOU WILL RECEIVE YOUR ORDERS REGULARLY, AND YOU WILL NOT FAIL TO CARRY THEM OUT.
THE KING IS DEGENERATE. SLOTHFUL. *DISSIPATED.*
IT SHOULD NOT BE HARD FOR YOU TO ACHIEVE COMPLETE DOMINANCE OVER HIM.
BUT LEST YOU BE TEMPTED TO DISOBEY, WHEN YOU FANCY YOURSELF OUT OF MY REACH, IN THE PALACE OF THE KING...
...I WILL DEMONSTRATE MY *POWER* TO YOU.

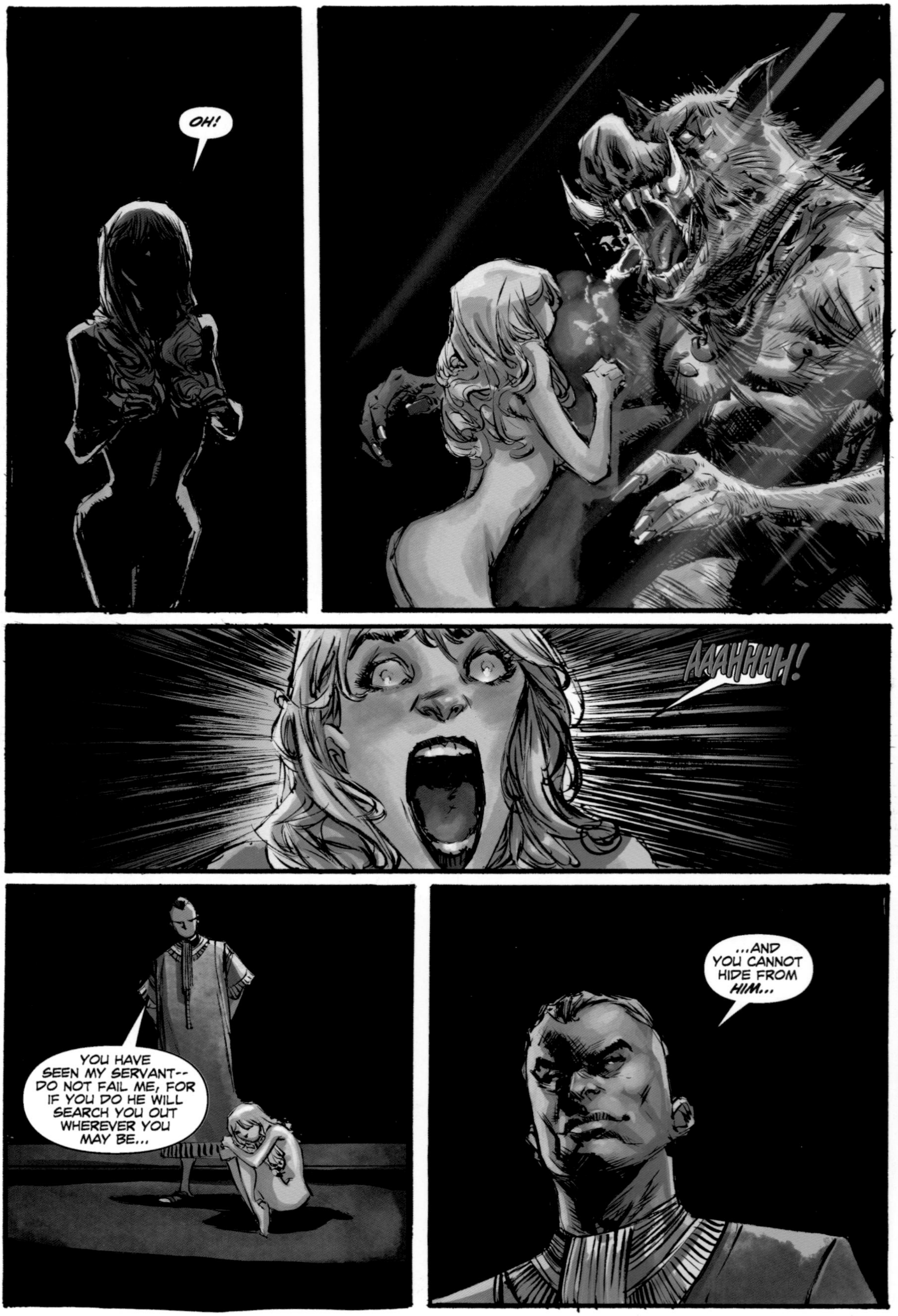
OH!
AAAHHHH!
YOU HAVE SEEN MY SERVANT-- DO NOT FAIL ME, FOR IF YOU DO HE WILL SEARCH YOU OUT WHEREVER YOU MAY BE...
...AND YOU CANNOT HIDE FROM *HIM*...

CHAPTER FOUR

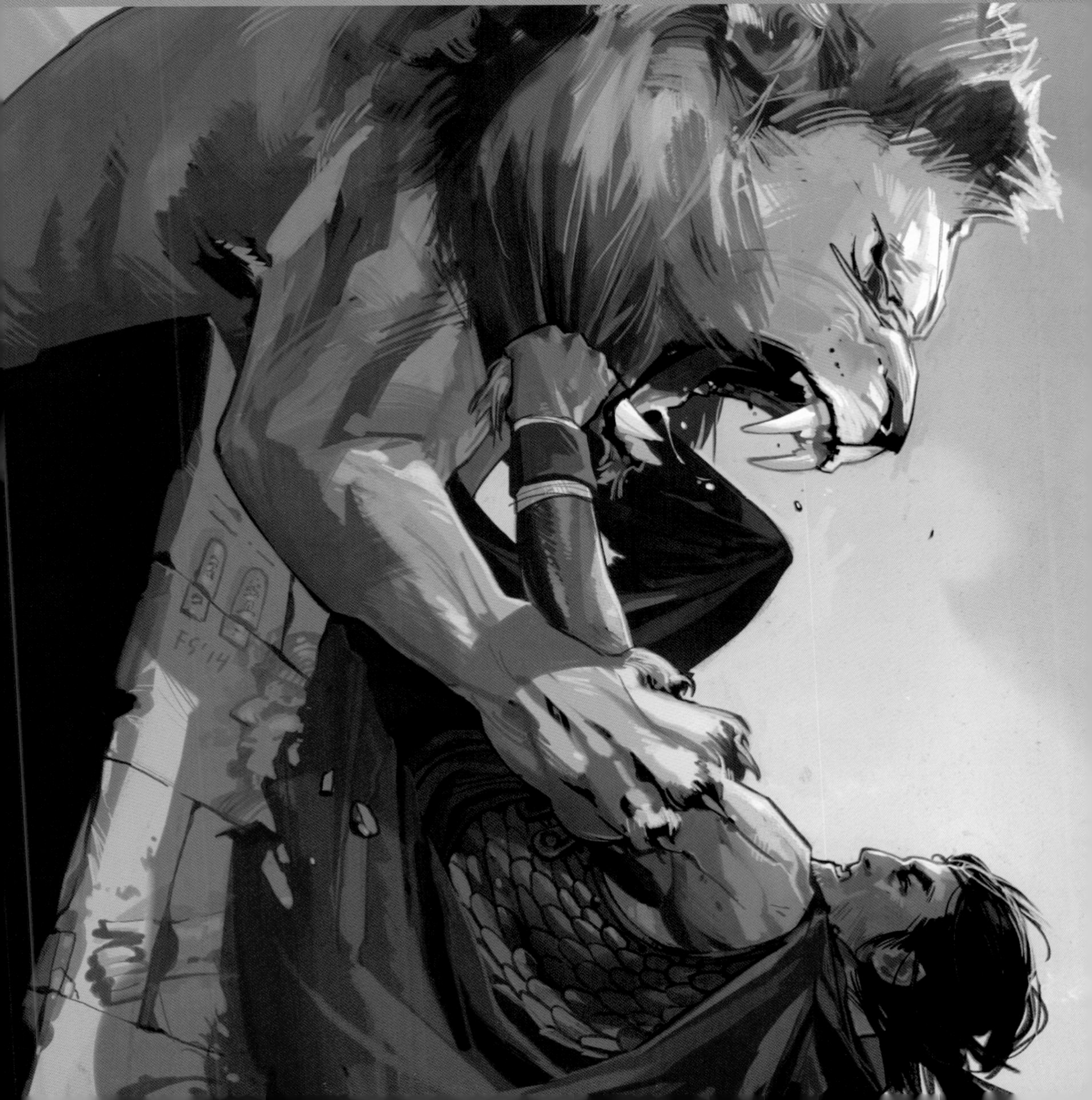

"I am *Cimmerian*. I have no *'honor.'*
'Honor' is the lie *civilized* dogs use to trick themselves
into thinking they are better than *beasts*."

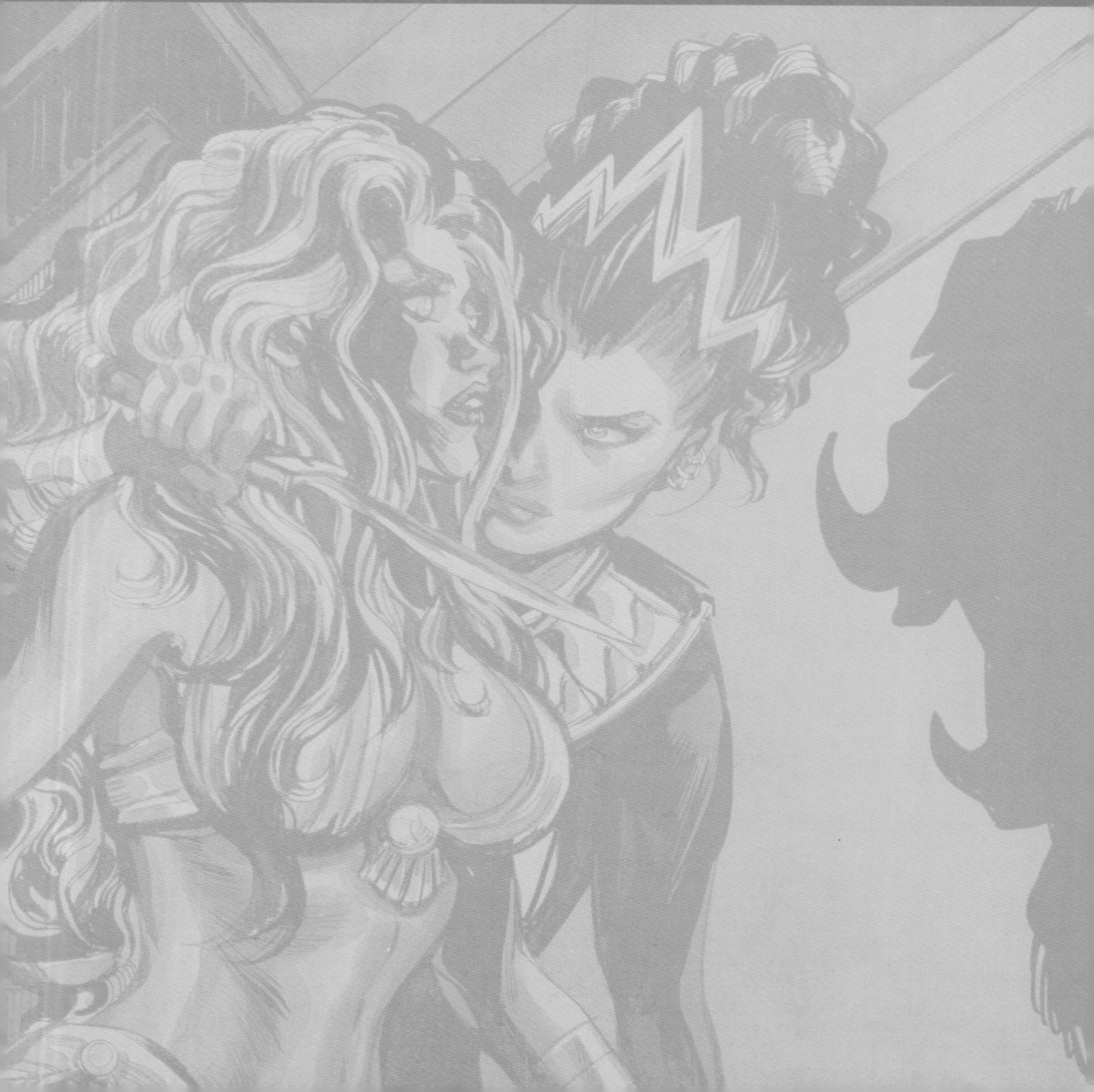

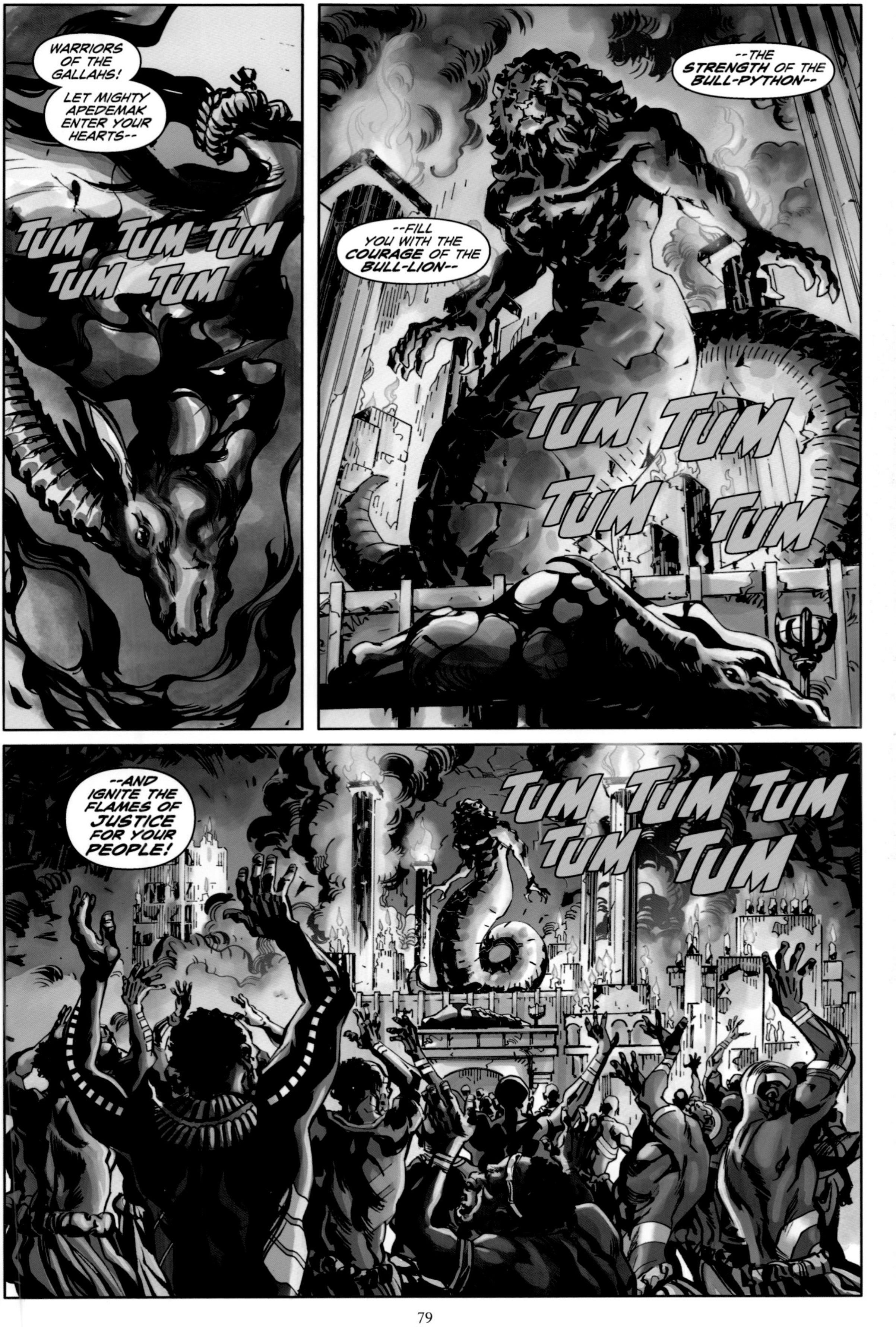
WARRIORS OF THE GALLAHS!
LET MIGHTY APEDEMAK ENTER YOUR HEARTS--
TUM, TUM TUM TUM TUM
--FILL YOU WITH THE COURAGE OF THE BULL-LION--
--THE STRENGTH OF THE BULL-PYTHON--
TUM TUM TUM TUM
--AND IGNITE THE FLAMES OF JUSTICE FOR YOUR PEOPLE!
TUM TUM TUM TUM TUM

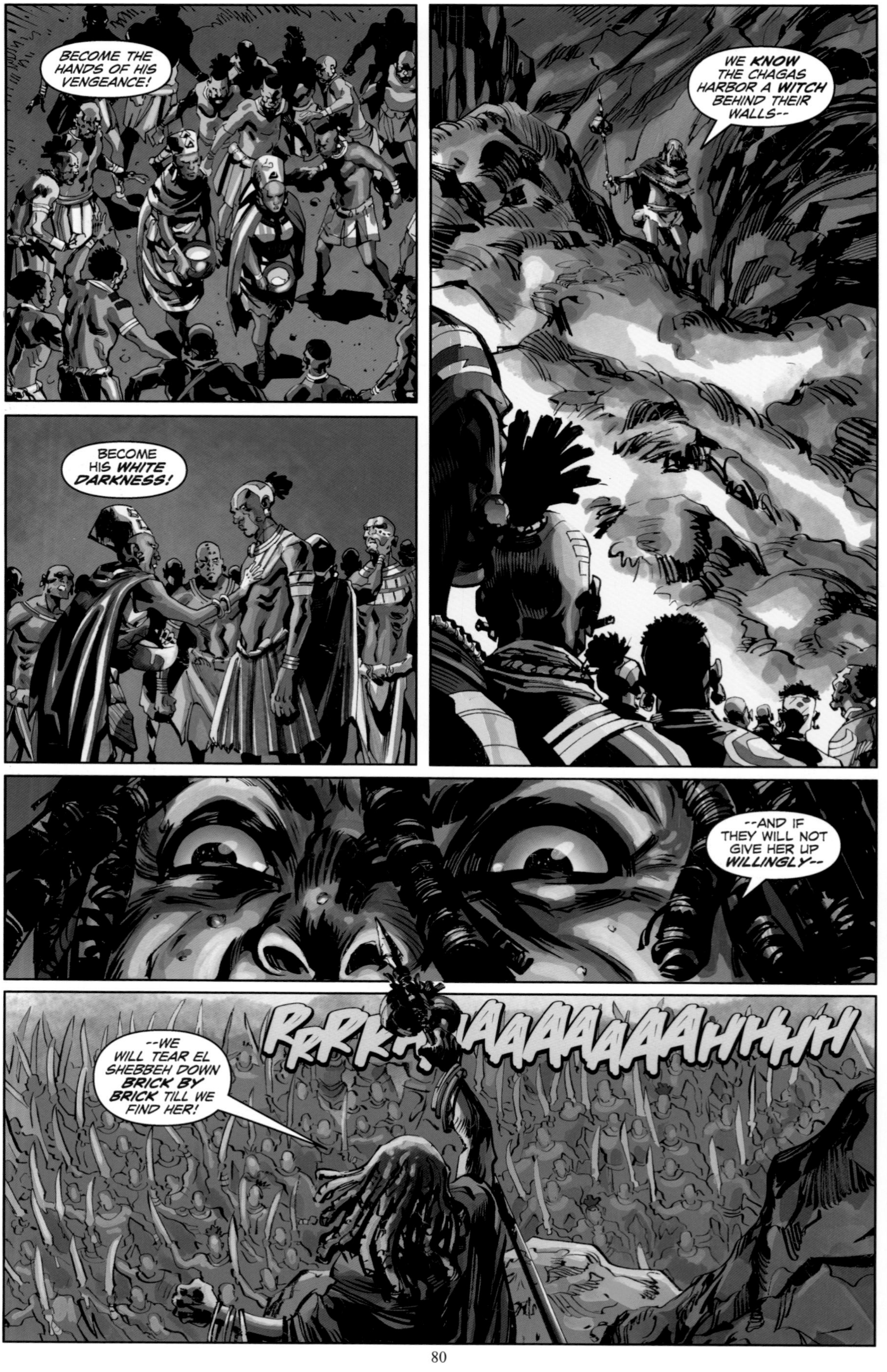
BECOME THE HANDS OF HIS VENGEANCE!
WE KNOW THE CHAGAS HARBOR A WITCH BEHIND THEIR WALLS--
BECOME HIS WHITE DARKNESS!
--AND IF THEY WILL NOT GIVE HER UP WILLINGLY--
--WE WILL TEAR EL SHEBBEH DOWN BRICK BY BRICK TILL WE FIND HER!
RRRRAAAAAAAAAAHHHHH

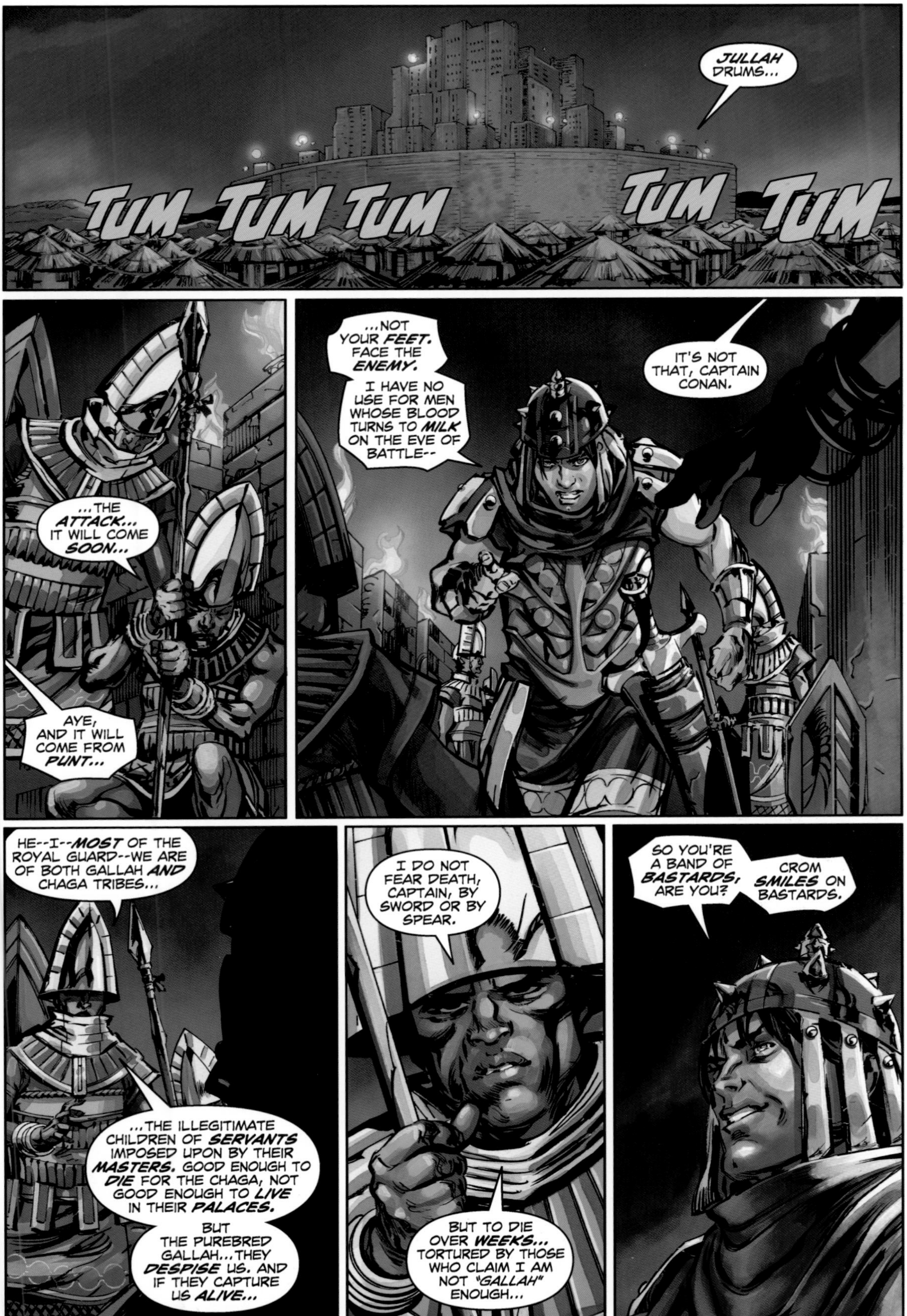
JULLAH DRUMS...
TUM TUM TUM TUM TUM
...THE ATTACK... IT WILL COME SOON...
AYE, AND IT WILL COME FROM PUNT...
...NOT YOUR FEET. FACE THE ENEMY.
I HAVE NO USE FOR MEN WHOSE BLOOD TURNS TO MILK ON THE EVE OF BATTLE--
IT'S NOT THAT, CAPTAIN CONAN.
HE--I--MOST OF THE ROYAL GUARD--WE ARE OF BOTH GALLAH AND CHAGA TRIBES...
...THE ILLEGITIMATE CHILDREN OF SERVANTS IMPOSED UPON BY THEIR MASTERS. GOOD ENOUGH TO DIE FOR THE CHAGA, NOT GOOD ENOUGH TO LIVE IN THEIR PALACES.
BUT THE PUREBRED GALLAH...THEY DESPISE US. AND IF THEY CAPTURE US ALIVE...
I DO NOT FEAR DEATH, CAPTAIN, BY SWORD OR BY SPEAR.
BUT TO DIE OVER WEEKS... TORTURED BY THOSE WHO CLAIM I AM NOT "GALLAH" ENOUGH...
SO YOU'RE A BAND OF BASTARDS, ARE YOU?
CROM SMILES ON BASTARDS.

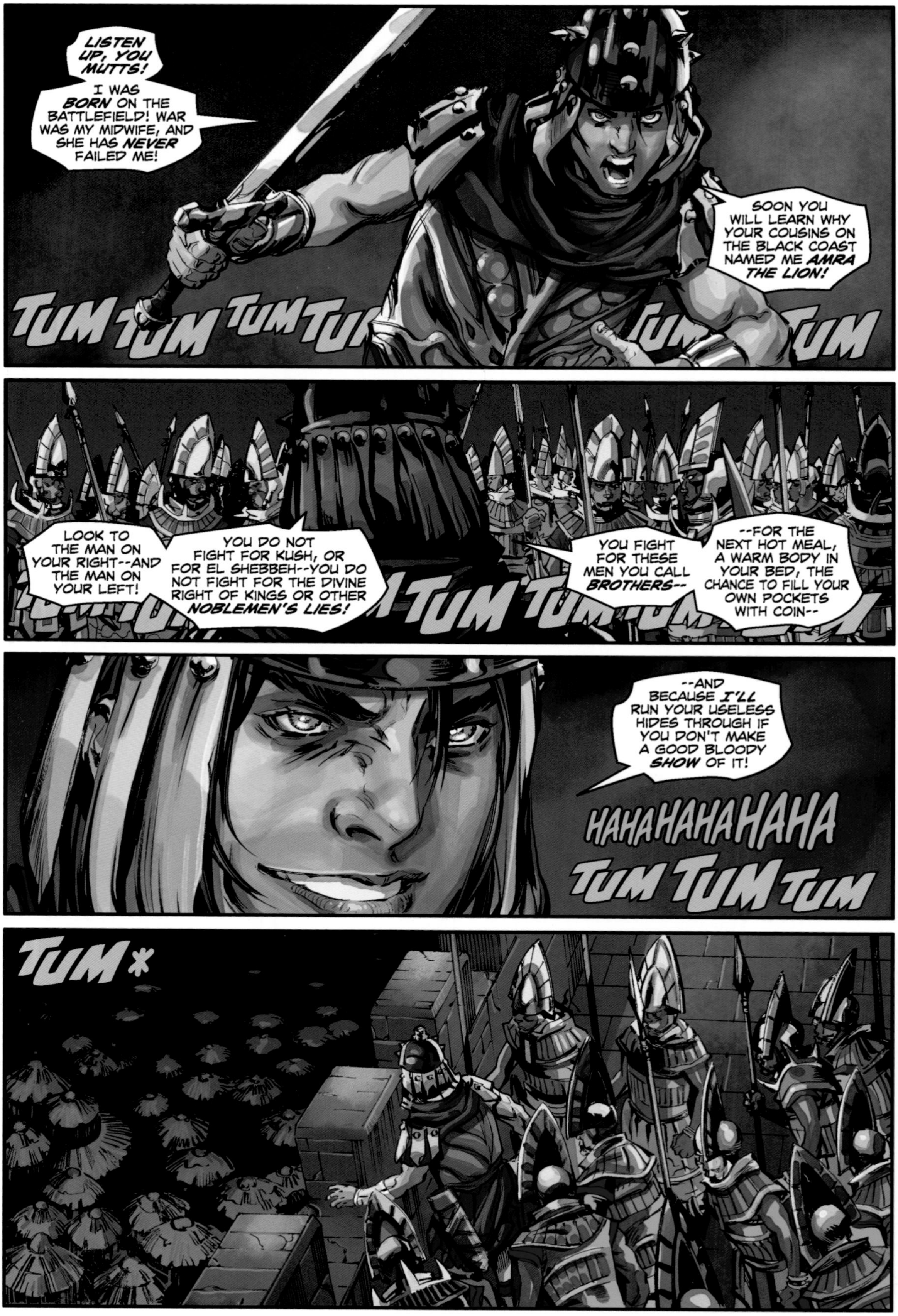
LISTEN UP, YOU MUTTS!
I WAS BORN ON THE BATTLEFIELD! WAR WAS MY MIDWIFE, AND SHE HAS NEVER FAILED ME!
SOON YOU WILL LEARN WHY YOUR COUSINS ON THE BLACK COAST NAMED ME AMRA THE LION!
TUM TUM TUM TUM TUM
LOOK TO THE MAN ON YOUR RIGHT--AND THE MAN ON YOUR LEFT!
YOU DO NOT FIGHT FOR KUSH, OR FOR EL SHEBBEH--YOU DO NOT FIGHT FOR THE DIVINE RIGHT OF KINGS OR OTHER NOBLEMEN'S LIES!
YOU FIGHT FOR THESE MEN YOU CALL BROTHERS--
--FOR THE NEXT HOT MEAL, A WARM BODY IN YOUR BED, THE CHANCE TO FILL YOUR OWN POCKETS WITH COIN--
TUM TUM
--AND BECAUSE I'LL RUN YOUR USELESS HIDES THROUGH IF YOU DON'T MAKE A GOOD BLOODY SHOW OF IT!
HAHAHAHAHAHA
TUM TUM TUM
TUM*

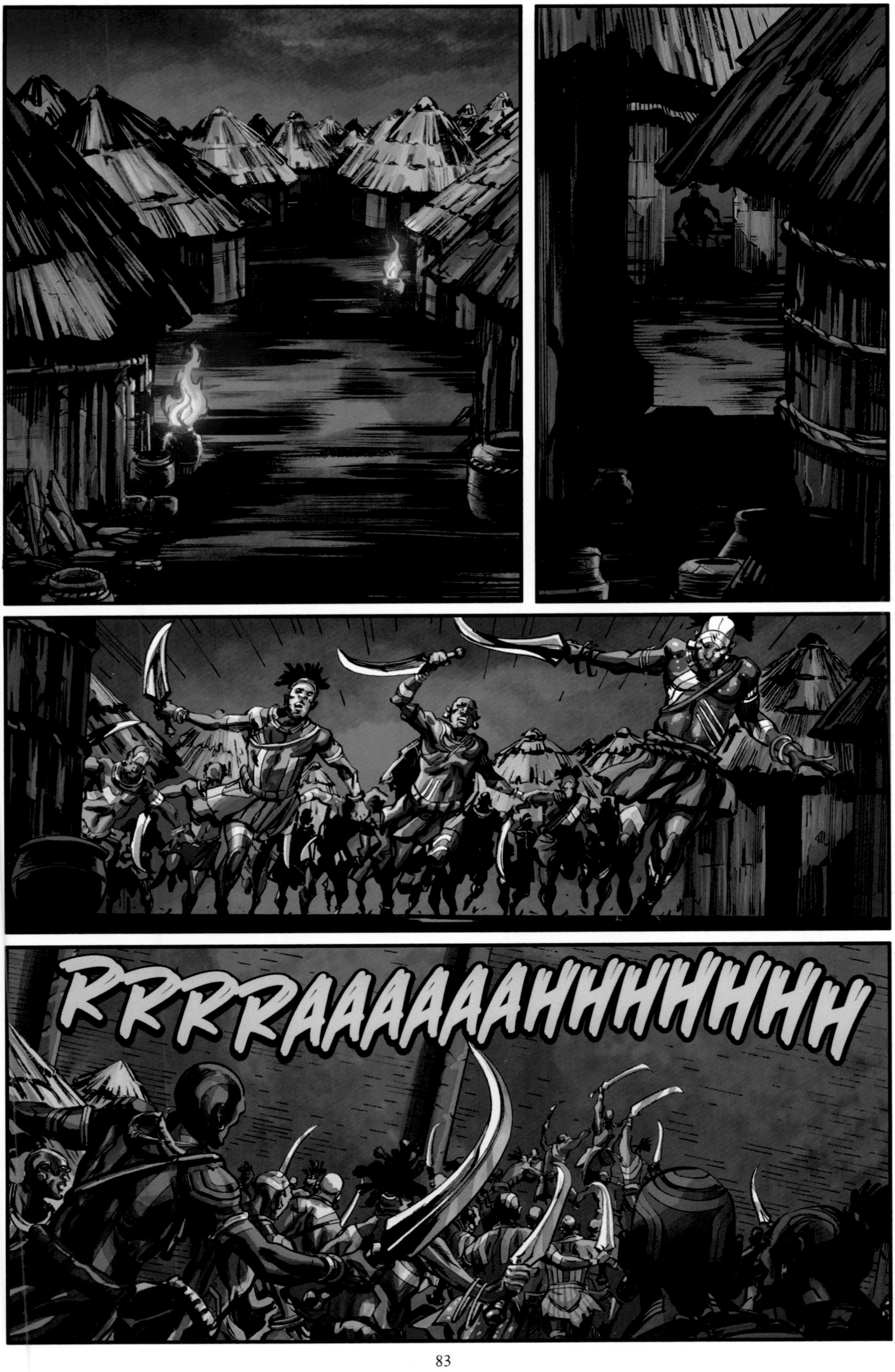
RRRRAAAAAAHHHHHHHH

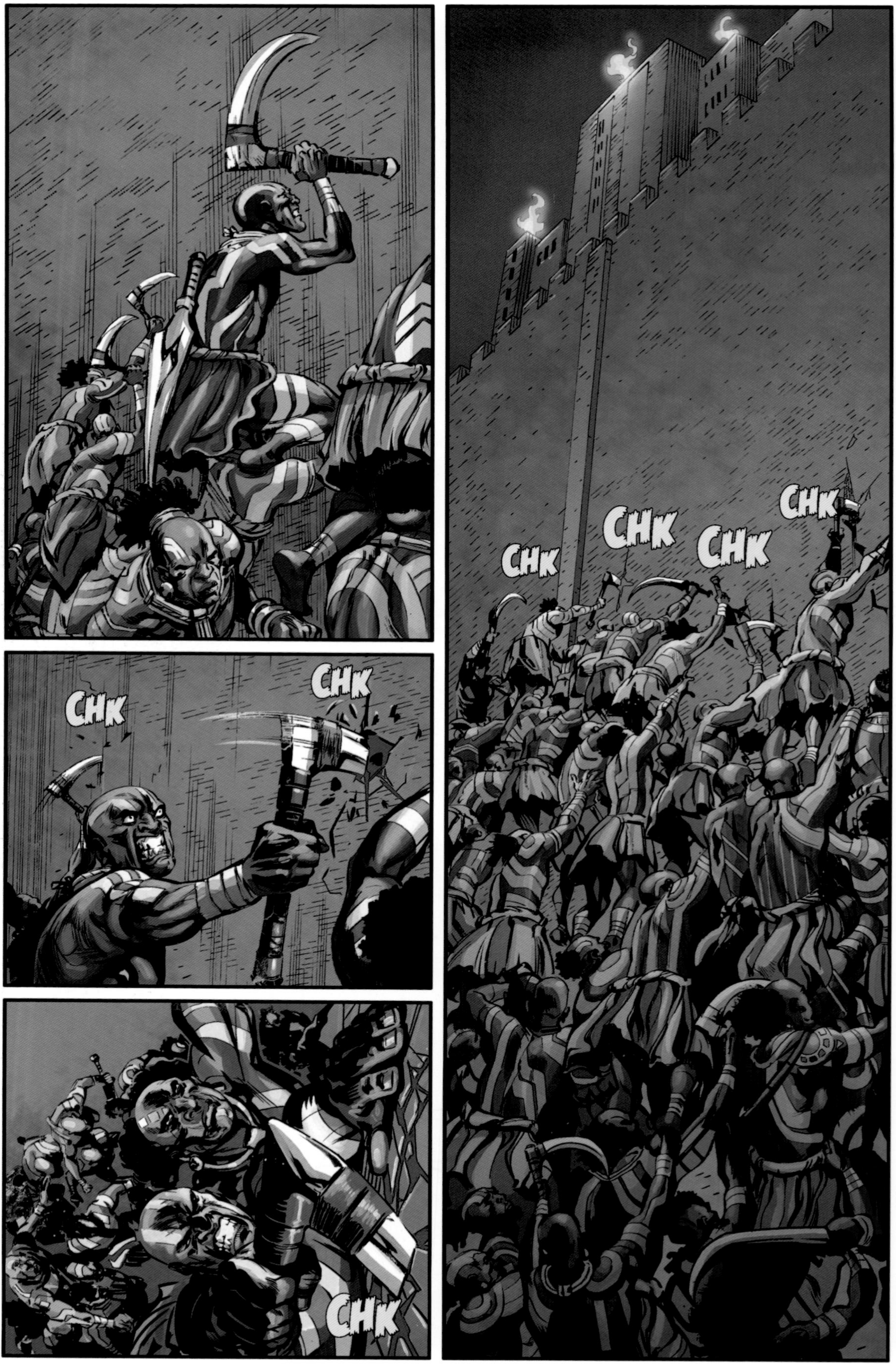
CHK
CHK
CHK
CHK
CHK
CHK
CHK

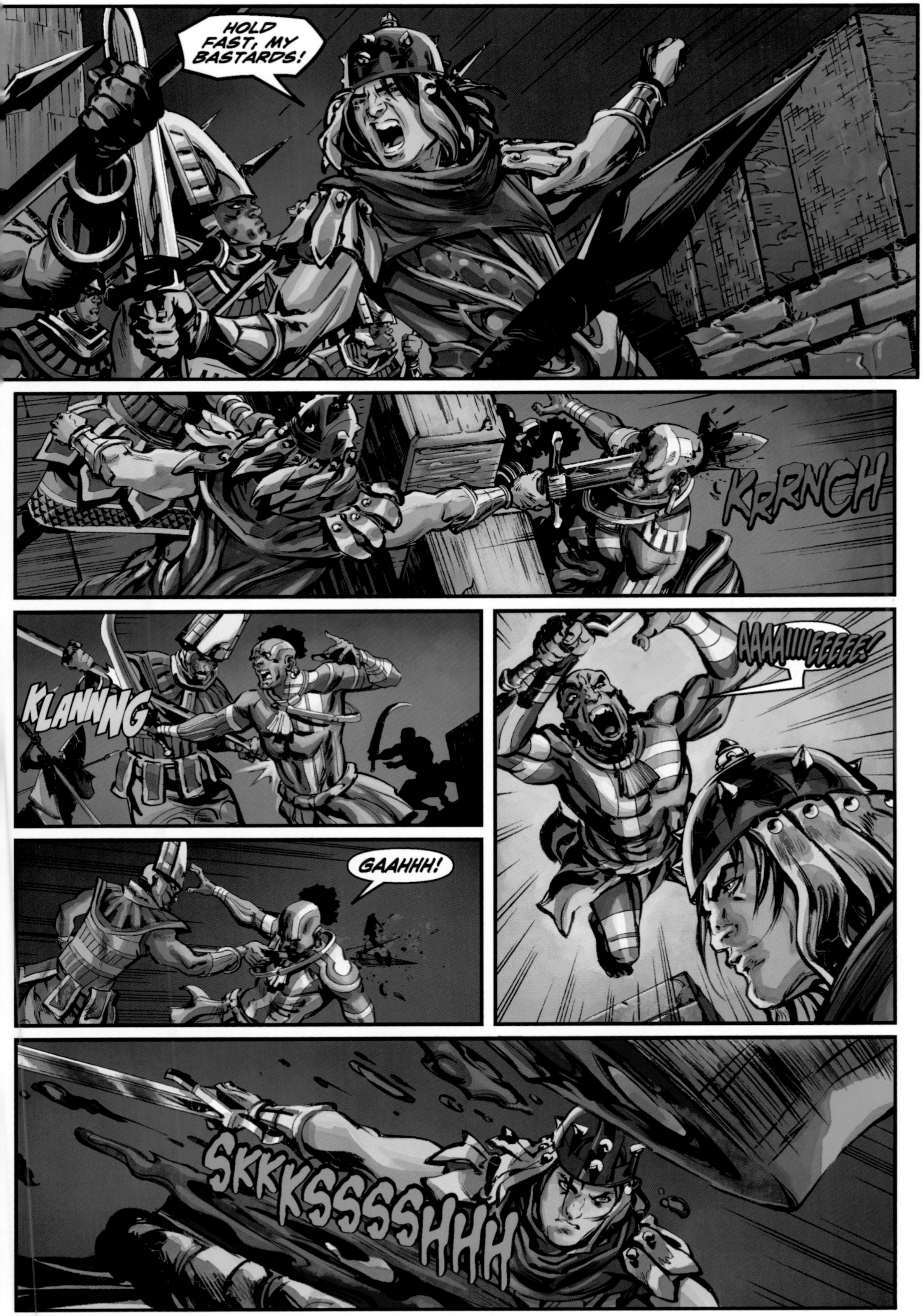
HOLD FAST, MY BASTARDS!
KRRNCH
KLANNNG
GAAHHH!
AAAAIIIIEEEEE!
SKKKSSSSSHHH

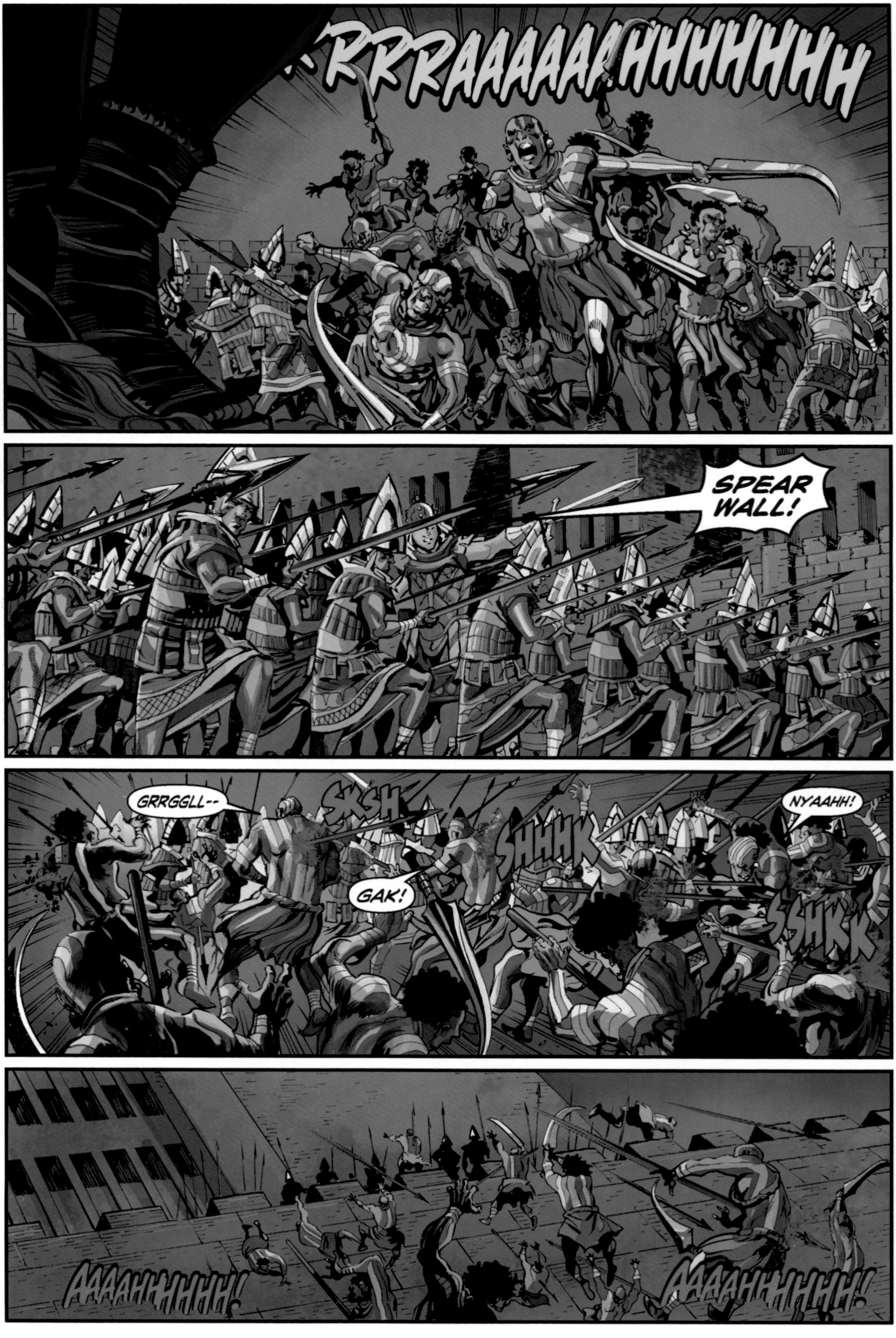
RRRAAAAAAHHHHHHHH
SPEAR WALL!
GRRGGLL--
SKSH
SHHK
GAK!
NYAAHH!
SHKK
AAAAHHHHHH!
AAAAHHHHHHH!

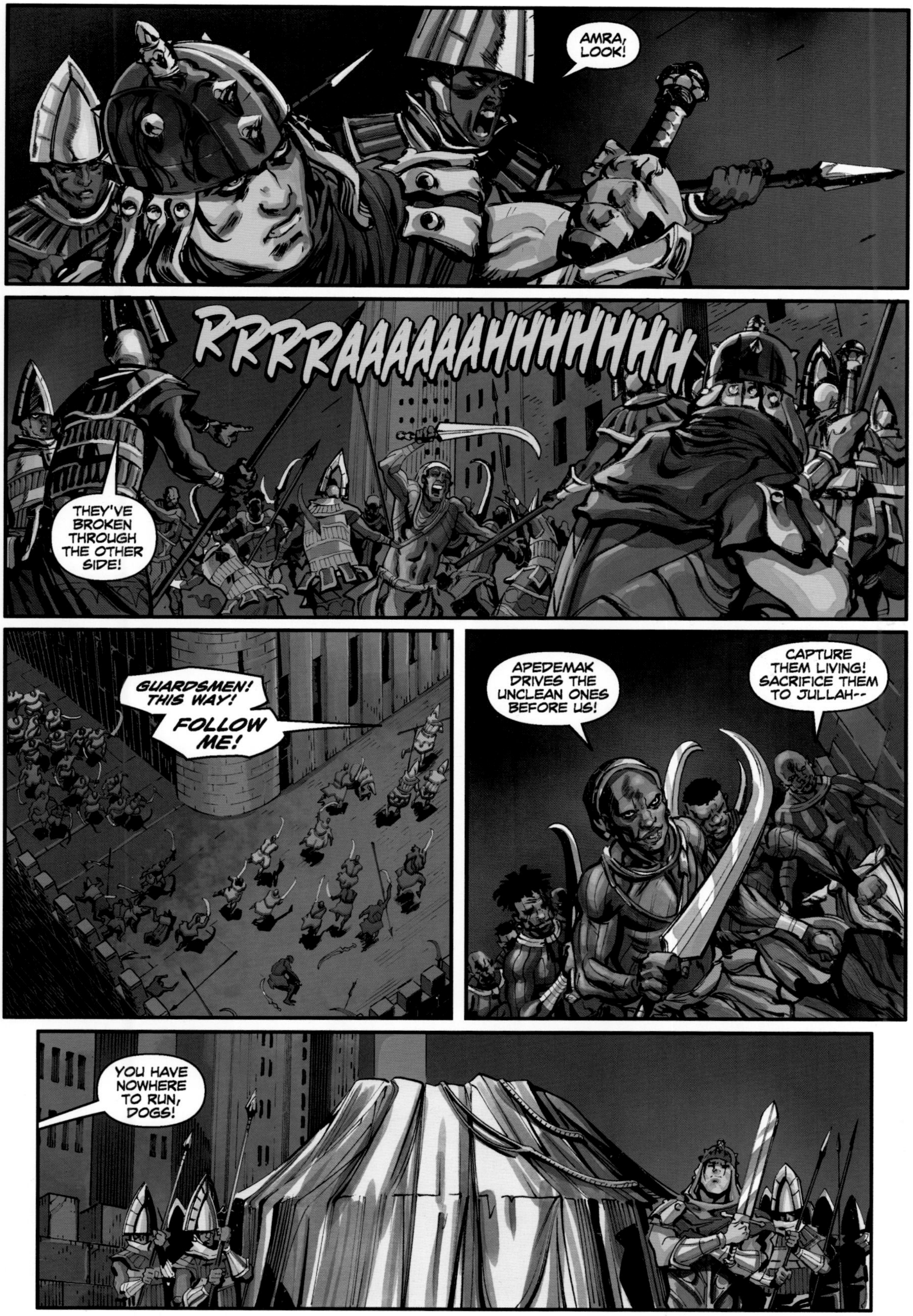
AMRA, LOOK!
RRRRAAAAAAHHHHHHH
THEY'VE BROKEN THROUGH THE OTHER SIDE!
GUARDSMEN! THIS WAY!
FOLLOW ME!
APEDEMAK DRIVES THE UNCLEAN ONES BEFORE US!
CAPTURE THEM LIVING! SACRIFICE THEM TO JULLAH--
YOU HAVE NOWHERE TO RUN, DOGS!

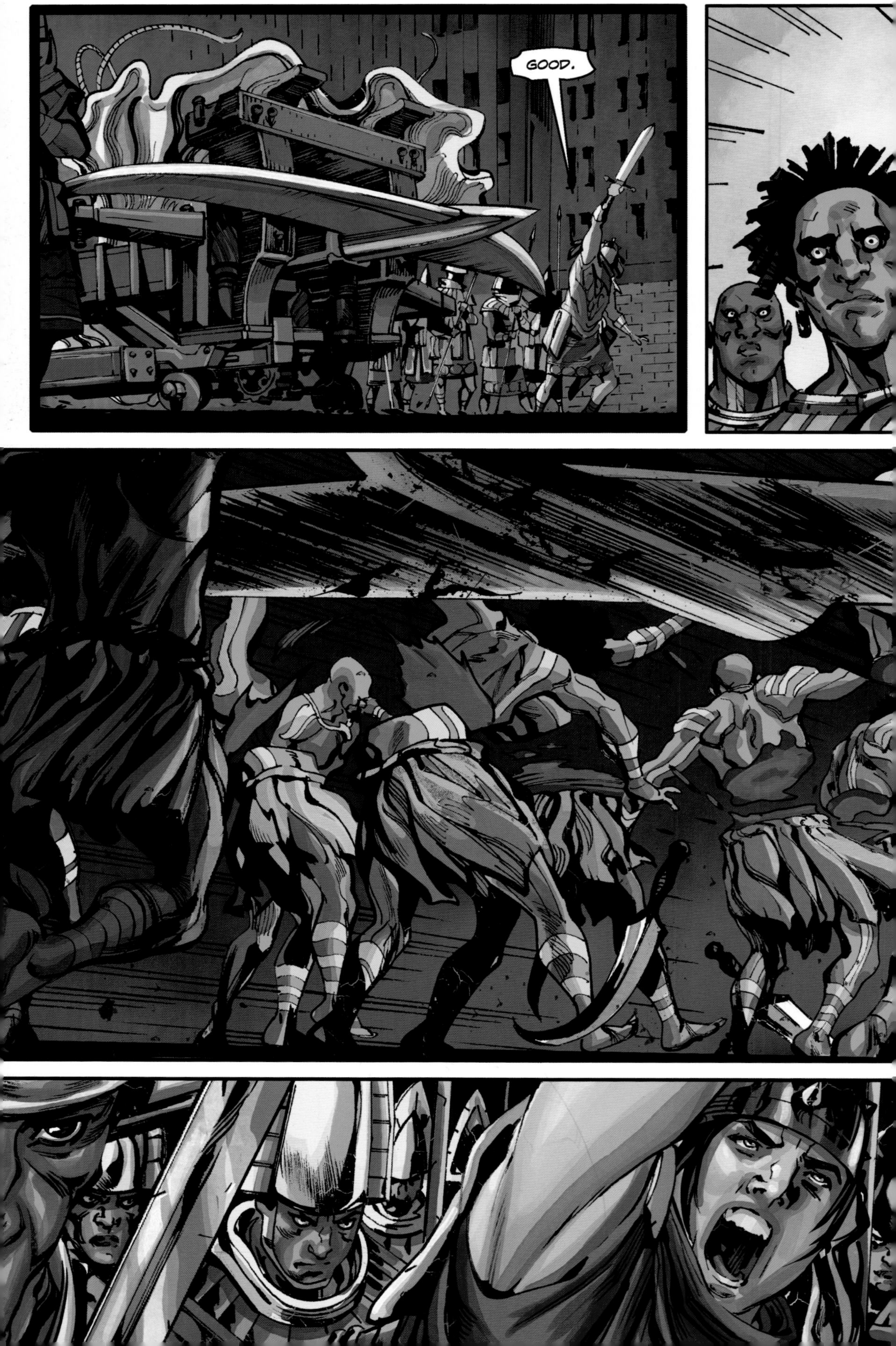
GOOD.

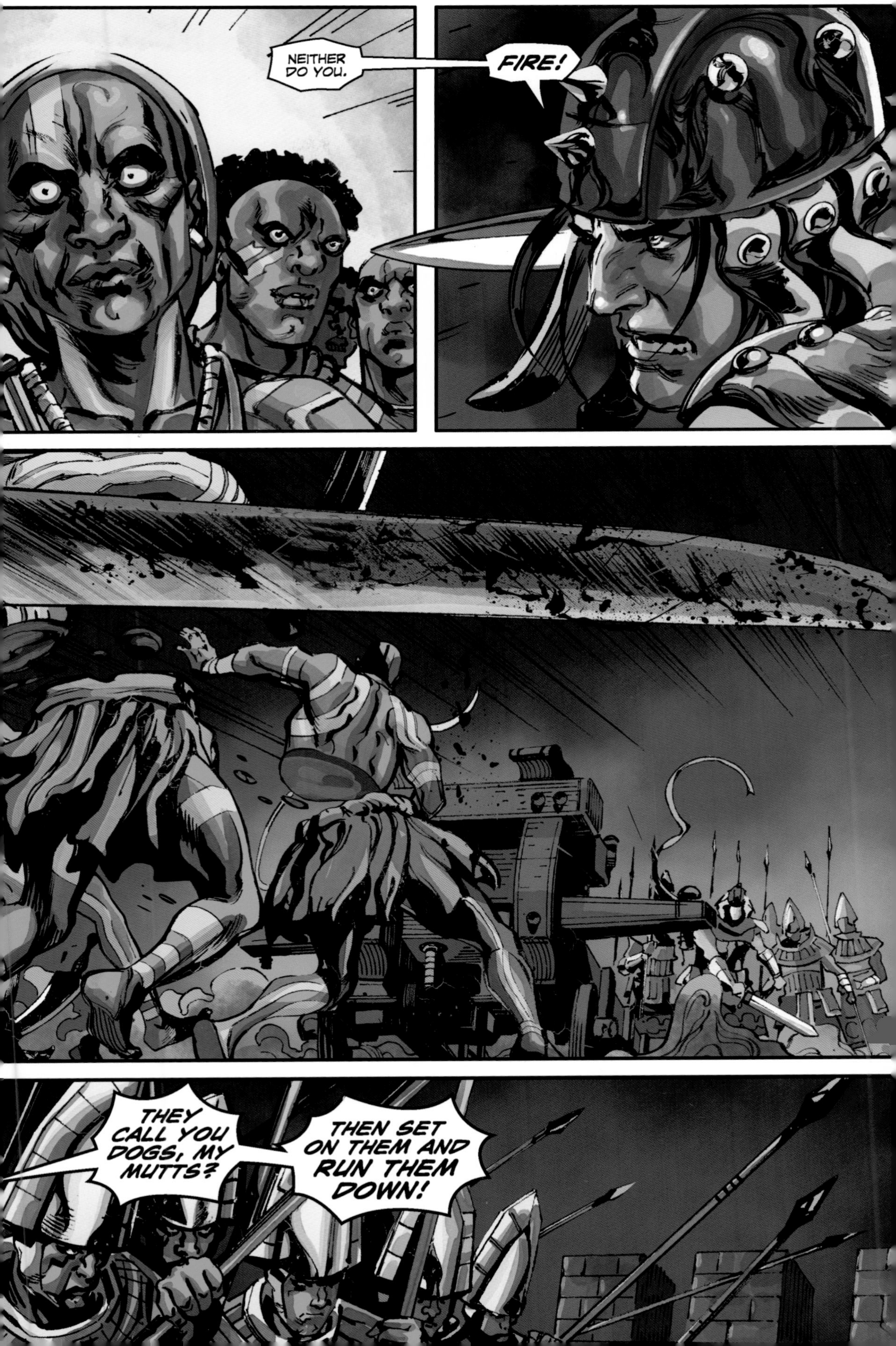
NEITHER DO YOU.
FIRE!
THEY CALL YOU DOGS, MY MUTTS?
THEN SET ON THEM AND RUN THEM DOWN!

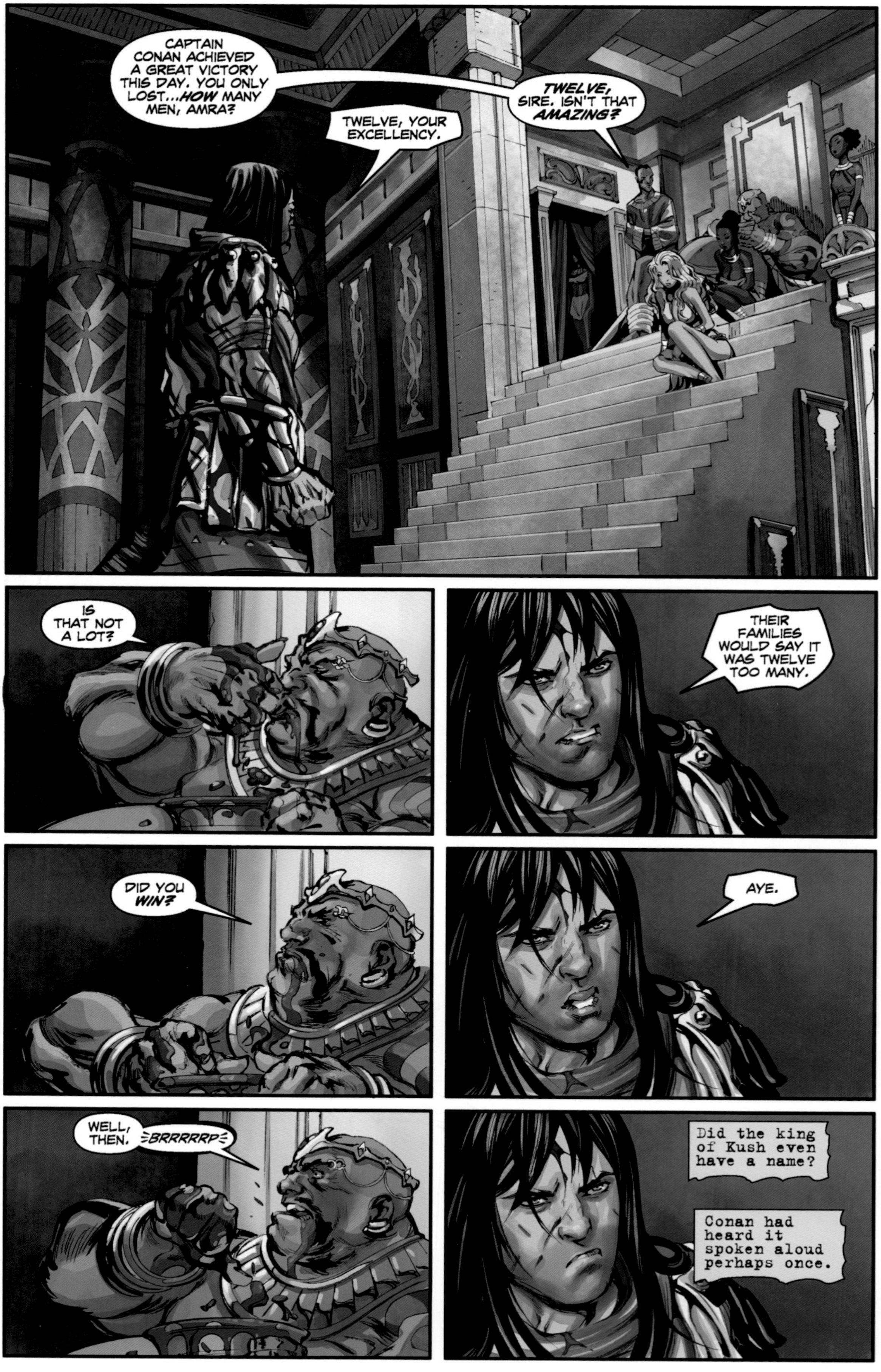

CAPTAIN CONAN ACHIEVED A GREAT VICTORY THIS DAY. YOU ONLY LOST...HOW MANY MEN, AMRA?
TWELVE, YOUR EXCELLENCY.
TWELVE, SIRE. ISN'T THAT AMAZING?
IS THAT NOT A LOT?
THEIR FAMILIES WOULD SAY IT WAS TWELVE TOO MANY.
DID YOU WIN?
AYE.
WELL, THEN.
BRRRRRP
Did the king of Kush even have a name?
Conan had heard it spoken aloud perhaps once.

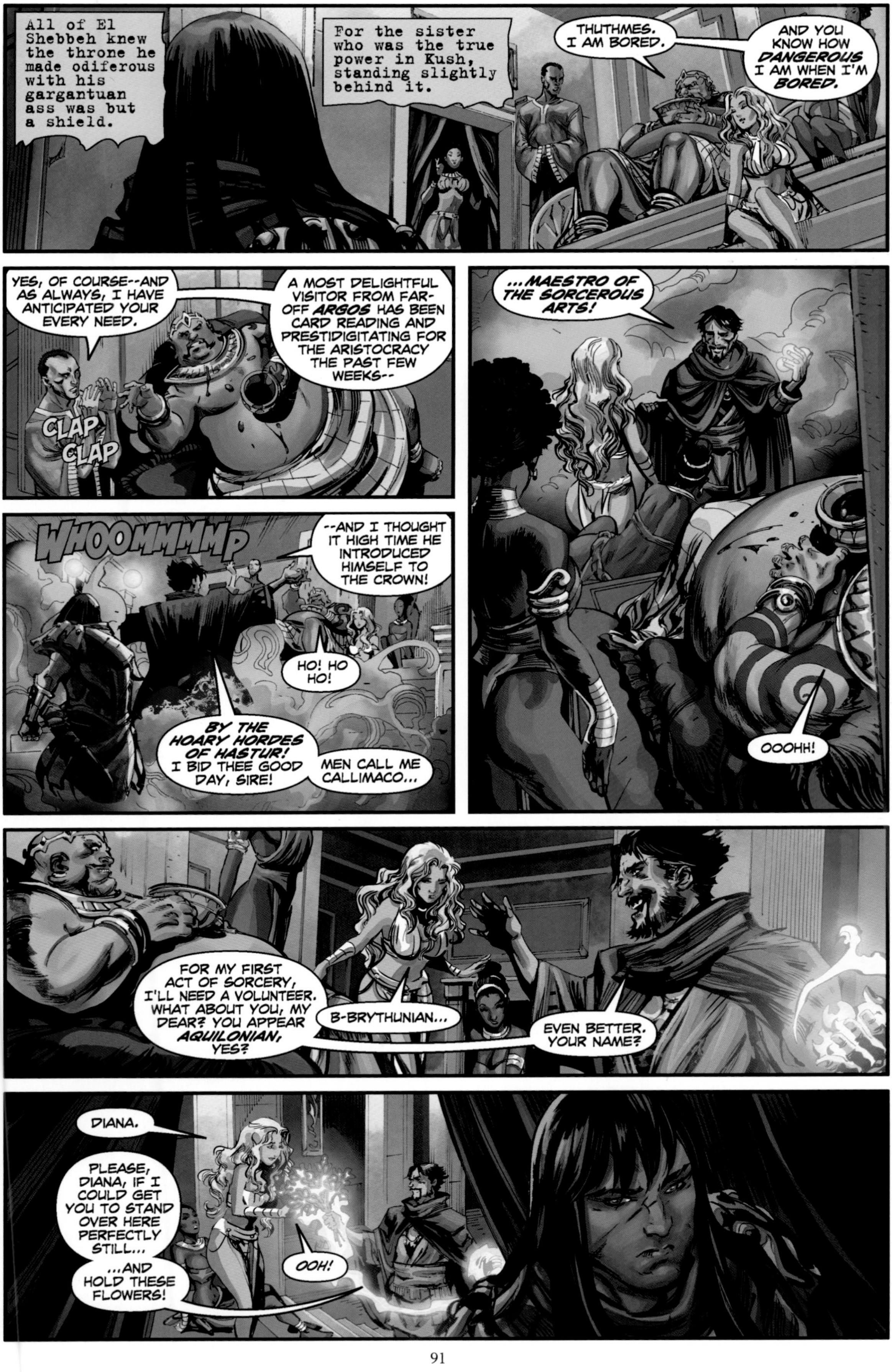
All of El Shebbeh knew the throne he made odiferous with his gargantuan ass was but a shield.
For the sister who was the true power in Kush, standing slightly behind it.
THUTHMES. I AM BORED.
AND YOU KNOW HOW DANGEROUS I AM WHEN I'M BORED.
YES, OF COURSE--AND AS ALWAYS, I HAVE ANTICIPATED YOUR EVERY NEED.
A MOST DELIGHTFUL VISITOR FROM FAR-OFF ARGOS HAS BEEN CARD READING AND PRESTIDIGITATING FOR THE ARISTOCRACY THE PAST FEW WEEKS--
CLAP CLAP
WHOOMMMMP
--AND I THOUGHT IT HIGH TIME HE INTRODUCED HIMSELF TO THE CROWN!
HO! HO HO!
BY THE HOARY HORDES OF HASTUR! I BID THEE GOOD DAY, SIRE!
MEN CALL ME CALLIMACO...
...MAESTRO OF THE SORCEROUS ARTS!
OOOHH!
FOR MY FIRST ACT OF SORCERY, I'LL NEED A VOLUNTEER. WHAT ABOUT YOU, MY DEAR? YOU APPEAR AQUILONIAN, YES?
B-BRYTHUNIAN...
EVEN BETTER. YOUR NAME?
DIANA.
PLEASE, DIANA, IF I COULD GET YOU TO STAND OVER HERE PERFECTLY STILL...
...AND HOLD THESE FLOWERS!
OOH!

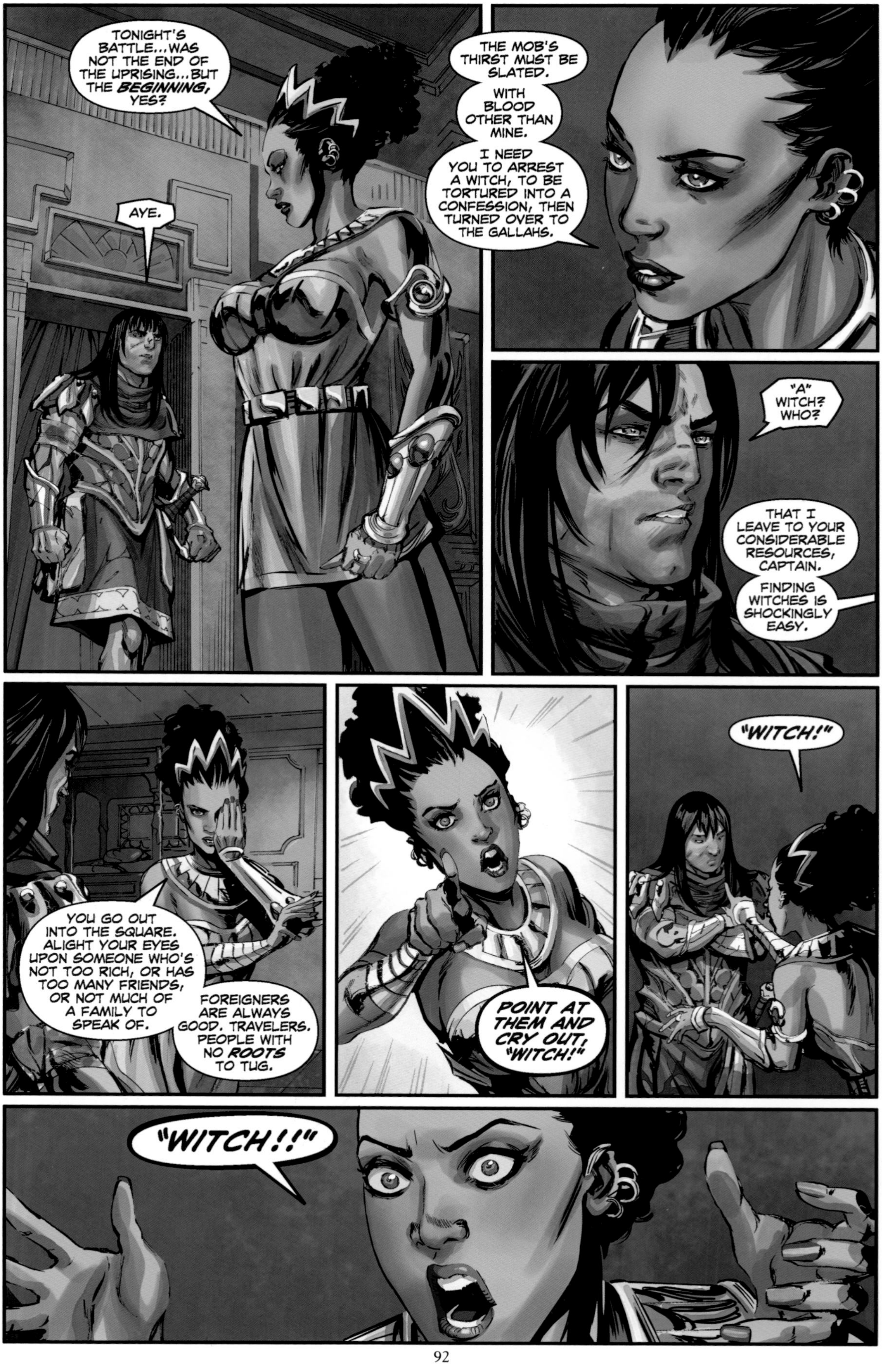
TONIGHT'S BATTLE...WAS NOT THE END OF THE UPRISING...BUT THE *BEGINNING,* YES?
AYE.
THE MOB'S THIRST MUST BE SLATED.
WITH BLOOD OTHER THAN MINE.
I NEED YOU TO ARREST A WITCH, TO BE TORTURED INTO A CONFESSION, THEN TURNED OVER TO THE GALLAHS.
"A" WITCH? WHO?
THAT I LEAVE TO YOUR CONSIDERABLE RESOURCES, CAPTAIN.
FINDING WITCHES IS SHOCKINGLY EASY.
YOU GO OUT INTO THE SQUARE. ALIGHT YOUR EYES UPON SOMEONE WHO'S NOT TOO RICH, OR HAS TOO MANY FRIENDS, OR NOT MUCH OF A FAMILY TO SPEAK OF.
FOREIGNERS ARE ALWAYS GOOD. TRAVELERS. PEOPLE WITH NO *ROOTS* TO TUG.
POINT AT THEM AND CRY OUT, "WITCH!"
"WITCH!"
"WITCH!!"

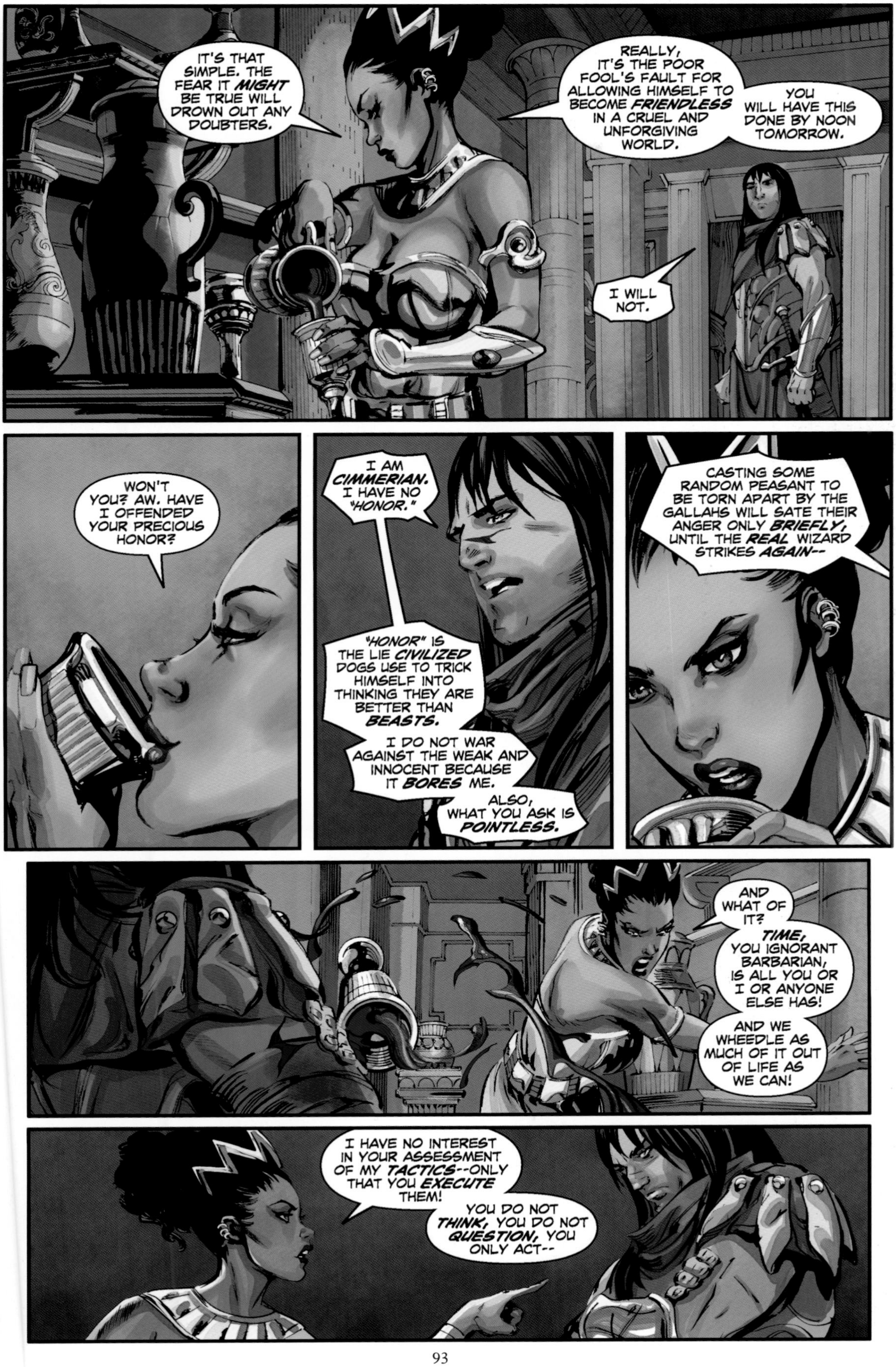
IT'S THAT SIMPLE. THE FEAR IT MIGHT BE TRUE WILL DROWN OUT ANY DOUBTERS.
REALLY, IT'S THE POOR FOOL'S FAULT FOR ALLOWING HIMSELF TO BECOME FRIENDLESS IN A CRUEL AND UNFORGIVING WORLD.
YOU WILL HAVE THIS DONE BY NOON TOMORROW.
I WILL NOT.
WON'T YOU? AW. HAVE I OFFENDED YOUR PRECIOUS HONOR?
I AM CIMMERIAN. I HAVE NO "HONOR."
"HONOR" IS THE LIE CIVILIZED DOGS USE TO TRICK HIMSELF INTO THINKING THEY ARE BETTER THAN BEASTS.
I DO NOT WAR AGAINST THE WEAK AND INNOCENT BECAUSE IT BORES ME.
ALSO, WHAT YOU ASK IS POINTLESS.
CASTING SOME RANDOM PEASANT TO BE TORN APART BY THE GALLAHS WILL SATE THEIR ANGER ONLY BRIEFLY, UNTIL THE REAL WIZARD STRIKES AGAIN--
AND WHAT OF IT? TIME, YOU IGNORANT BARBARIAN, IS ALL YOU OR I OR ANYONE ELSE HAS!
AND WE WHEEDLE AS MUCH OF IT OUT OF LIFE AS WE CAN!
I HAVE NO INTEREST IN YOUR ASSESSMENT OF MY TACTICS--ONLY THAT YOU EXECUTE THEM!
YOU DO NOT THINK, YOU DO NOT QUESTION, YOU ONLY ACT--

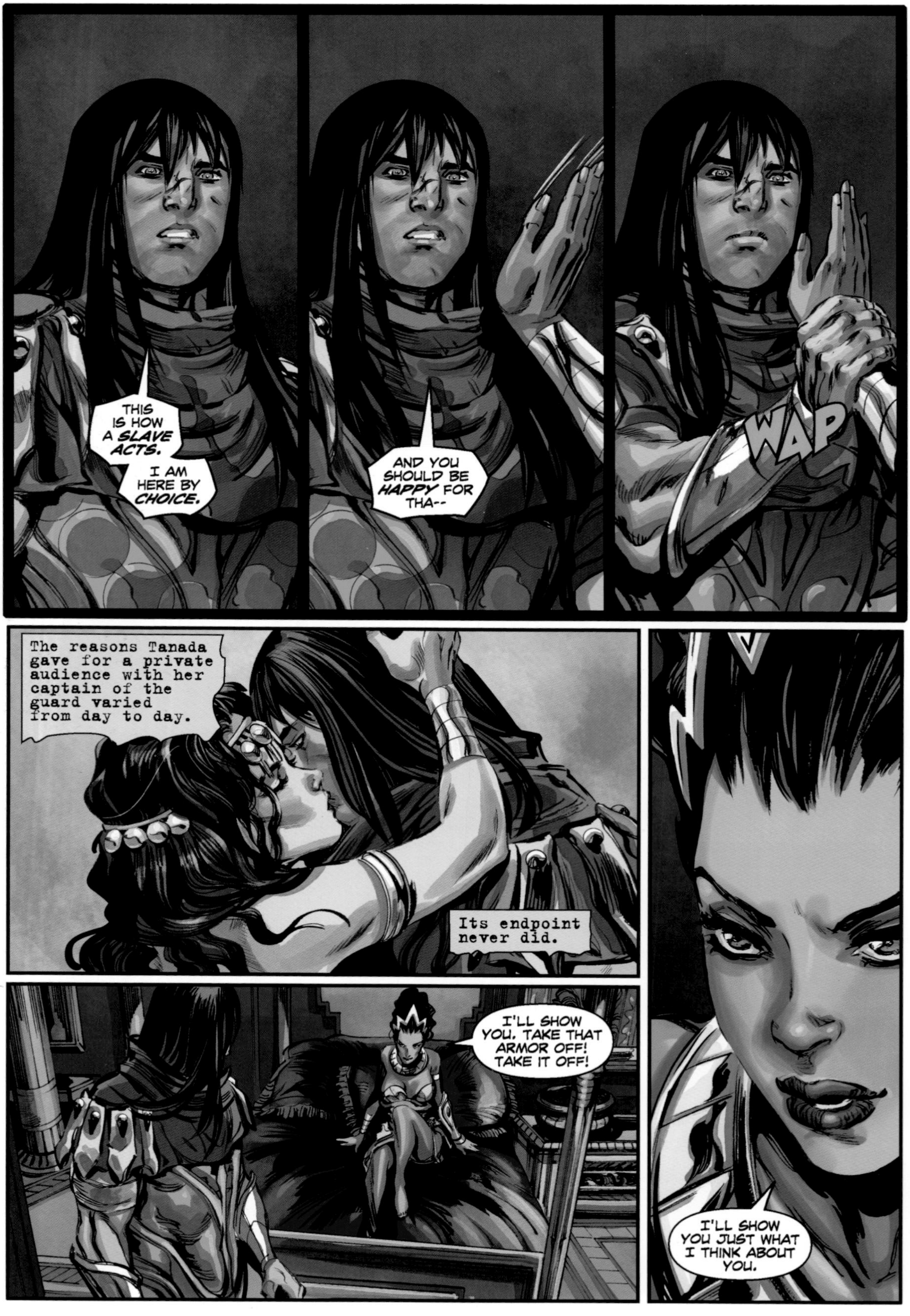

THIS IS HOW A SLAVE ACTS.
I AM HERE BY CHOICE.
AND YOU SHOULD BE HAPPY FOR THA--
WAP
The reasons Tanada gave for a private audience with her captain of the guard varied from day to day.
Its endpoint never did.
I'LL SHOW YOU. TAKE THAT ARMOR OFF! TAKE IT OFF!
I'LL SHOW YOU JUST WHAT I THINK ABOUT YOU.

They did not "make love."

This was another civilized lie.

He did not look at her while they did this.

He closed his eyes and thought of another.

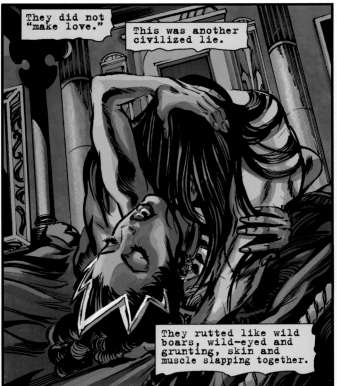

They rutted like wild boars, wild-eyed and grunting, skin and muscle slapping together.

Bêlit and Tanada were both beautiful killers, it was true.

But Tanada never had to steady her feet on a blood-slick deck or break through a sailor's rib cage with her blade.

Bêlit thought of men as flesh and bone, not as inconveniences to be squashed.

And the longer he spent in Tanada of Kush's service...

...the less Conan was able to see the Queen of the Black Coast in her.

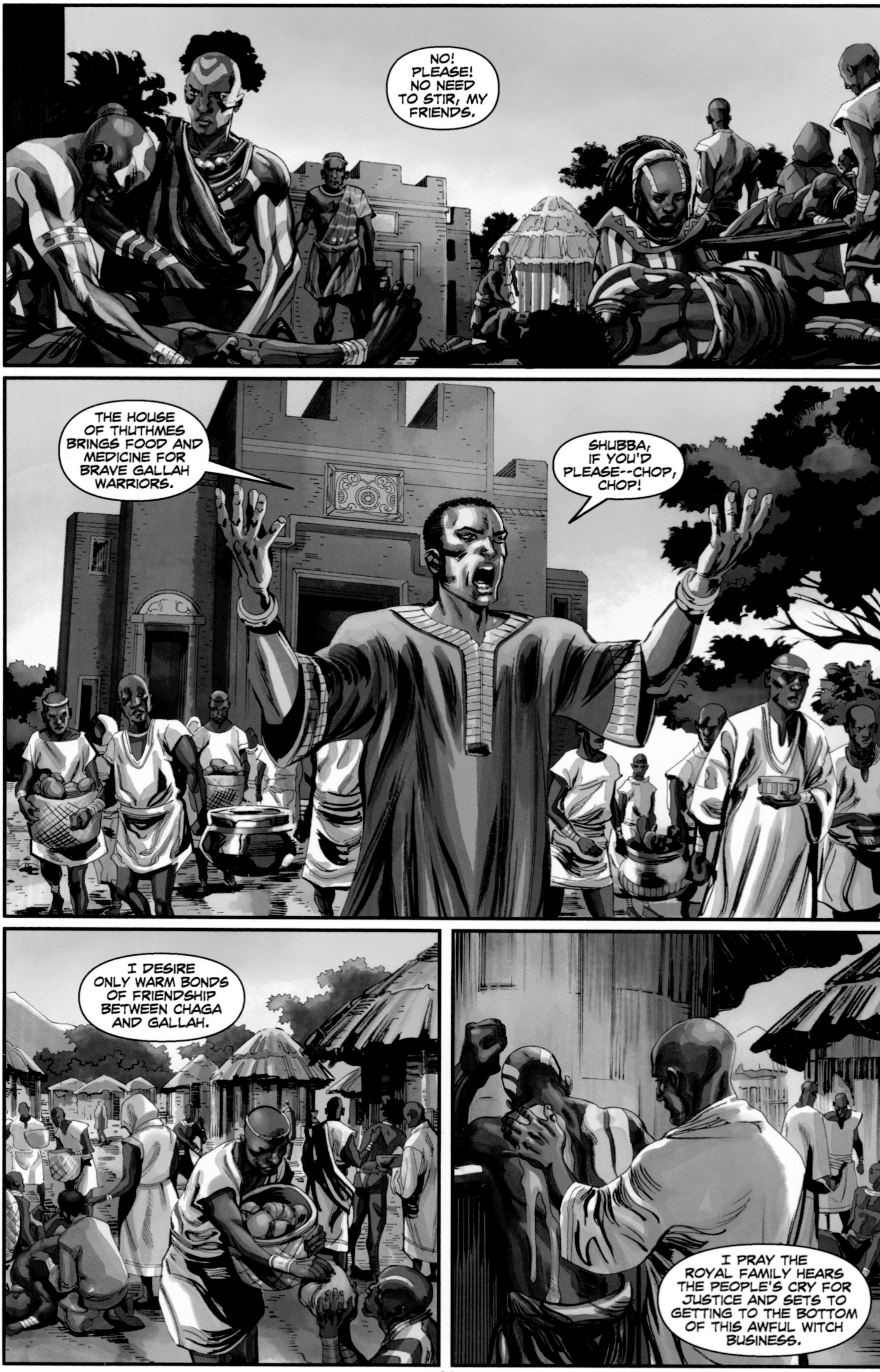
NO! PLEASE! NO NEED TO STIR, MY FRIENDS.
THE HOUSE OF THUTHMES BRINGS FOOD AND MEDICINE FOR BRAVE GALLAH WARRIORS.
SHUBBA, IF YOU'D PLEASE--CHOP, CHOP!
I DESIRE ONLY WARM BONDS OF FRIENDSHIP BETWEEN CHAGA AND GALLAH.
I PRAY THE ROYAL FAMILY HEARS THE PEOPLE'S CRY FOR JUSTICE AND SETS TO GETTING TO THE BOTTOM OF THIS AWFUL WITCH BUSINESS.

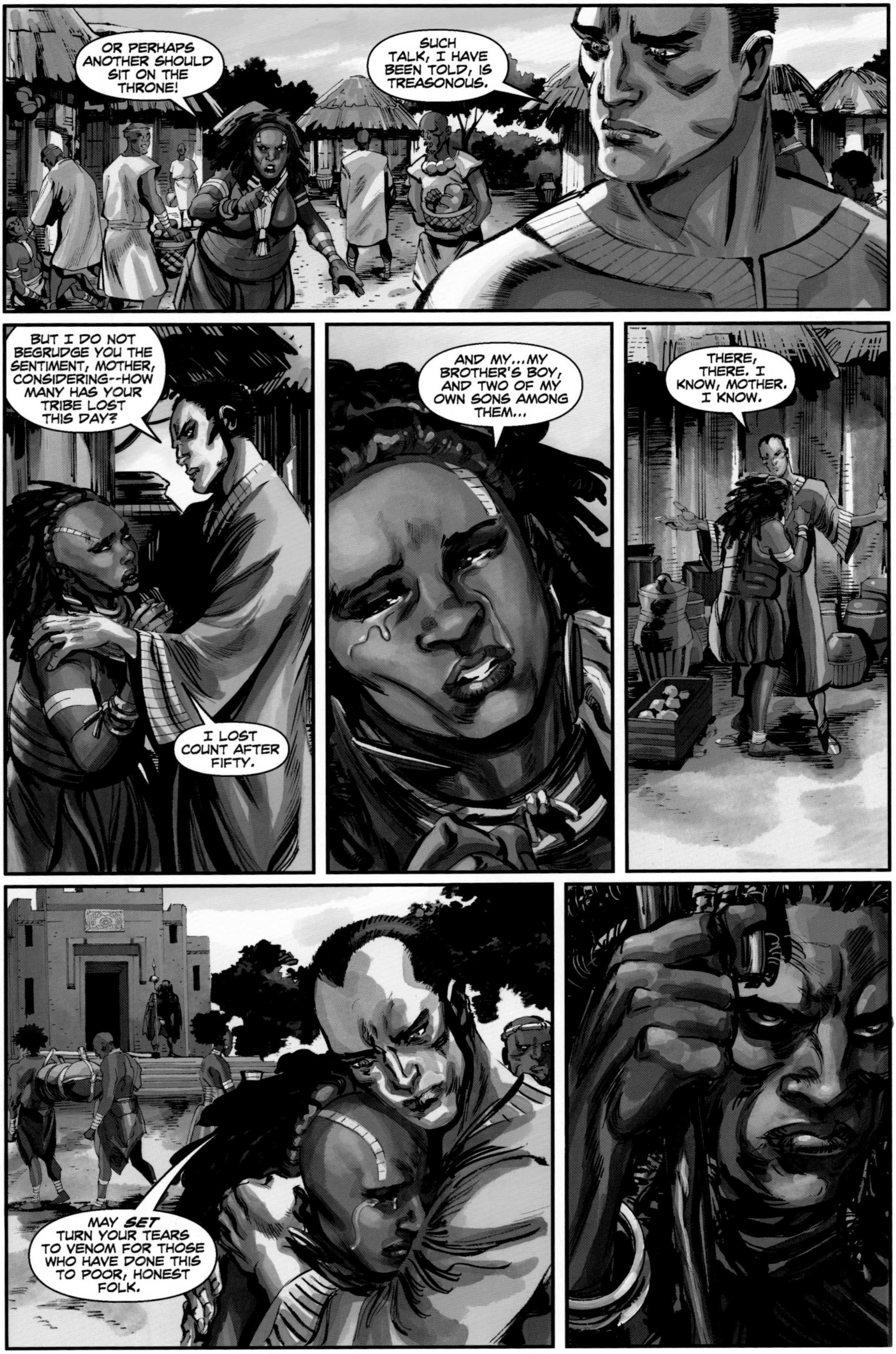
OR PERHAPS ANOTHER SHOULD SIT ON THE THRONE!
SUCH TALK, I HAVE BEEN TOLD, IS TREASONOUS.
BUT I DO NOT BEGRUDGE YOU THE SENTIMENT, MOTHER, CONSIDERING--HOW MANY HAS YOUR TRIBE LOST THIS DAY?
I LOST COUNT AFTER FIFTY.
AND MY...MY BROTHER'S BOY, AND TWO OF MY OWN SONS AMONG THEM...
THERE, THERE. I KNOW, MOTHER. I KNOW.
MAY *SET* TURN YOUR TEARS TO VENOM FOR THOSE WHO HAVE DONE THIS TO POOR, HONEST FOLK.

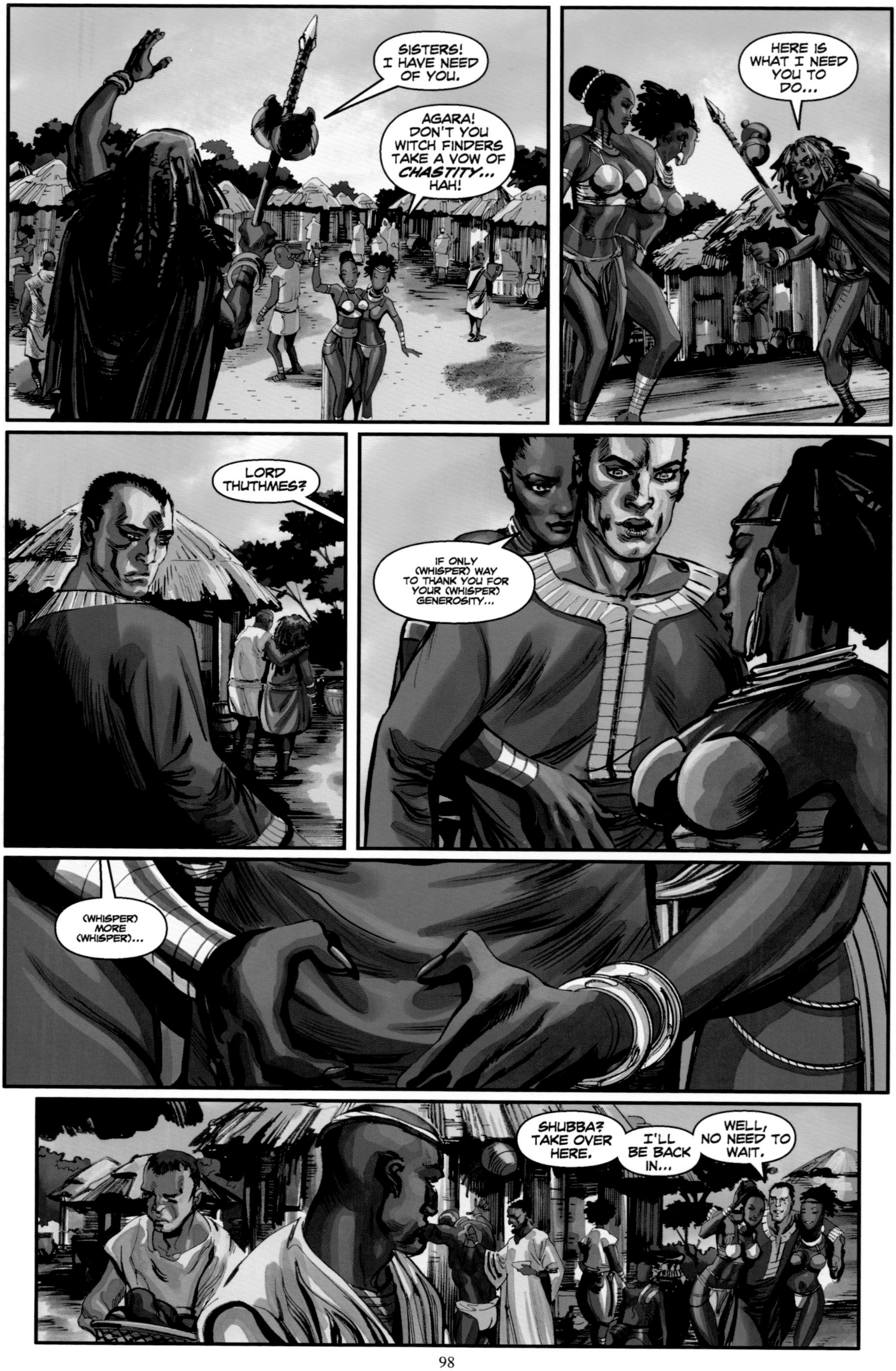
SISTERS! I HAVE NEED OF YOU.
AGARA! DON'T YOU WITCH FINDERS TAKE A VOW OF *CHASTITY*... HAH!
HERE IS WHAT I NEED YOU TO DO...
LORD THUTHMES?
IF ONLY (WHISPER) WAY TO THANK YOU FOR YOUR (WHISPER) GENEROSITY...
(WHISPER) MORE (WHISPER)...
SHUBBA? TAKE OVER HERE.
I'LL BE BACK IN...
WELL, NO NEED TO WAIT.

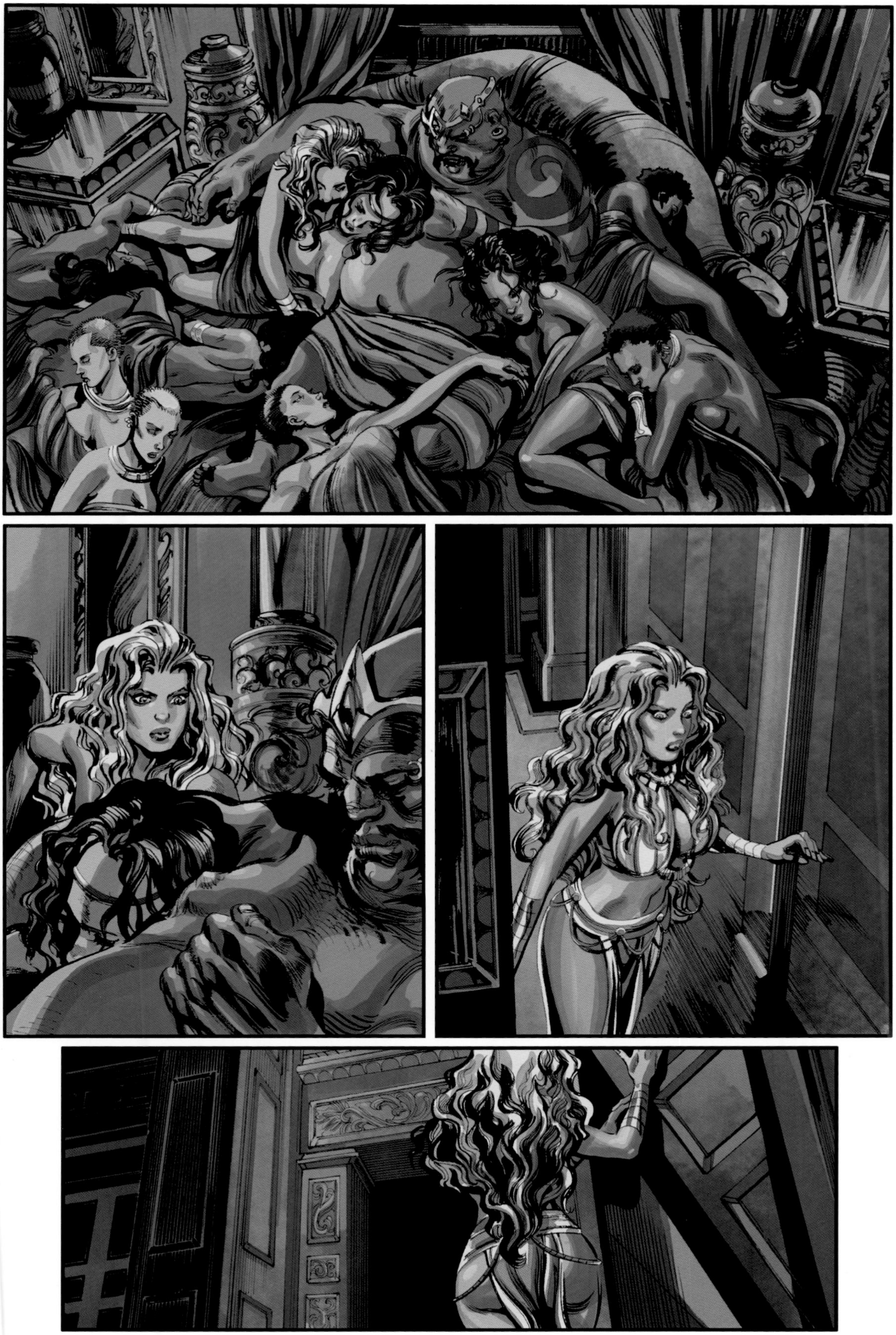

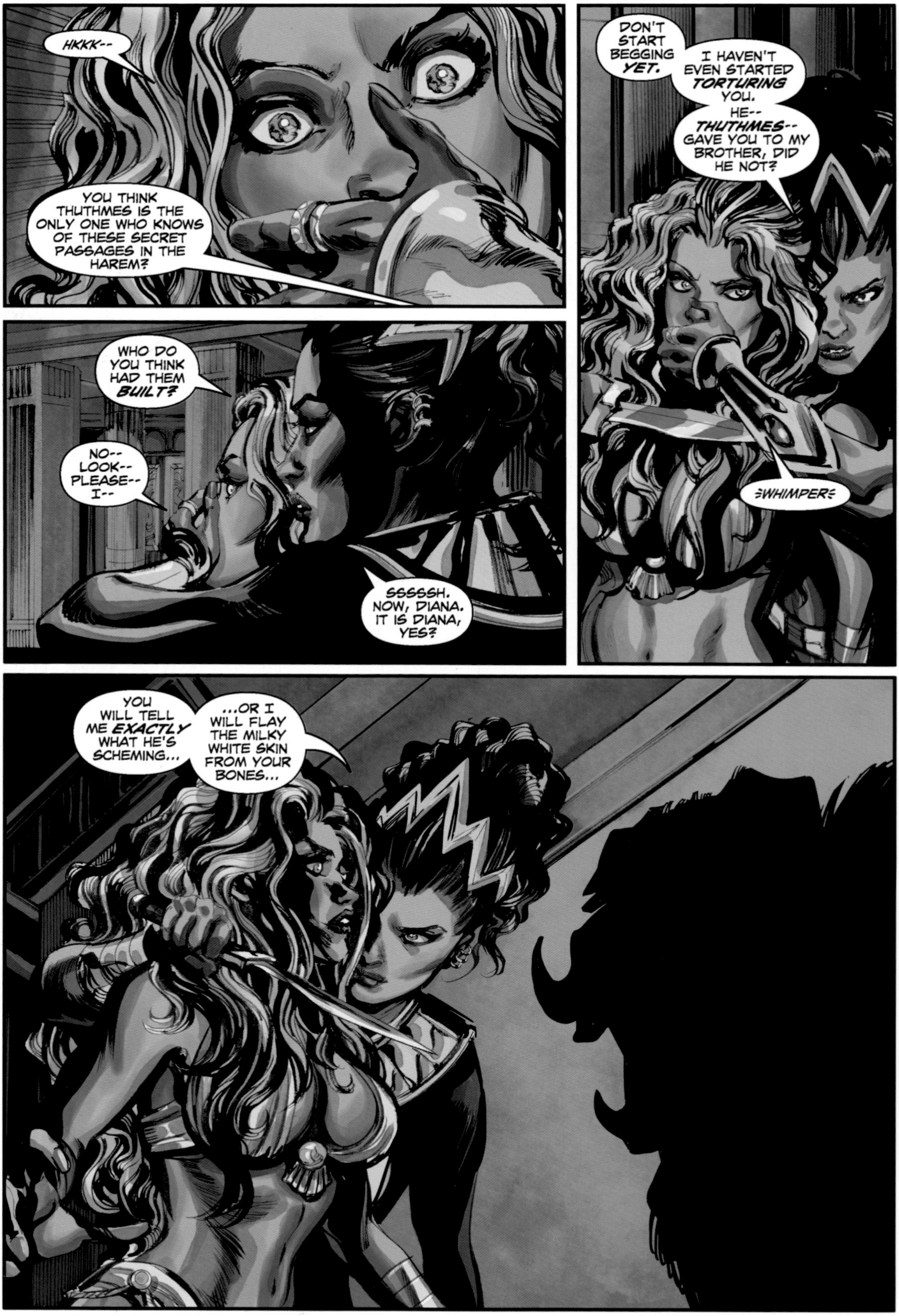

HKKK--
YOU THINK THUTHMES IS THE ONLY ONE WHO KNOWS OF THESE SECRET PASSAGES IN THE HAREM?
DON'T START BEGGING *YET.*
I HAVEN'T EVEN STARTED *TORTURING* YOU.
HE-- *THUTHMES*-- GAVE YOU TO MY BROTHER, DID HE NOT?
WHO DO YOU THINK HAD THEM *BUILT?*
NO-- LOOK-- PLEASE-- I--
SSSSSH. NOW, DIANA. IT IS DIANA, YES?
≈WHIMPER≈
YOU WILL TELL ME *EXACTLY* WHAT HE'S SCHEMING...
...OR I WILL FLAY THE MILKY WHITE SKIN FROM YOUR BONES...

CHAPTER FIVE

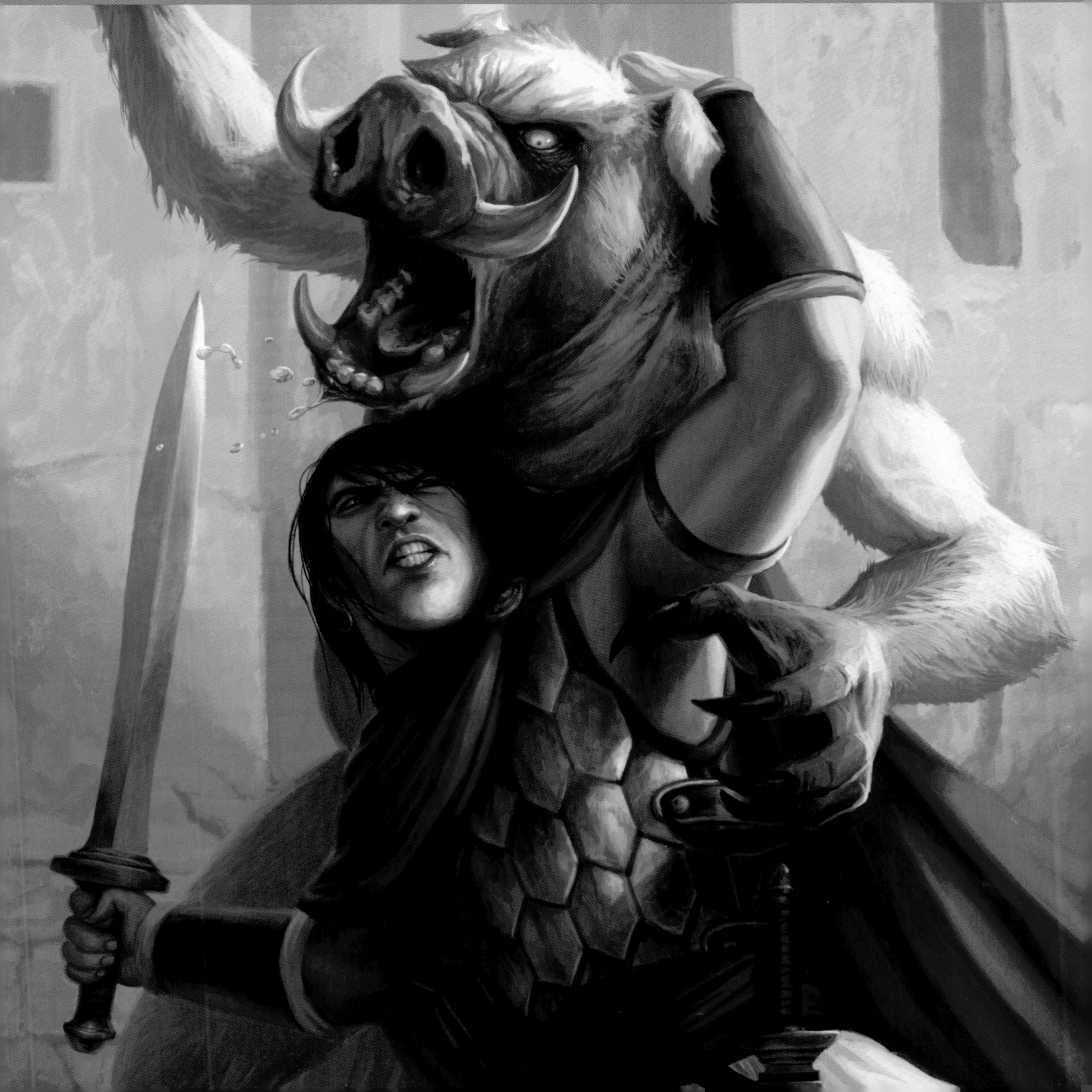

"I will steal the light from your eyes!"

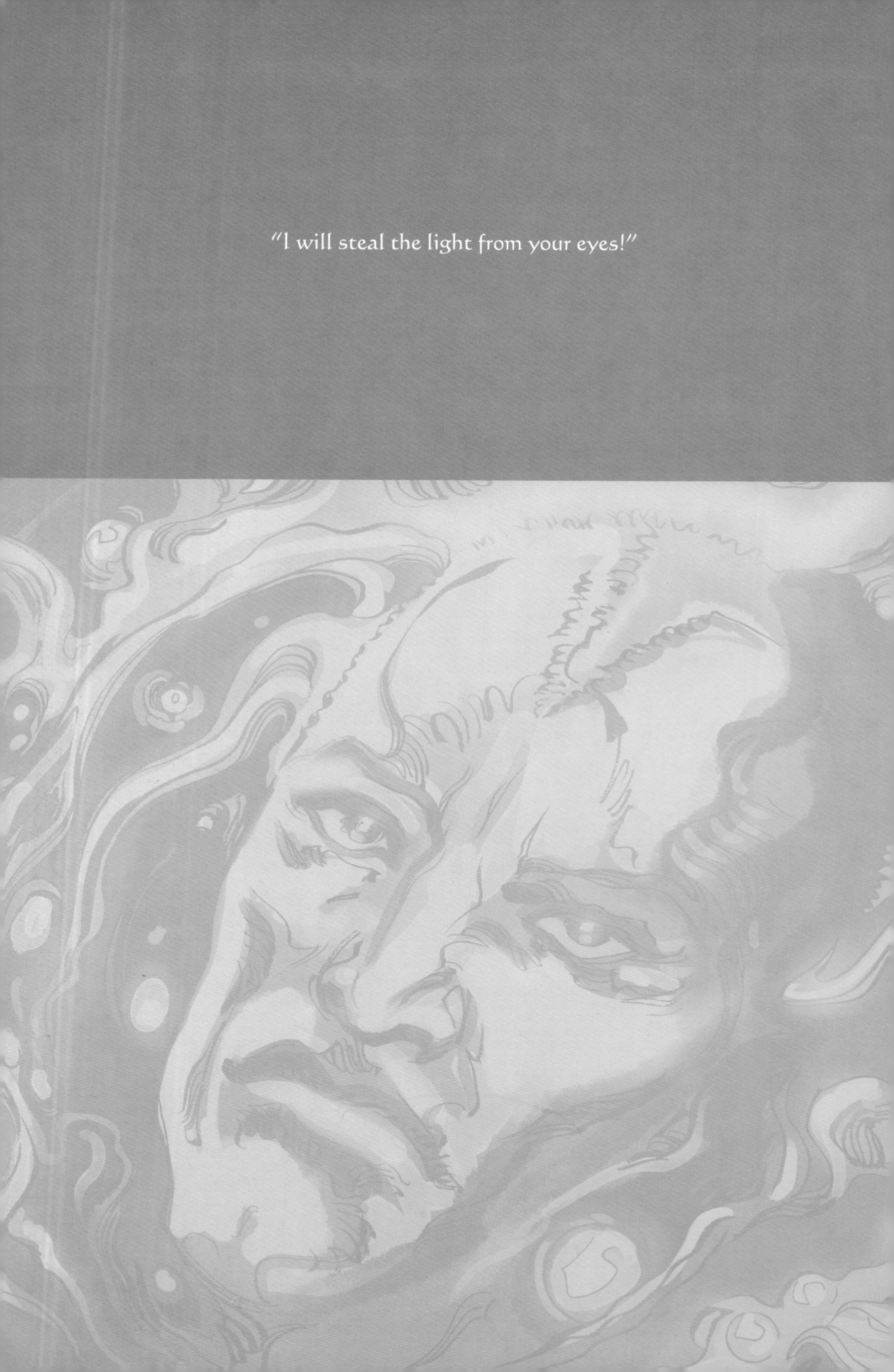

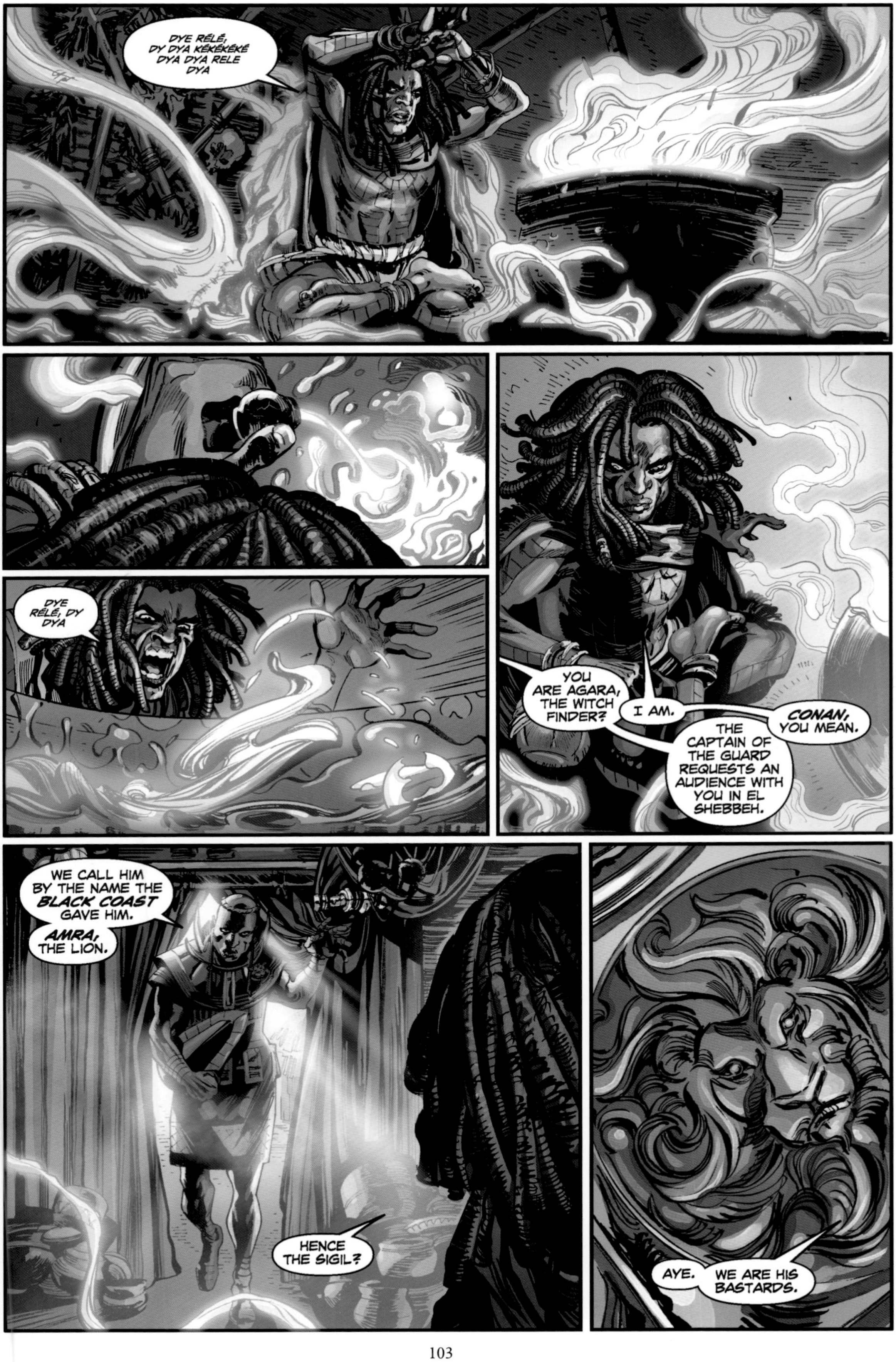
DYE RÉLÉ, DY DYA KÉKÉKÉKÉ DYA DYA RELE DYA
DYE RÉLÉ, DY DYA
YOU ARE AGARA, THE WITCH FINDER?
I AM.
CONAN, YOU MEAN.
THE CAPTAIN OF THE GUARD REQUESTS AN AUDIENCE WITH YOU IN EL SHEBBEH.
WE CALL HIM BY THE NAME THE BLACK COAST GAVE HIM.
AMRA, THE LION.
HENCE THE SIGIL?
AYE.
WE ARE HIS BASTARDS.

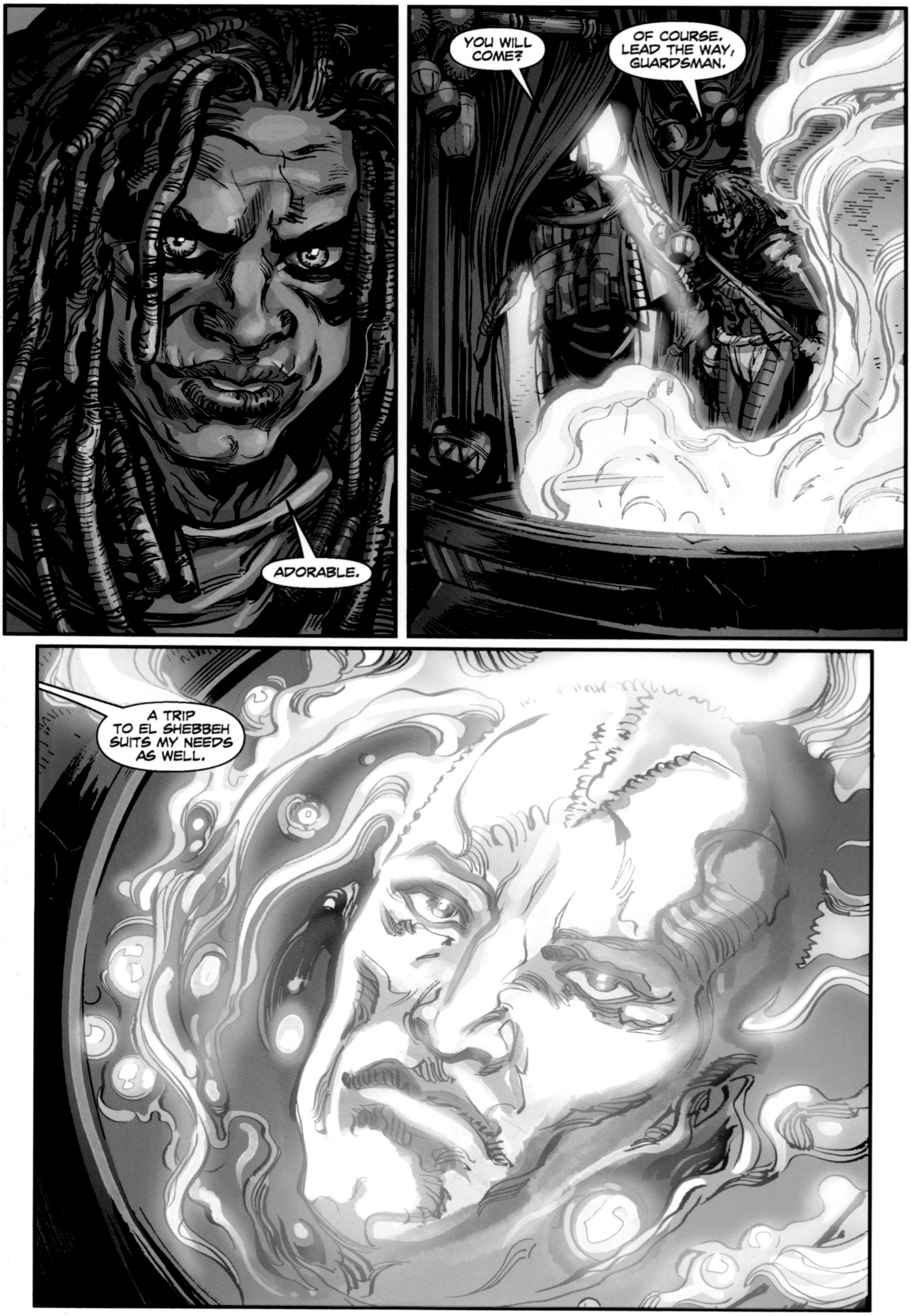
ADORABLE.
YOU WILL COME?
OF COURSE. LEAD THE WAY, GUARDSMAN.
A TRIP TO EL SHEBBEH SUITS MY NEEDS AS WELL.

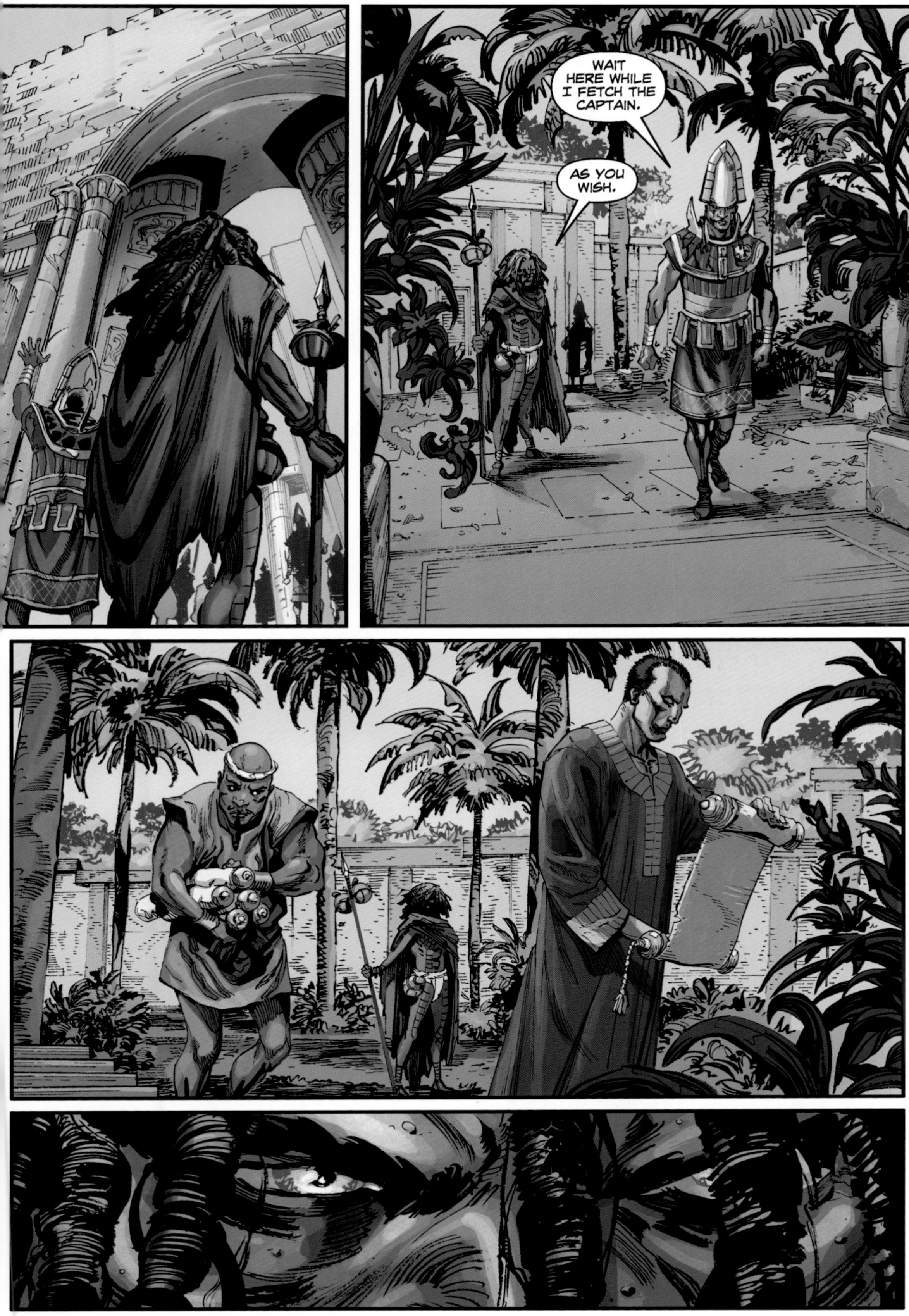
WAIT HERE WHILE I FETCH THE CAPTAIN.
AS YOU WISH.

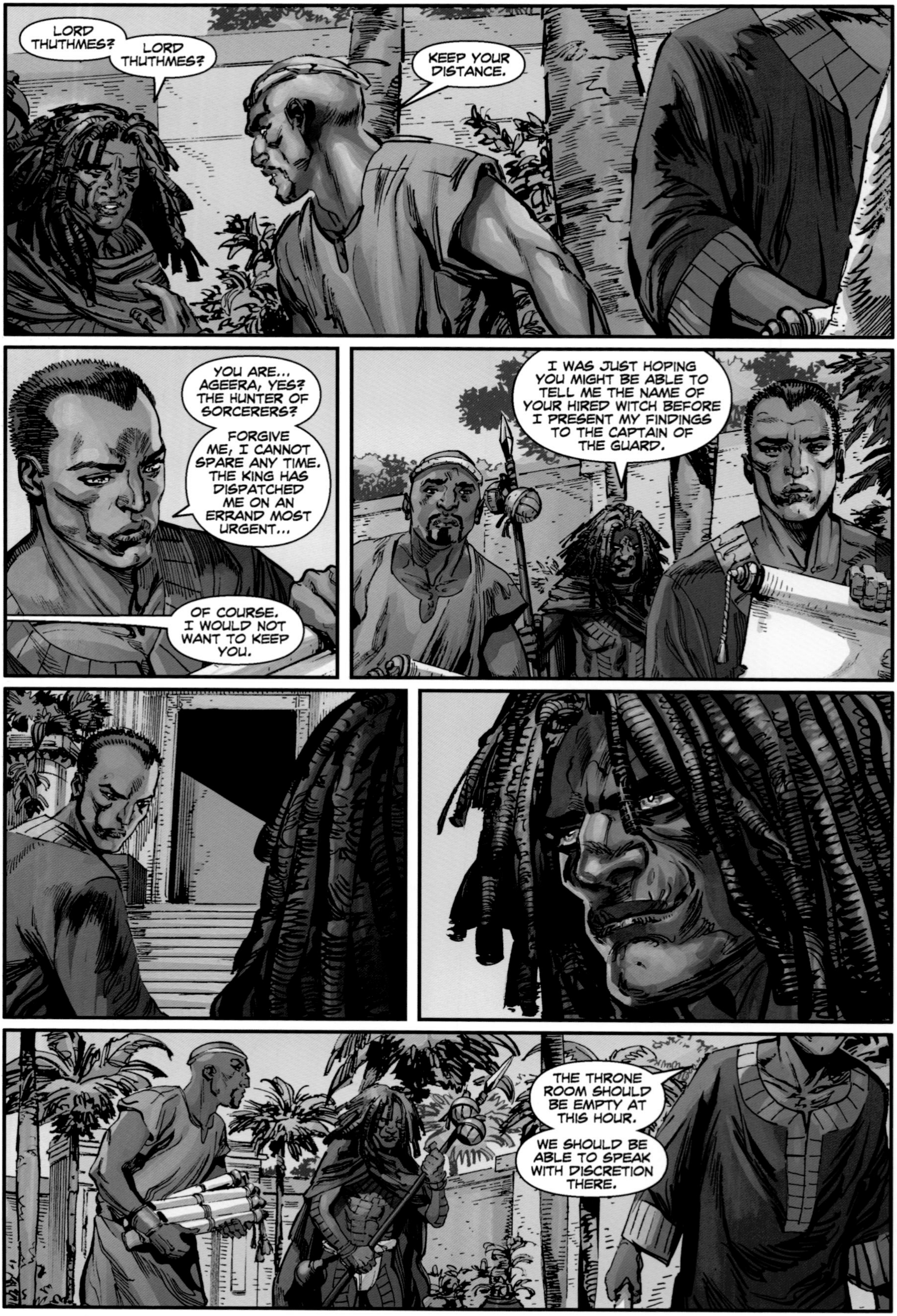
LORD THUTHMES?
LORD THUTHMES?
KEEP YOUR DISTANCE.
YOU ARE... AGEERA, YES? THE HUNTER OF SORCERERS?
FORGIVE ME, I CANNOT SPARE ANY TIME. THE KING HAS DISPATCHED ME ON AN ERRAND MOST URGENT...
OF COURSE. I WOULD NOT WANT TO KEEP YOU.
I WAS JUST HOPING YOU MIGHT BE ABLE TO TELL ME THE NAME OF YOUR HIRED WITCH BEFORE I PRESENT MY FINDINGS TO THE CAPTAIN OF THE GUARD.
THE THRONE ROOM SHOULD BE EMPTY AT THIS HOUR.
WE SHOULD BE ABLE TO SPEAK WITH DISCRETION THERE.

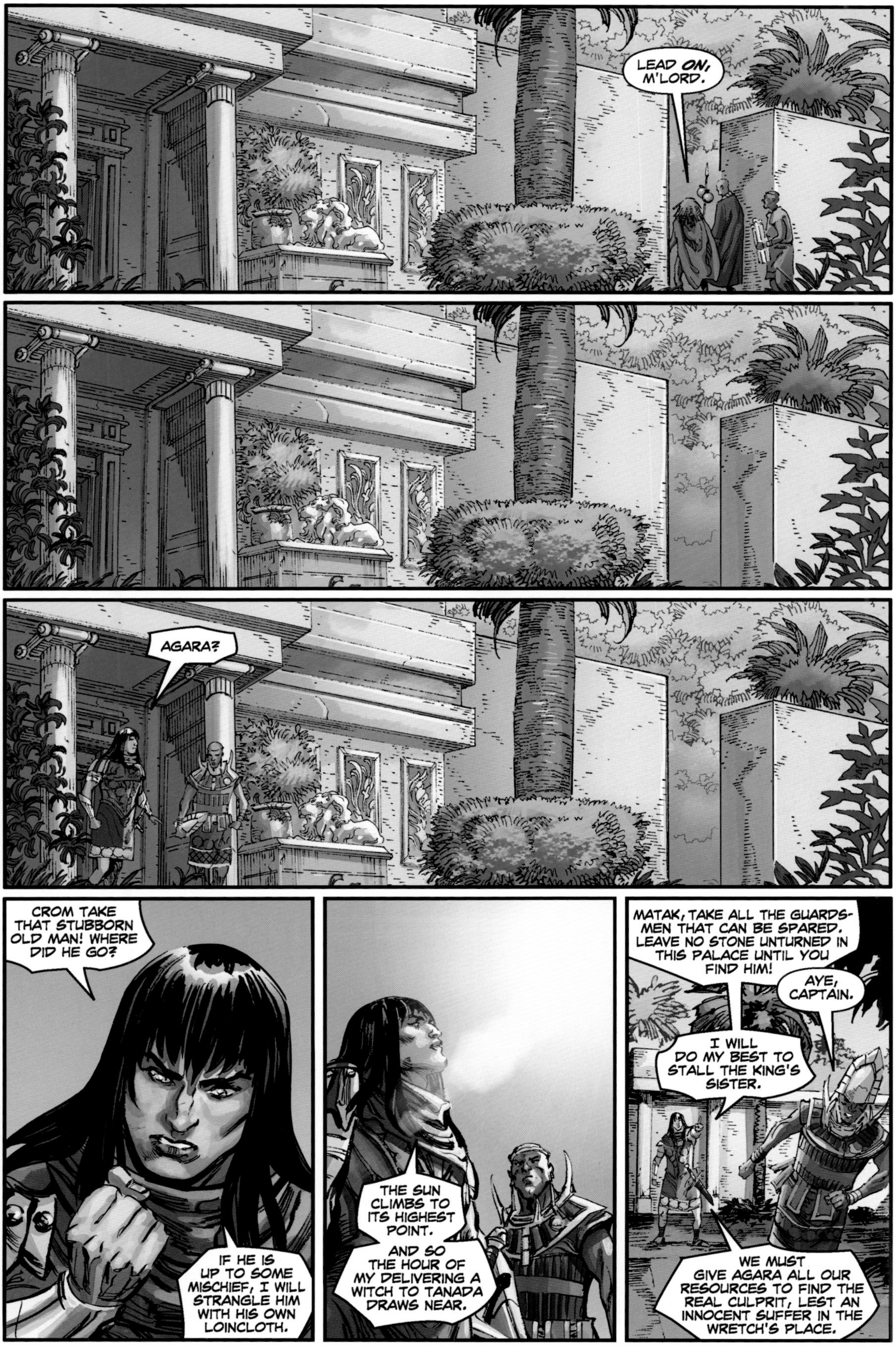
LEAD ON, M'LORD.
AGARA?
CROM TAKE THAT STUBBORN OLD MAN! WHERE DID HE GO?
IF HE IS UP TO SOME MISCHIEF, I WILL STRANGLE HIM WITH HIS OWN LOINCLOTH.
THE SUN CLIMBS TO ITS HIGHEST POINT.
AND SO THE HOUR OF MY DELIVERING A WITCH TO TANADA DRAWS NEAR.
MATAK, TAKE ALL THE GUARDSMEN THAT CAN BE SPARED. LEAVE NO STONE UNTURNED IN THIS PALACE UNTIL YOU FIND HIM!
AYE, CAPTAIN.
I WILL DO MY BEST TO STALL THE KING'S SISTER.
WE MUST GIVE AGARA ALL OUR RESOURCES TO FIND THE REAL CULPRIT, LEST AN INNOCENT SUFFER IN THE WRETCH'S PLACE.

YOU ARE RESPECTED AMONG THE GALLAHS, OLD MAN, OR I WOULD CLAP YOU IN IRONS FOR MAKING SUCH A RASH ACCUSATION AGAINST A MEMBER OF THE ROYAL HOUSEH--

NONSENSE.

YOU WANT TO KNOW HOW MUCH I KNOW.

WHICH IS *ENOUGH*.

THE WHORES WHOSE MINISTRATIONS YOU ENJOYED IN PUNT YESTERDAY WERE IN MY EMPLOY.

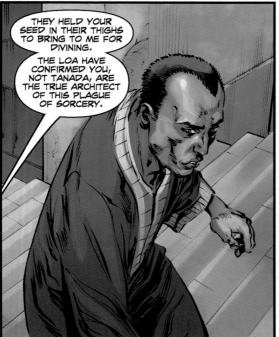

THEY HELD YOUR SEED IN THEIR THIGHS TO BRING TO ME FOR DIVINING.

THE LOA HAVE CONFIRMED YOU, NOT TANADA, ARE THE TRUE ARCHITECT OF THIS PLAGUE OF SORCERY.

YOU *FOOL*. YOU HAVE INJECTED FORCES YOU CANNOT POSSIBLY *UNDERSTAND*, MUCH LESS *CONTROL*, INTO YOUR PETTY *INTRIGUES!*

DELIVER YOUR SELL MAGE UNTO *ME* AND I MAY *NOT* TELL THE KING AND HIS SISTER THEY EMPLOY A SENESCHAL WHOSE ARROGANCE AND AMBITION ARE MATCHED ONLY BY HIS RECKLESS *STUPIDITY*--

YOU WOULD LECTURE ME ON ARROGANCE, OLD MAN?

CONFRONTING ME IN THE PALACE THAT WILL SOON BE MINE?

108

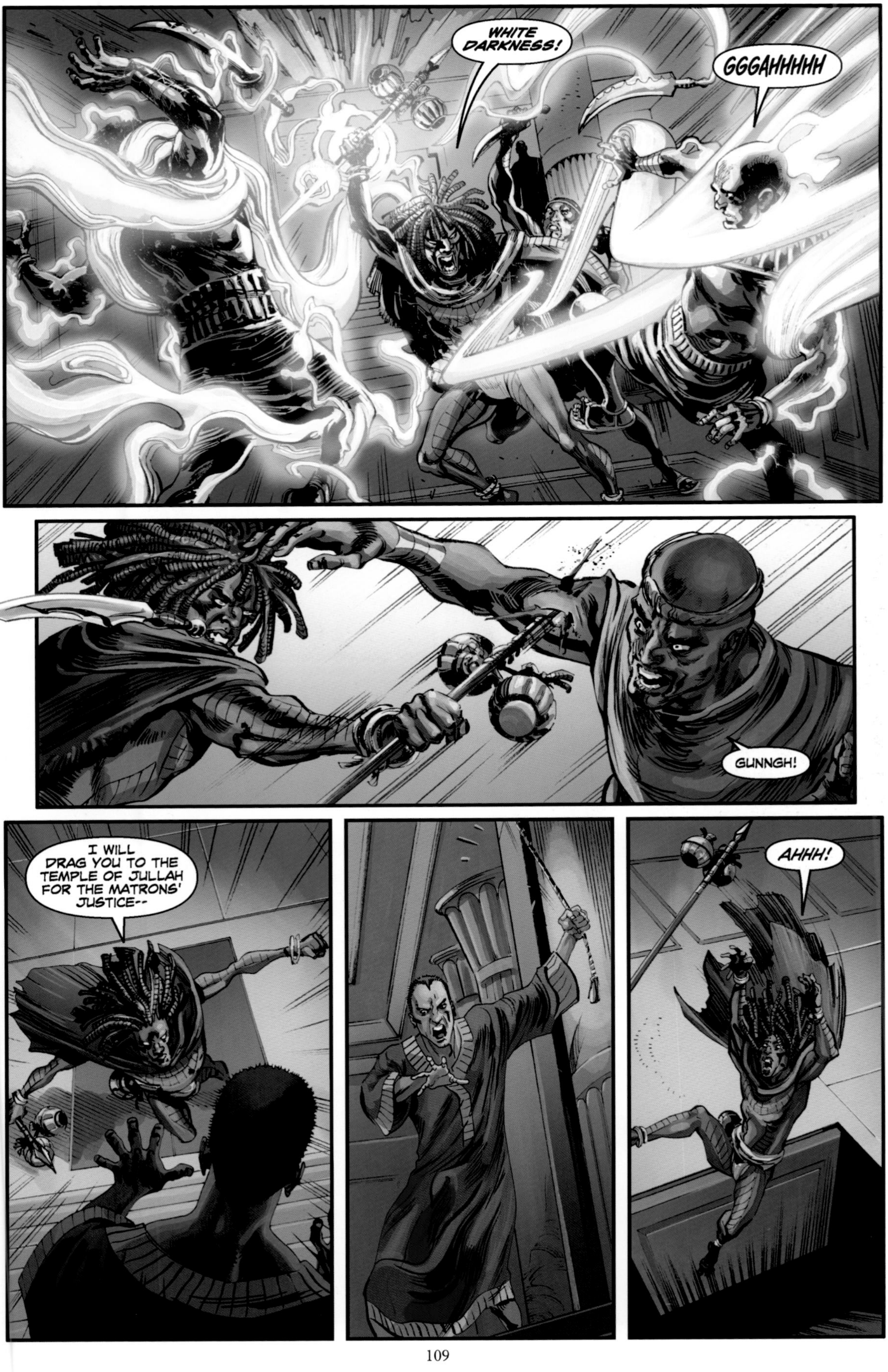
WHITE DARKNESS!
GGGAHHHHH
GUNNGH!
I WILL DRAG YOU TO THE TEMPLE OF JULLAH FOR THE MATRONS' JUSTICE--
AHHH!

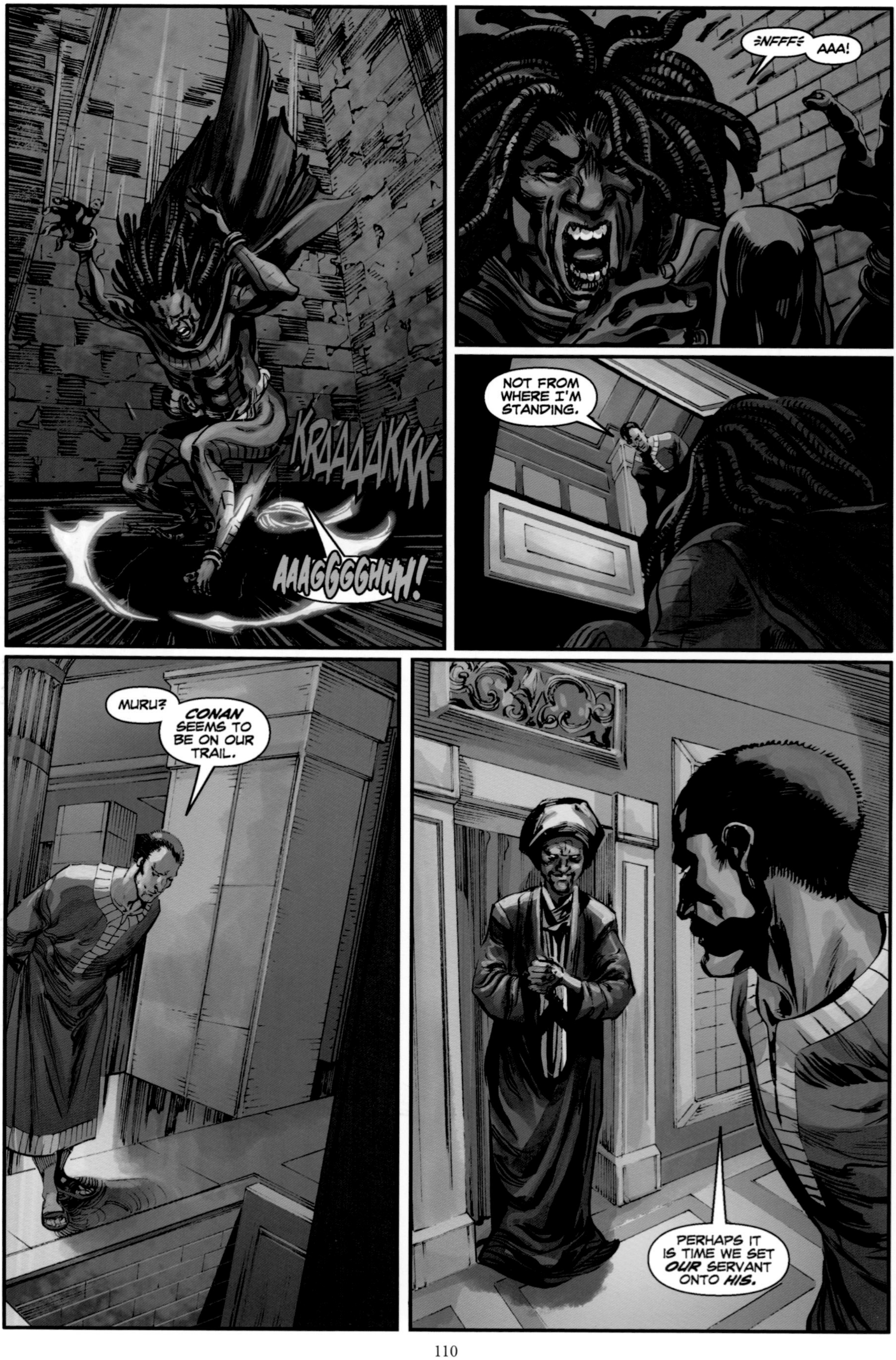
KRAAAAKKK
AAAGGGGHHH!
=NFFF= AAA!
NOT FROM WHERE I'M STANDING.
MURU?
CONAN SEEMS TO BE ON OUR TRAIL.
PERHAPS IT IS TIME WE SET OUR SERVANT ONTO HIS.

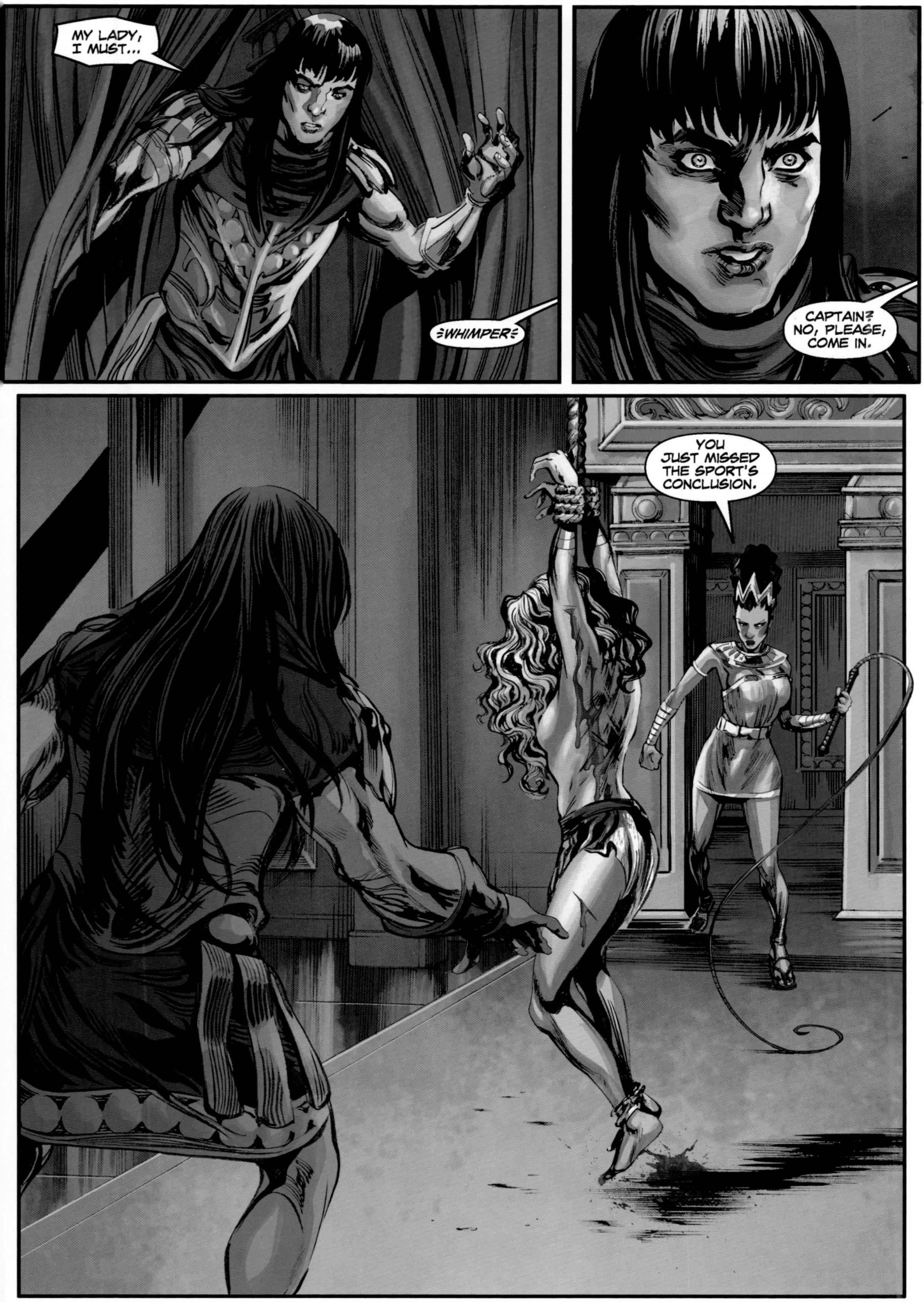
MY LADY, I MUST...
WHIMPER
CAPTAIN? NO, PLEASE, COME IN.
YOU JUST MISSED THE SPORT'S CONCLUSION.

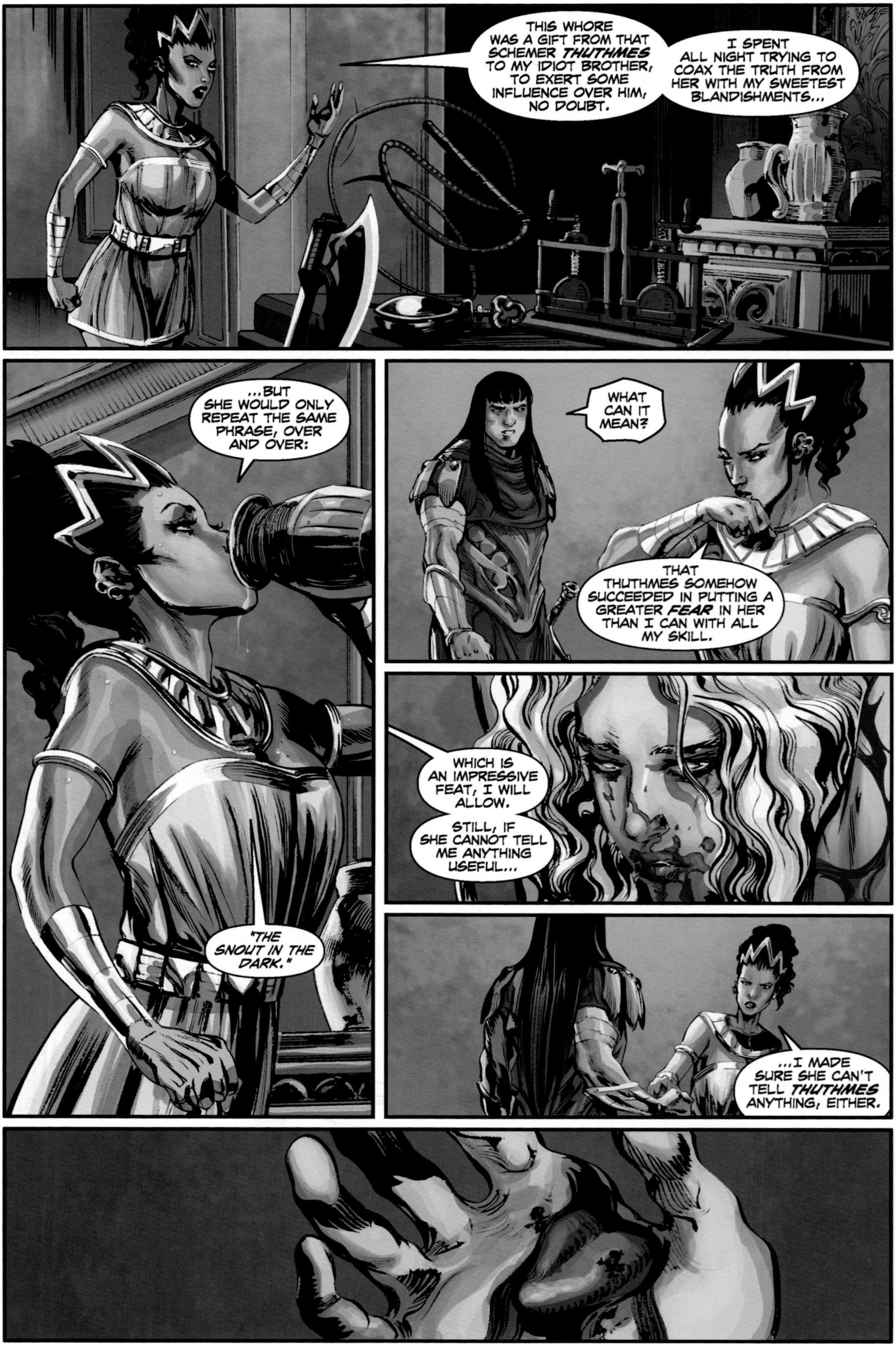
THIS WHORE WAS A GIFT FROM THAT SCHEMER *THUTHMES* TO MY IDIOT BROTHER, TO EXERT SOME INFLUENCE OVER HIM, NO DOUBT.
I SPENT ALL NIGHT TRYING TO COAX THE TRUTH FROM HER WITH MY SWEETEST BLANDISHMENTS...
...BUT SHE WOULD ONLY REPEAT THE SAME PHRASE, OVER AND OVER:
"THE SNOUT IN THE DARK."
WHAT CAN IT MEAN?
THAT THUTHMES SOMEHOW SUCCEEDED IN PUTTING A GREATER *FEAR* IN HER THAN I CAN WITH ALL MY SKILL.
WHICH IS AN IMPRESSIVE FEAT, I WILL ALLOW.
STILL, IF SHE CANNOT TELL ME ANYTHING USEFUL...
...I MADE SURE SHE CAN'T TELL *THUTHMES* ANYTHING, EITHER.

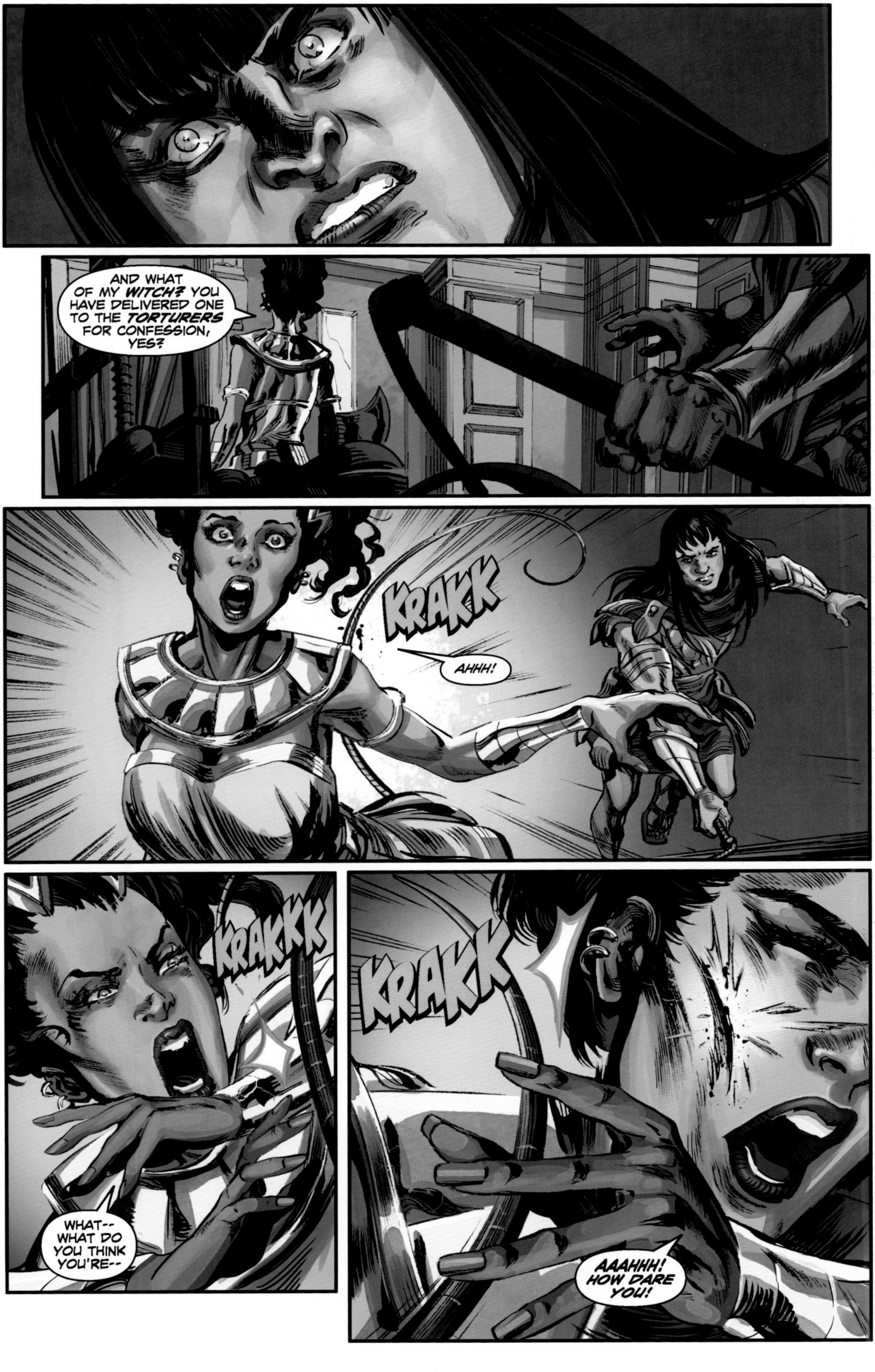
AND WHAT OF MY WITCH? YOU HAVE DELIVERED ONE TO THE TORTURERS FOR CONFESSION, YES?
KRAKK
AHHH!
KRAKKK
WHAT-- WHAT DO YOU THINK YOU'RE--
KRAKK
AAAHHH! HOW DARE YOU!

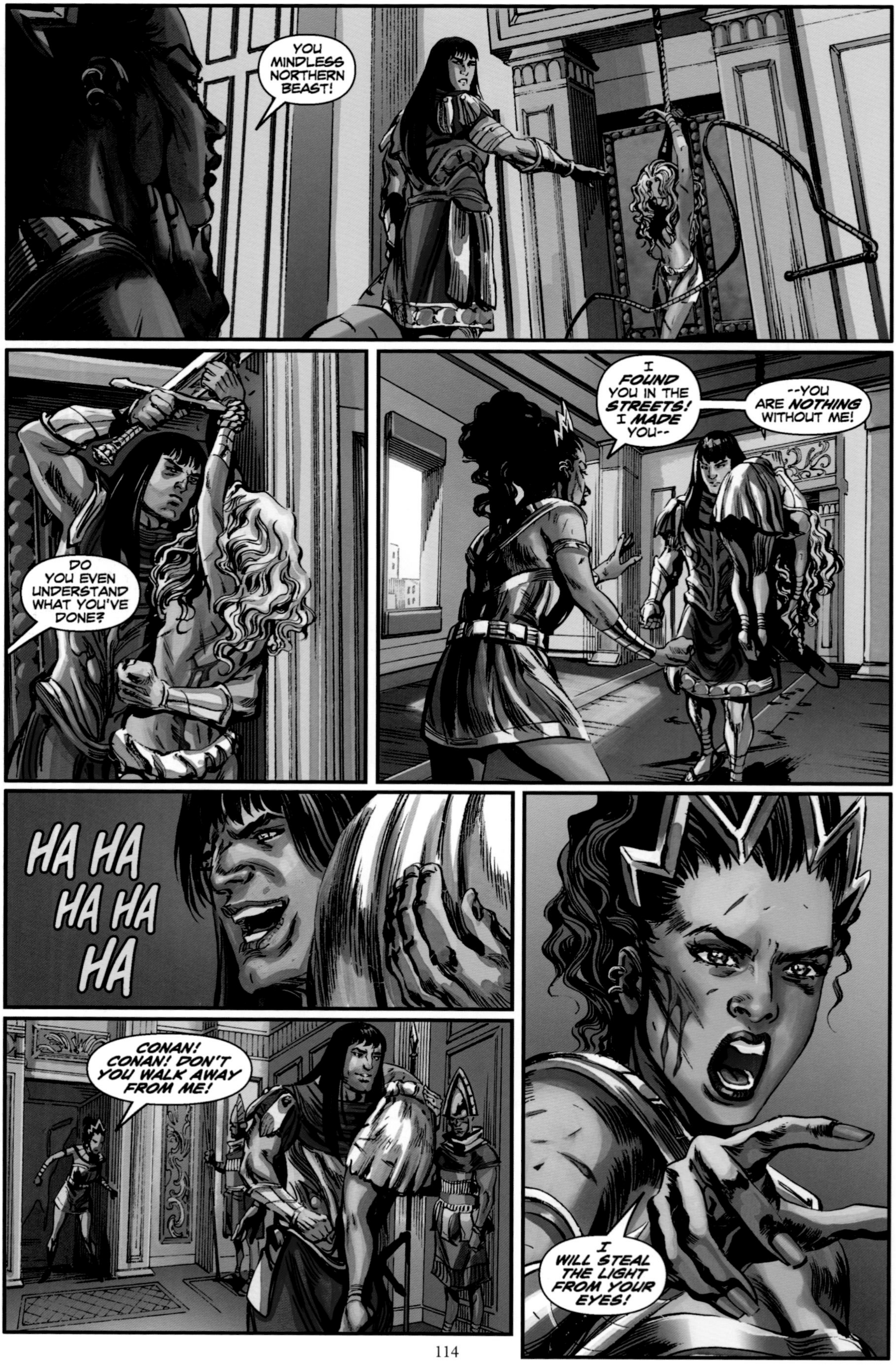
YOU MINDLESS NORTHERN BEAST!
DO YOU EVEN UNDERSTAND WHAT YOU'VE DONE?
I FOUND YOU IN THE STREETS! I MADE YOU--
--YOU ARE NOTHING WITHOUT ME!
HA HA HA HA HA
CONAN! CONAN! DON'T YOU WALK AWAY FROM ME!
I WILL STEAL THE LIGHT FROM YOUR EYES!

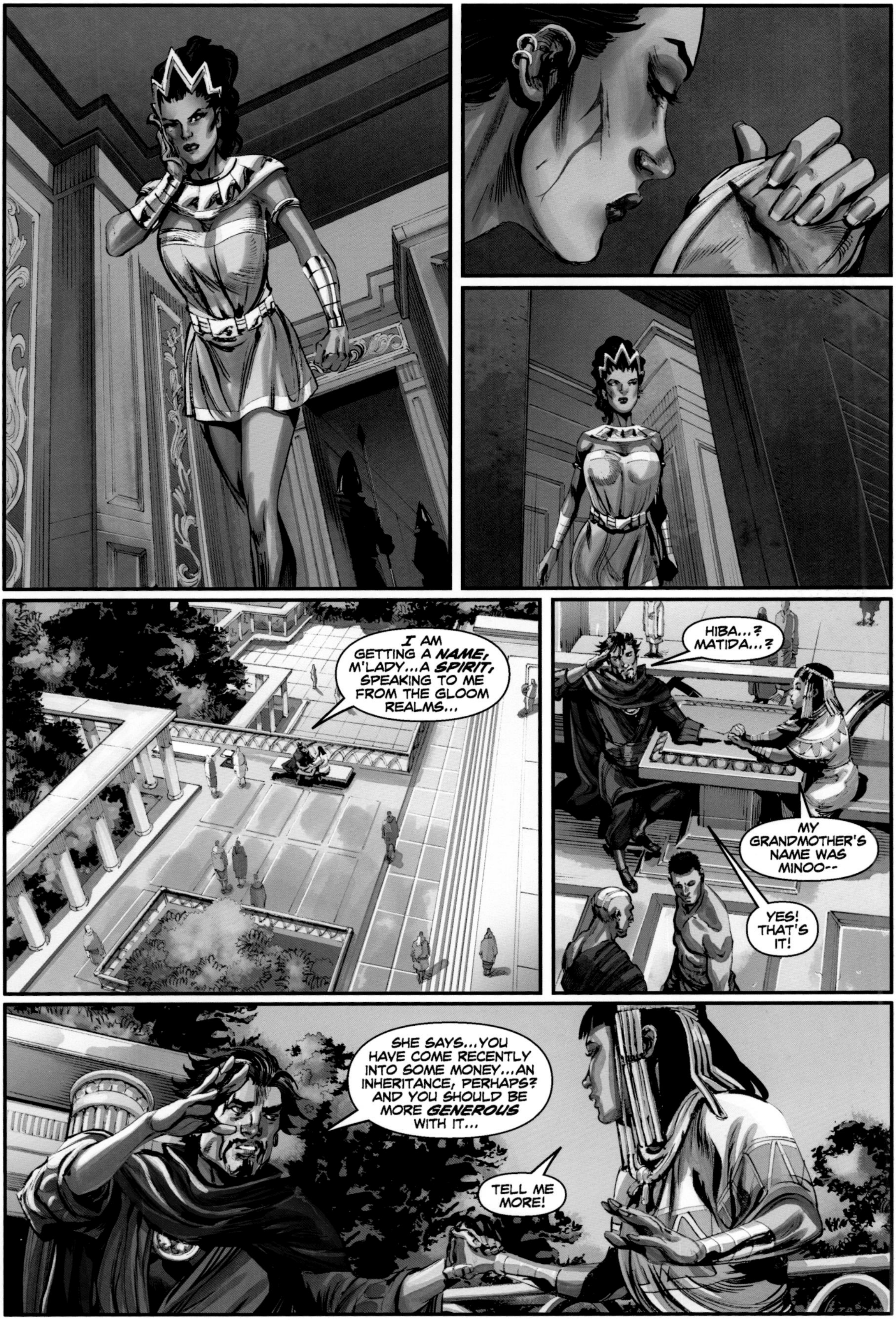
I AM GETTING A NAME, M'LADY...A SPIRIT, SPEAKING TO ME FROM THE GLOOM REALMS...
HIBA...? MATIDA...?
MY GRANDMOTHER'S NAME WAS MINOO--
YES! THAT'S IT!
SHE SAYS...YOU HAVE COME RECENTLY INTO SOME MONEY...AN INHERITANCE, PERHAPS? AND YOU SHOULD BE MORE GENEROUS WITH IT...
TELL ME MORE!

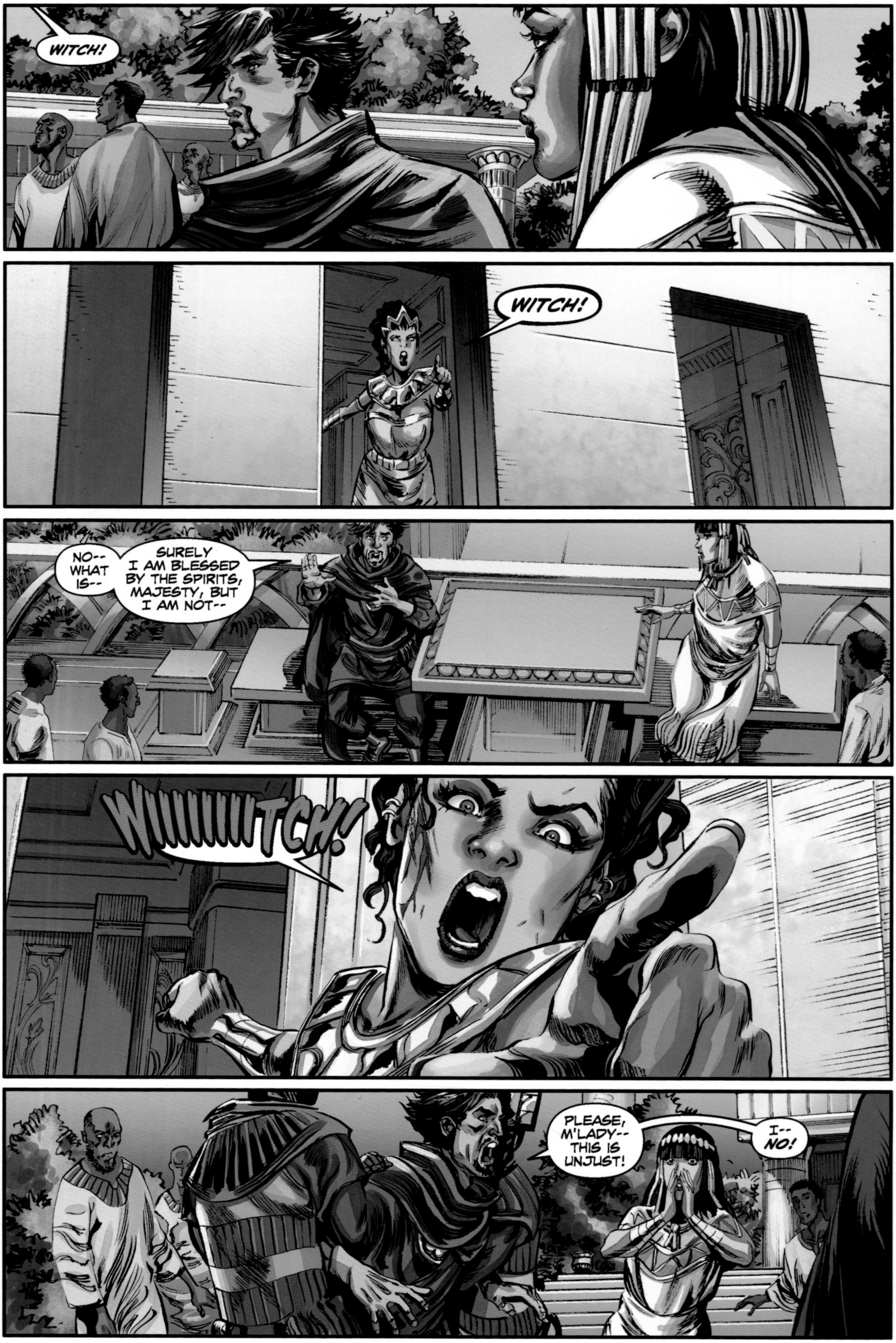
WITCH!
WITCH!
NO-- WHAT IS--
SURELY I AM BLESSED BY THE SPIRITS, MAJESTY, BUT I AM NOT--
WIIIIIIIIITCH!
PLEASE, M'LADY-- THIS IS UNJUST!
I-- NO!

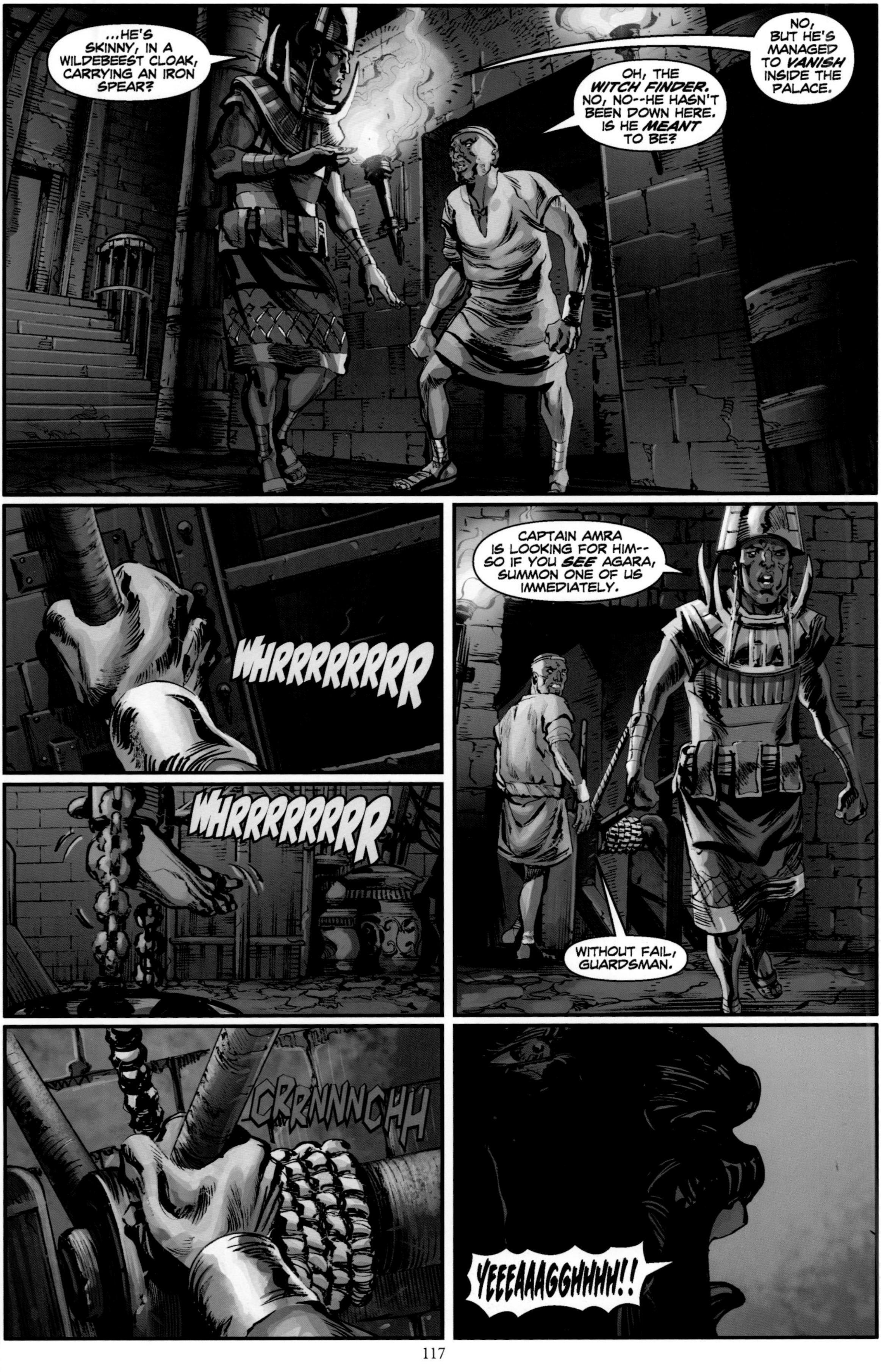
...HE'S SKINNY, IN A WILDEBEEST CLOAK, CARRYING AN IRON SPEAR?
OH, THE WITCH FINDER. NO, NO--HE HASN'T BEEN DOWN HERE. IS HE MEANT TO BE?
NO, BUT HE'S MANAGED TO VANISH INSIDE THE PALACE.
WHRRRRRRRR
CAPTAIN AMRA IS LOOKING FOR HIM--SO IF YOU SEE AGARA, SUMMON ONE OF US IMMEDIATELY.
WHRRRRRRRR
WITHOUT FAIL, GUARDSMAN.
CRRNNNCHH
YEEEAAAGGHHHH!!

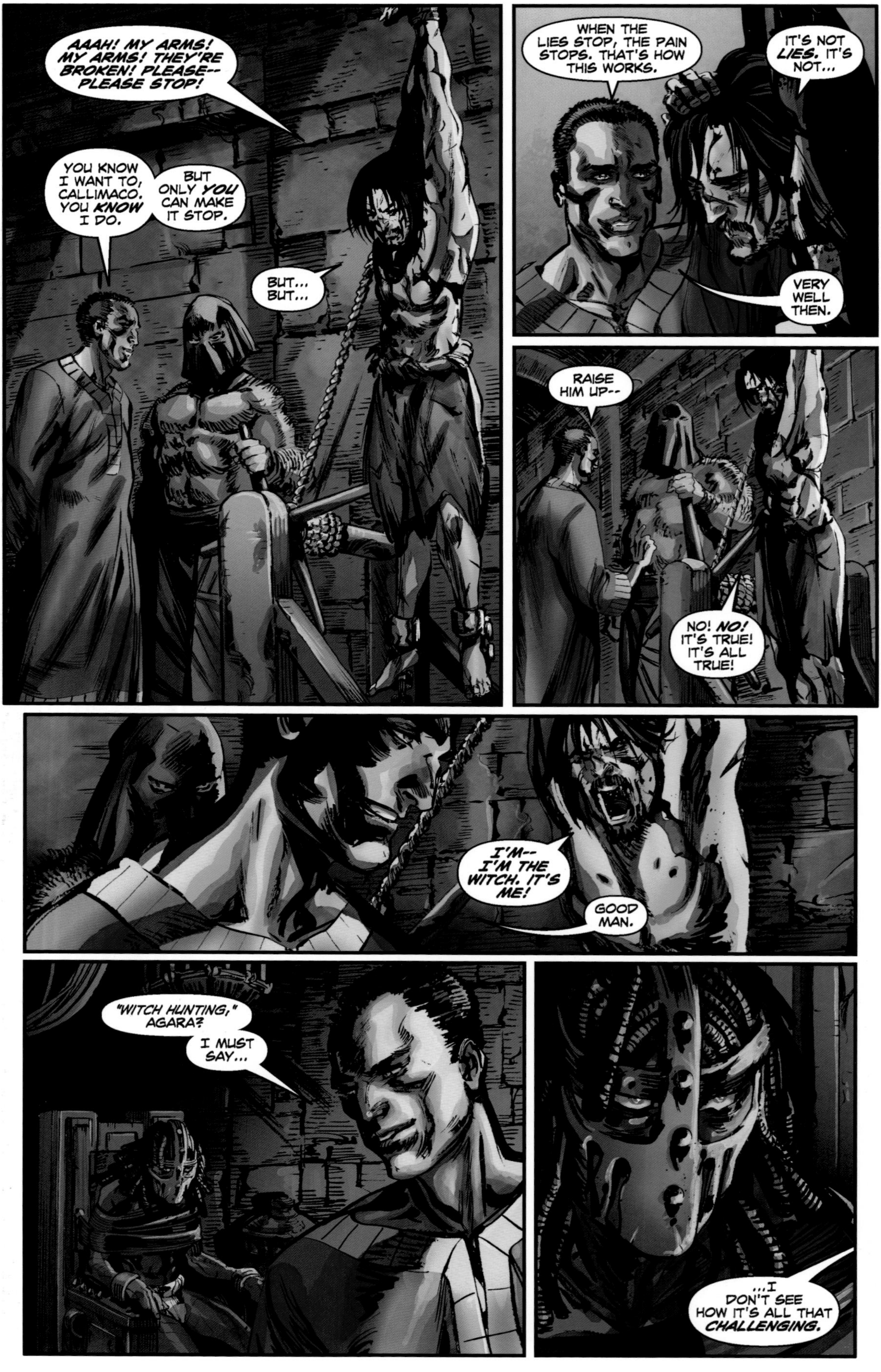
AAAH! MY ARMS! MY ARMS! THEY'RE BROKEN! PLEASE-- PLEASE STOP!
YOU KNOW I WANT TO, CALLIMACO. YOU KNOW I DO.
BUT ONLY YOU CAN MAKE IT STOP.
BUT... BUT...
WHEN THE LIES STOP, THE PAIN STOPS. THAT'S HOW THIS WORKS.
IT'S NOT LIES. IT'S NOT...
VERY WELL THEN.
RAISE HIM UP--
NO! NO! IT'S TRUE! IT'S ALL TRUE!
I'M-- I'M THE WITCH. IT'S ME!
GOOD MAN.
"WITCH HUNTING," AGARA?
I MUST SAY...
...I DON'T SEE HOW IT'S ALL THAT CHALLENGING.

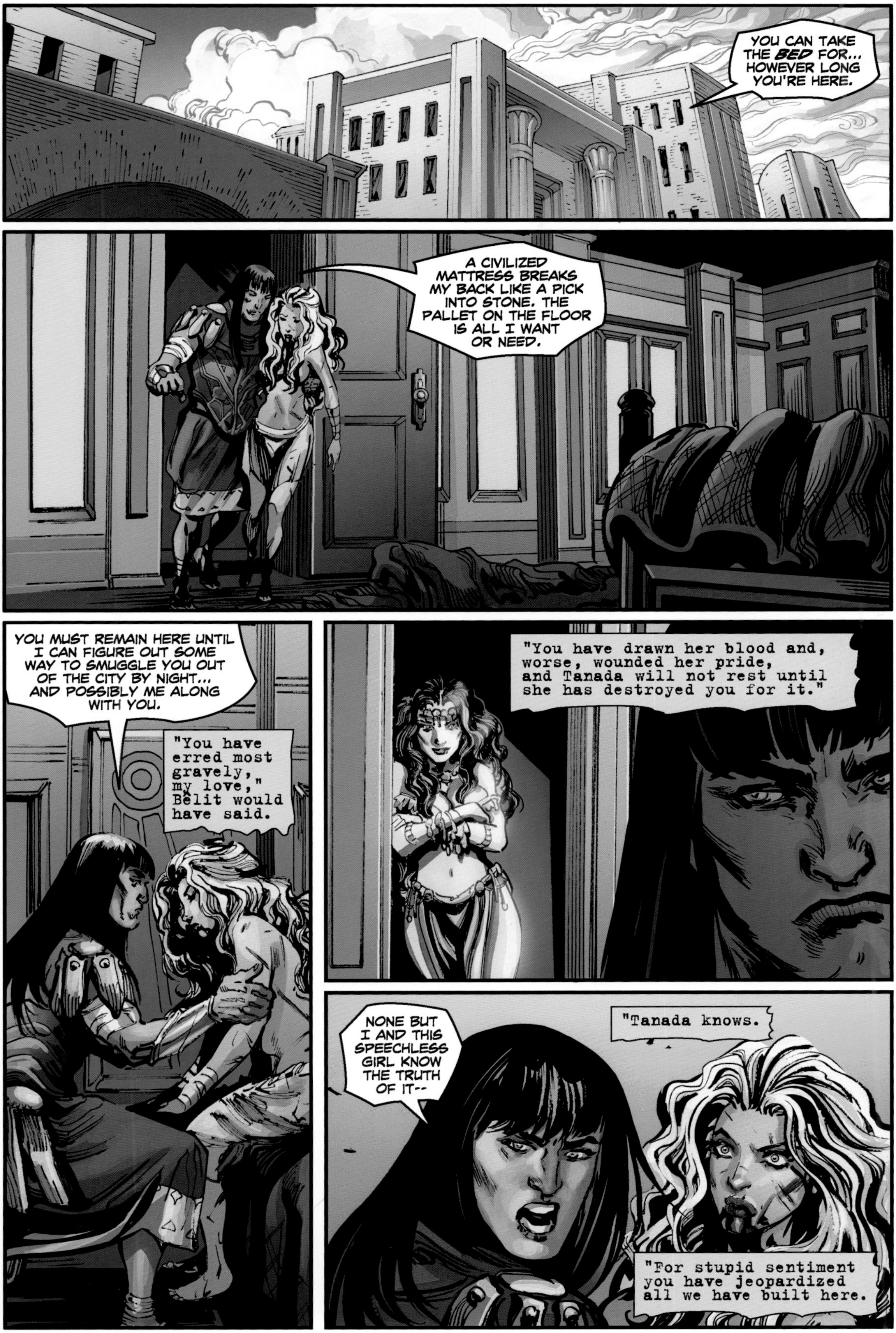
YOU CAN TAKE THE BED FOR... HOWEVER LONG YOU'RE HERE.
A CIVILIZED MATTRESS BREAKS MY BACK LIKE A PICK INTO STONE. THE PALLET ON THE FLOOR IS ALL I WANT OR NEED.
YOU MUST REMAIN HERE UNTIL I CAN FIGURE OUT SOME WAY TO SMUGGLE YOU OUT OF THE CITY BY NIGHT... AND POSSIBLY ME ALONG WITH YOU.
"You have erred most gravely, my love," Bêlit would have said.
"You have drawn her blood and, worse, wounded her pride, and Tanada will not rest until she has destroyed you for it."
NONE BUT I AND THIS SPEECHLESS GIRL KNOW THE TRUTH OF IT--
"Tanada knows.
"For stupid sentiment you have jeopardized all we have built here.

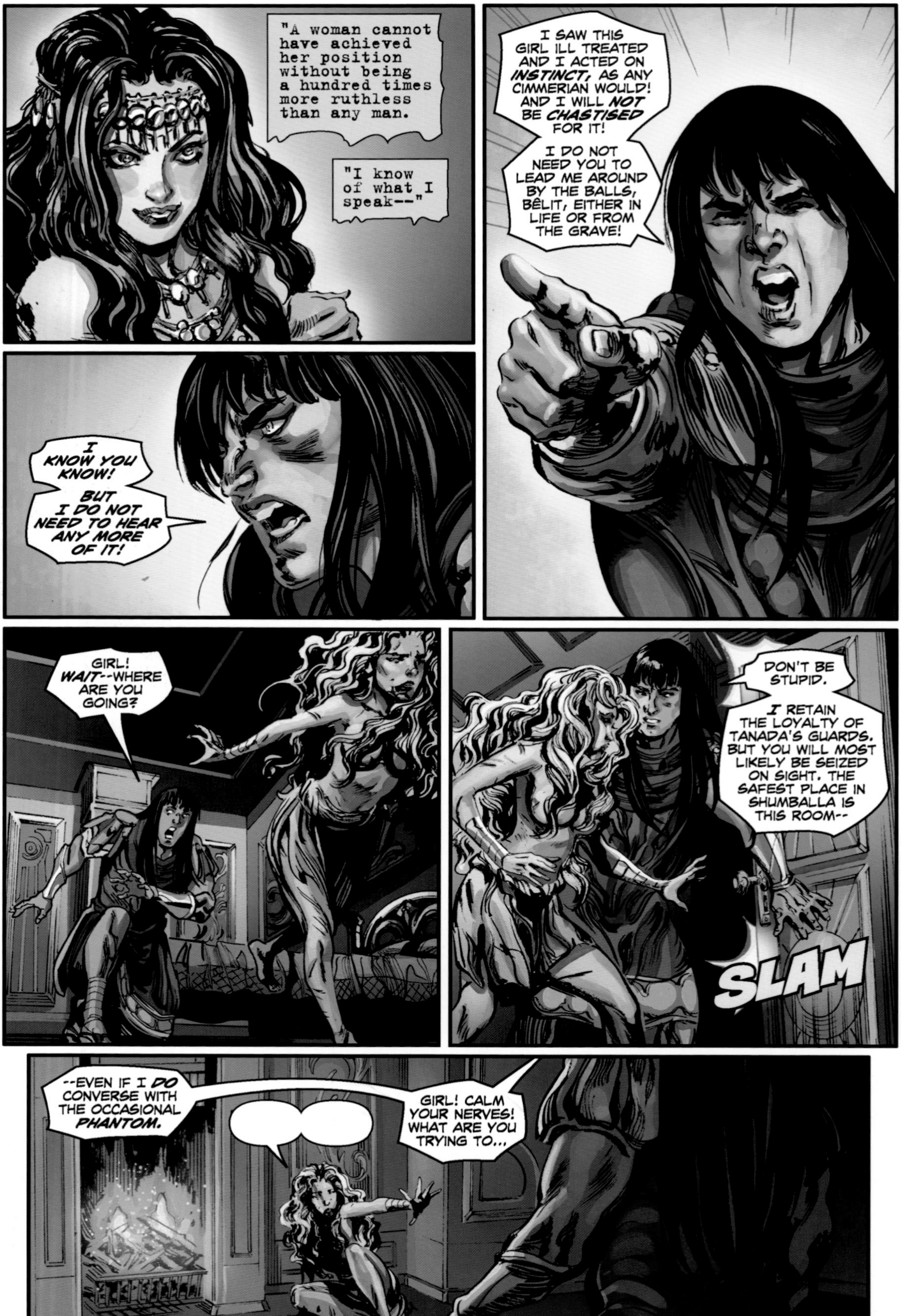

"A woman cannot have achieved her position without being a hundred times more ruthless than any man.
"I know of what I speak--"
I SAW THIS GIRL ILL TREATED AND I ACTED ON *INSTINCT,* AS ANY CIMMERIAN WOULD! AND I WILL *NOT* BE *CHASTISED* FOR IT!
I DO NOT NEED YOU TO LEAD ME AROUND BY THE BALLS, BÊLIT, EITHER IN LIFE OR FROM THE GRAVE!
I KNOW YOU KNOW!
BUT I DO NOT NEED TO HEAR ANY MORE OF IT!
GIRL! *WAIT*--WHERE ARE YOU GOING?
DON'T BE STUPID.
I RETAIN THE LOYALTY OF TANADA'S GUARDS. BUT YOU WILL MOST LIKELY BE SEIZED ON SIGHT. THE SAFEST PLACE IN SHUMBALLA IS THIS ROOM--
SLAM
--EVEN IF I *DO* CONVERSE WITH THE OCCASIONAL *PHANTOM.*
GIRL! CALM YOUR NERVES! WHAT ARE YOU TRYING TO...

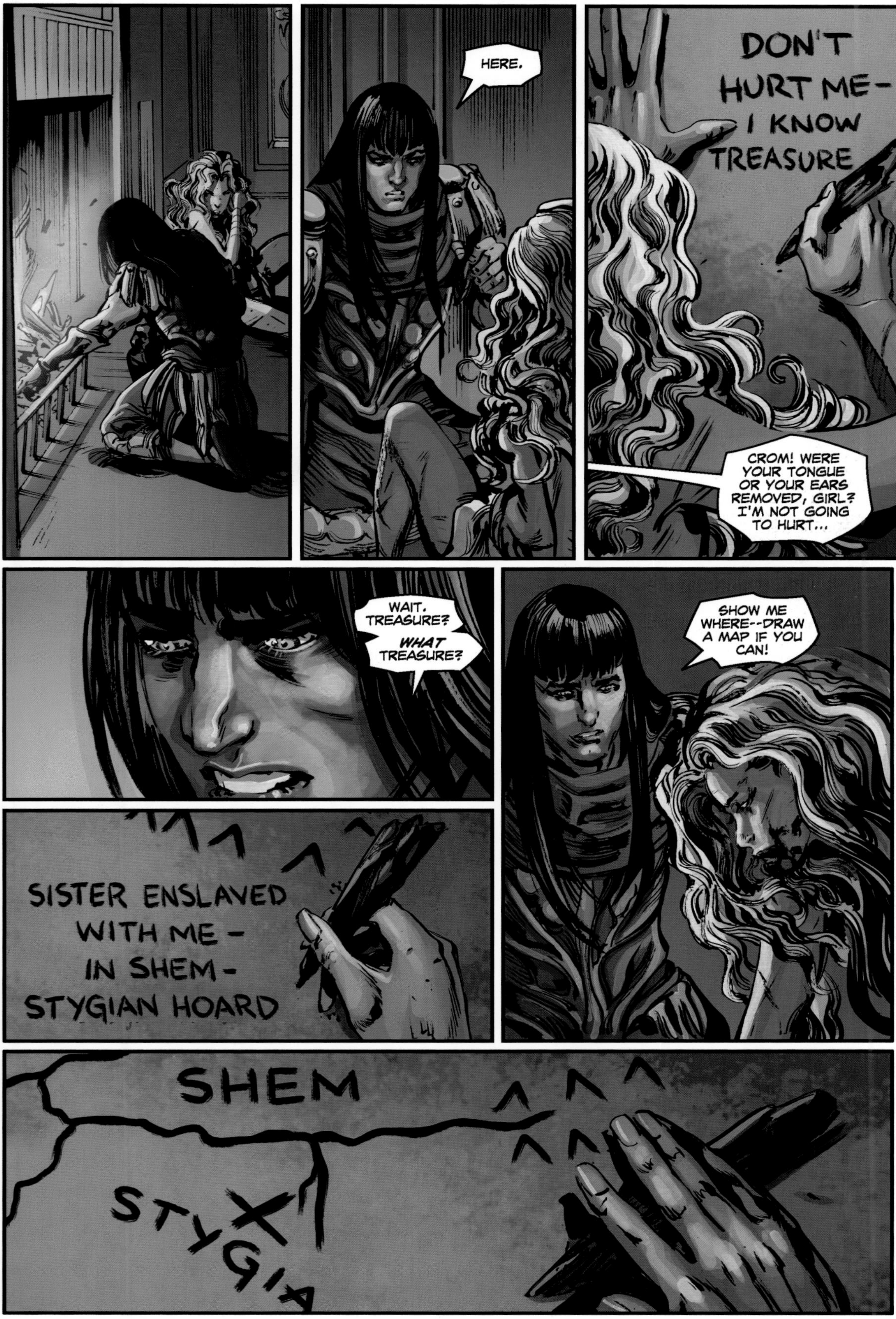

HERE.
DON'T HURT ME - I KNOW TREASURE
CROM! WERE YOUR TONGUE OR YOUR EARS REMOVED, GIRL? I'M NOT GOING TO HURT...
WAIT. TREASURE? *WHAT* TREASURE?
SHOW ME WHERE--DRAW A MAP IF YOU CAN!
SISTER ENSLAVED WITH ME - IN SHEM - STYGIAN HOARD
SHEM
STYGIA

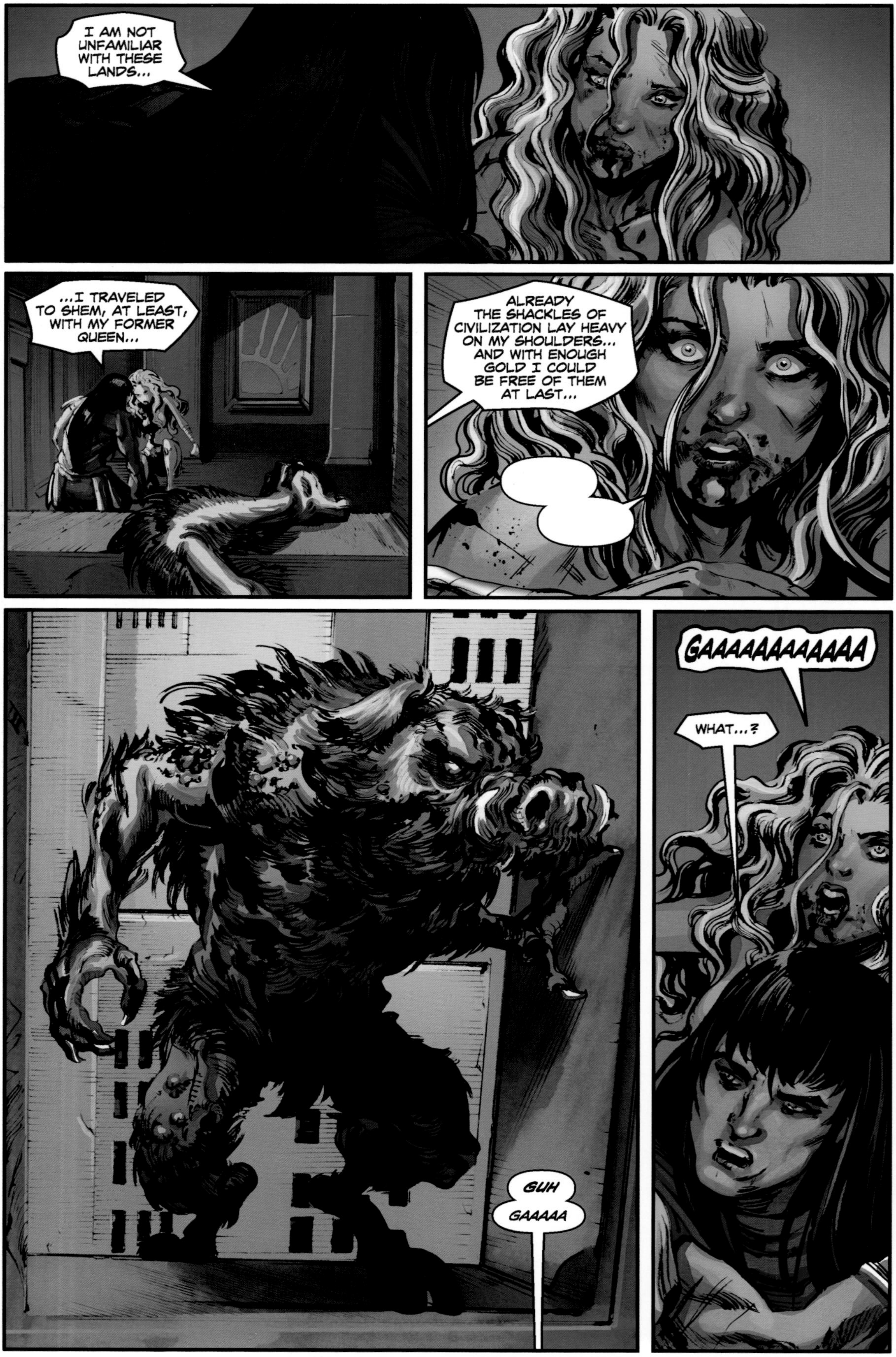
I AM NOT UNFAMILIAR WITH THESE LANDS...
...I TRAVELED TO SHEM, AT LEAST, WITH MY FORMER QUEEN...
ALREADY THE SHACKLES OF CIVILIZATION LAY HEAVY ON MY SHOULDERS... AND WITH ENOUGH GOLD I COULD BE FREE OF THEM AT LAST...
GAAAAAAAAAAA
WHAT...?
GUH
GAAAAA

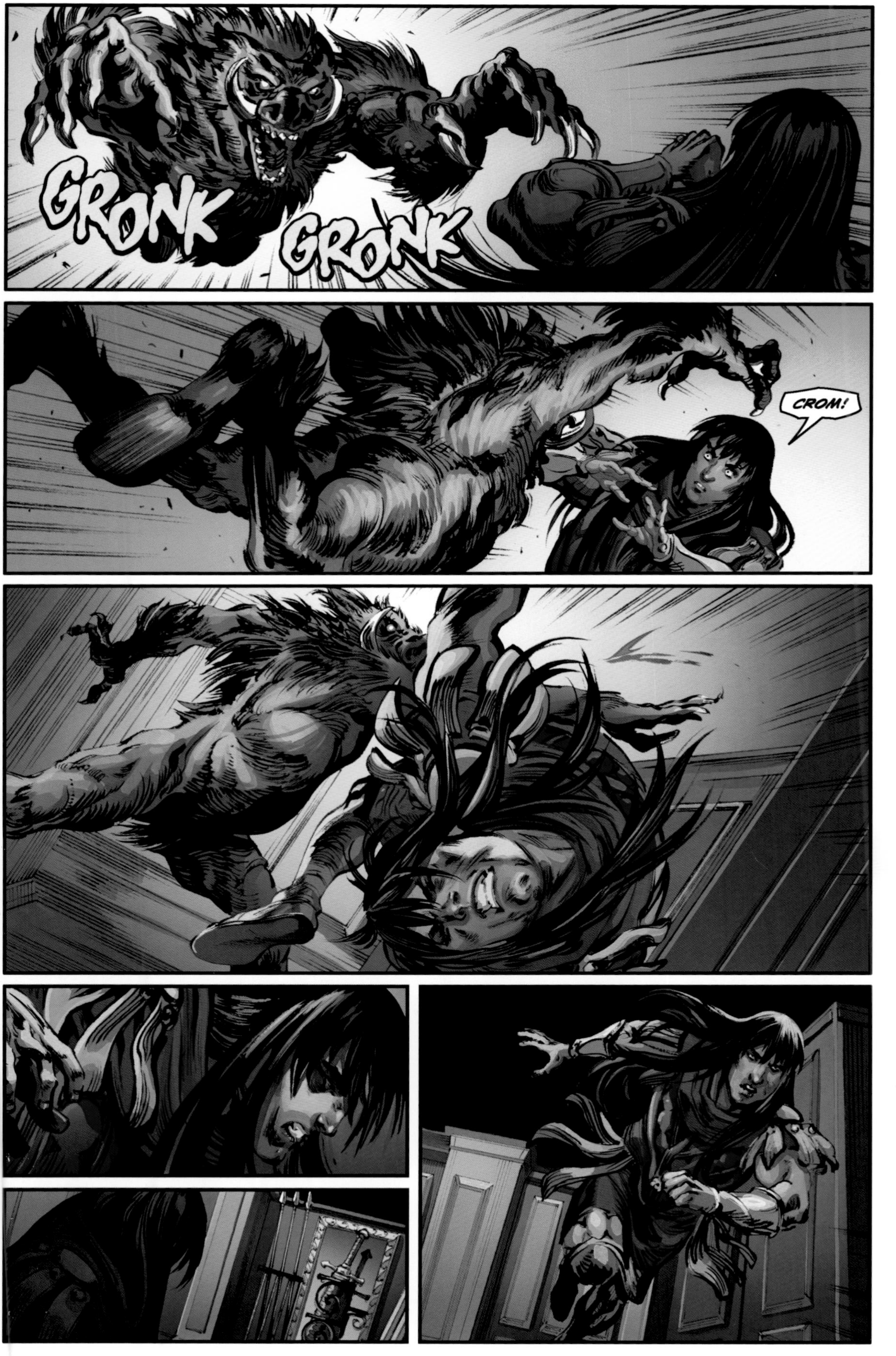
GRONK
GRONK
CROM!

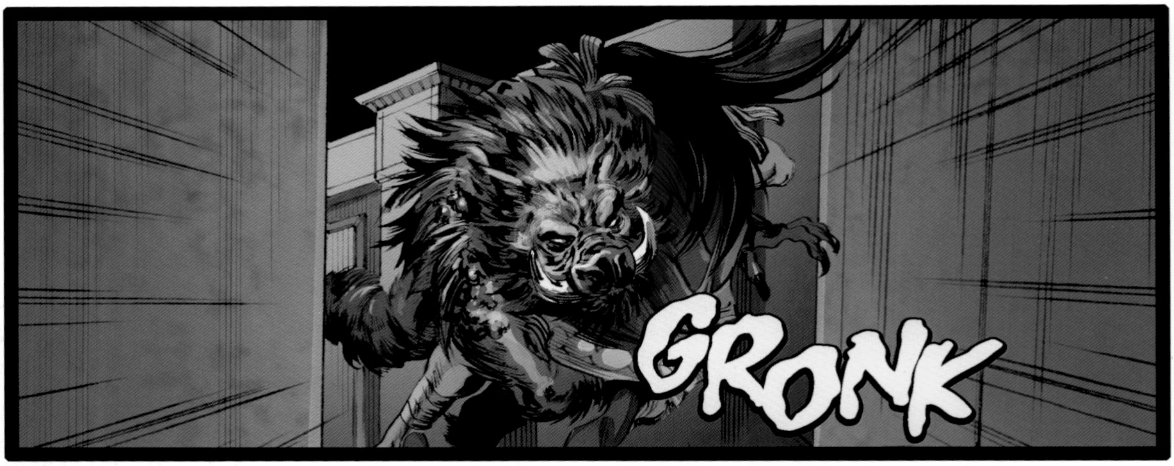
GRONK

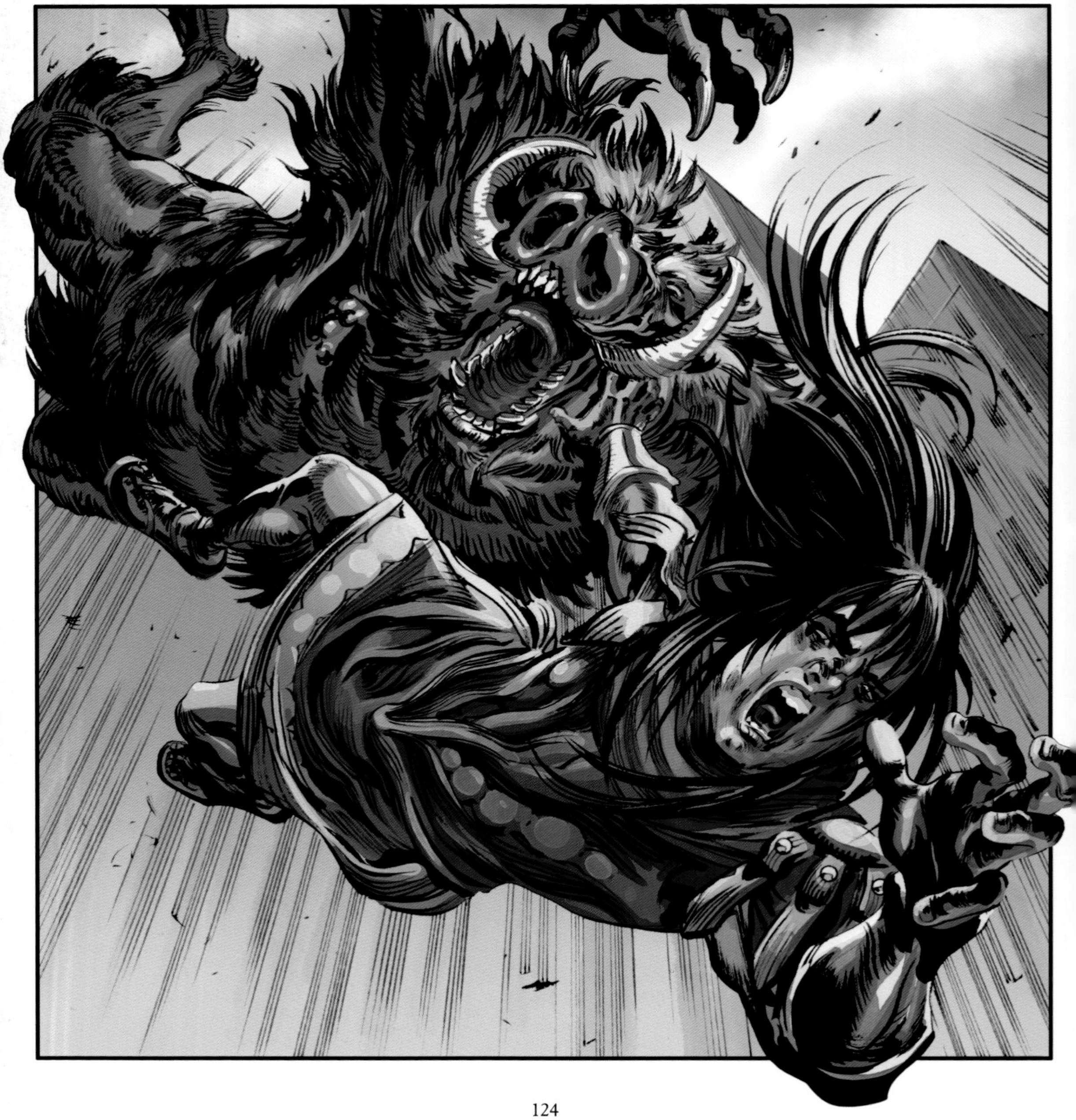

CHAPTER SIX

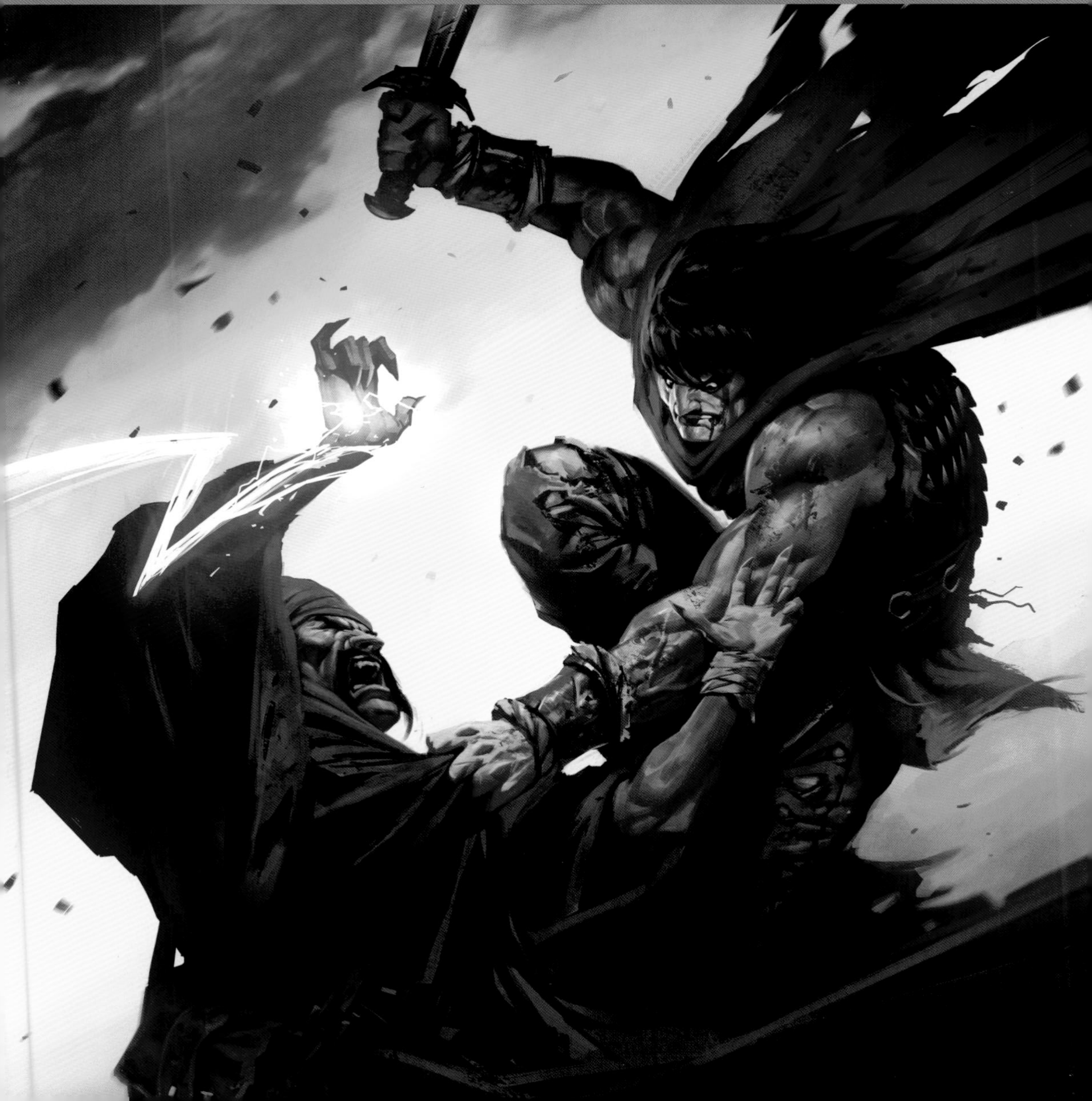

"Crom laughs at you all!
Only a strong arm bends the world!"

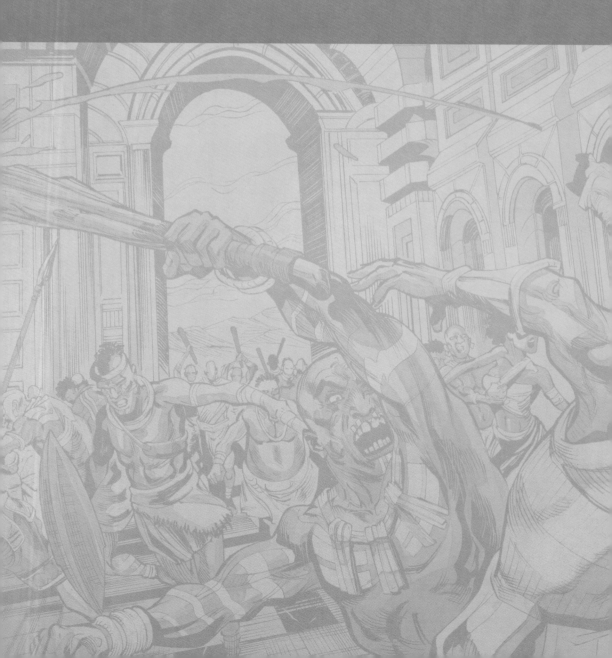

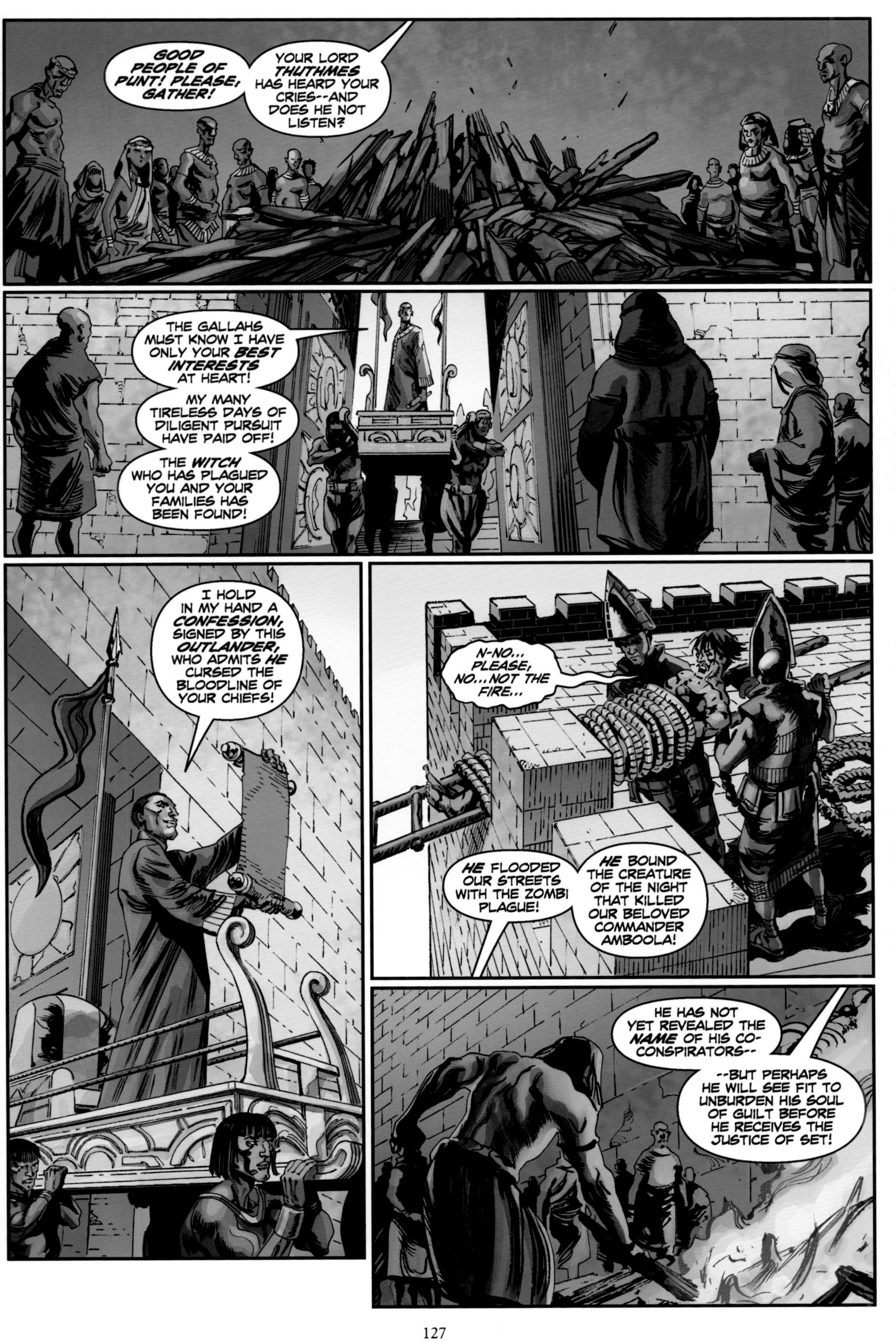

GOOD PEOPLE OF PUNT! PLEASE, GATHER!
YOUR LORD THUTHMES HAS HEARD YOUR CRIES--AND DOES HE NOT LISTEN?
THE GALLAHS MUST KNOW I HAVE ONLY YOUR BEST INTERESTS AT HEART!
MY MANY TIRELESS DAYS OF DILIGENT PURSUIT HAVE PAID OFF!
THE WITCH WHO HAS PLAGUED YOU AND YOUR FAMILIES HAS BEEN FOUND!
I HOLD IN MY HAND A CONFESSION, SIGNED BY THIS OUTLANDER, WHO ADMITS HE CURSED THE BLOODLINE OF YOUR CHIEFS!
N-NO... PLEASE, NO... NOT THE FIRE...
HE FLOODED OUR STREETS WITH THE ZOMBI PLAGUE!
HE BOUND THE CREATURE OF THE NIGHT THAT KILLED OUR BELOVED COMMANDER AMBOOLA!
HE HAS NOT YET REVEALED THE NAME OF HIS CO-CONSPIRATORS--
--BUT PERHAPS HE WILL SEE FIT TO UNBURDEN HIS SOUL OF GUILT BEFORE HE RECEIVES THE JUSTICE OF SET!

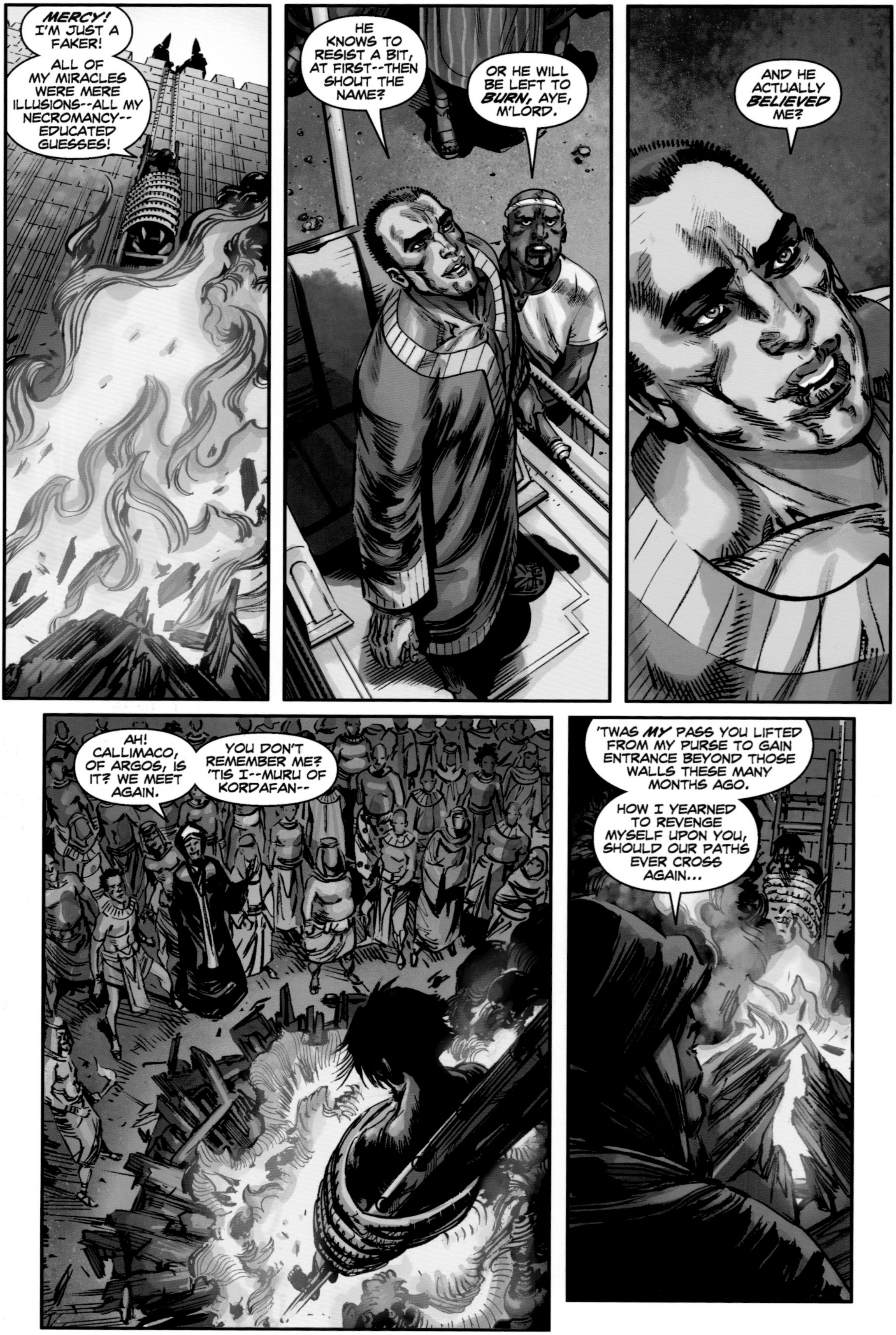
MERCY! I'M JUST A FAKER!
ALL OF MY MIRACLES WERE MERE ILLUSIONS--ALL MY NECROMANCY--EDUCATED GUESSES!
HE KNOWS TO RESIST A BIT, AT FIRST--THEN SHOUT THE NAME?
OR HE WILL BE LEFT TO BURN, AYE, M'LORD.
AND HE ACTUALLY BELIEVED ME?
AH! CALLIMACO, OF ARGOS, IS IT? WE MEET AGAIN.
YOU DON'T REMEMBER ME? 'TIS I--MURU OF KORDAFAN--
'TWAS MY PASS YOU LIFTED FROM MY PURSE TO GAIN ENTRANCE BEYOND THOSE WALLS THESE MANY MONTHS AGO.
HOW I YEARNED TO REVENGE MYSELF UPON YOU, SHOULD OUR PATHS EVER CROSS AGAIN...

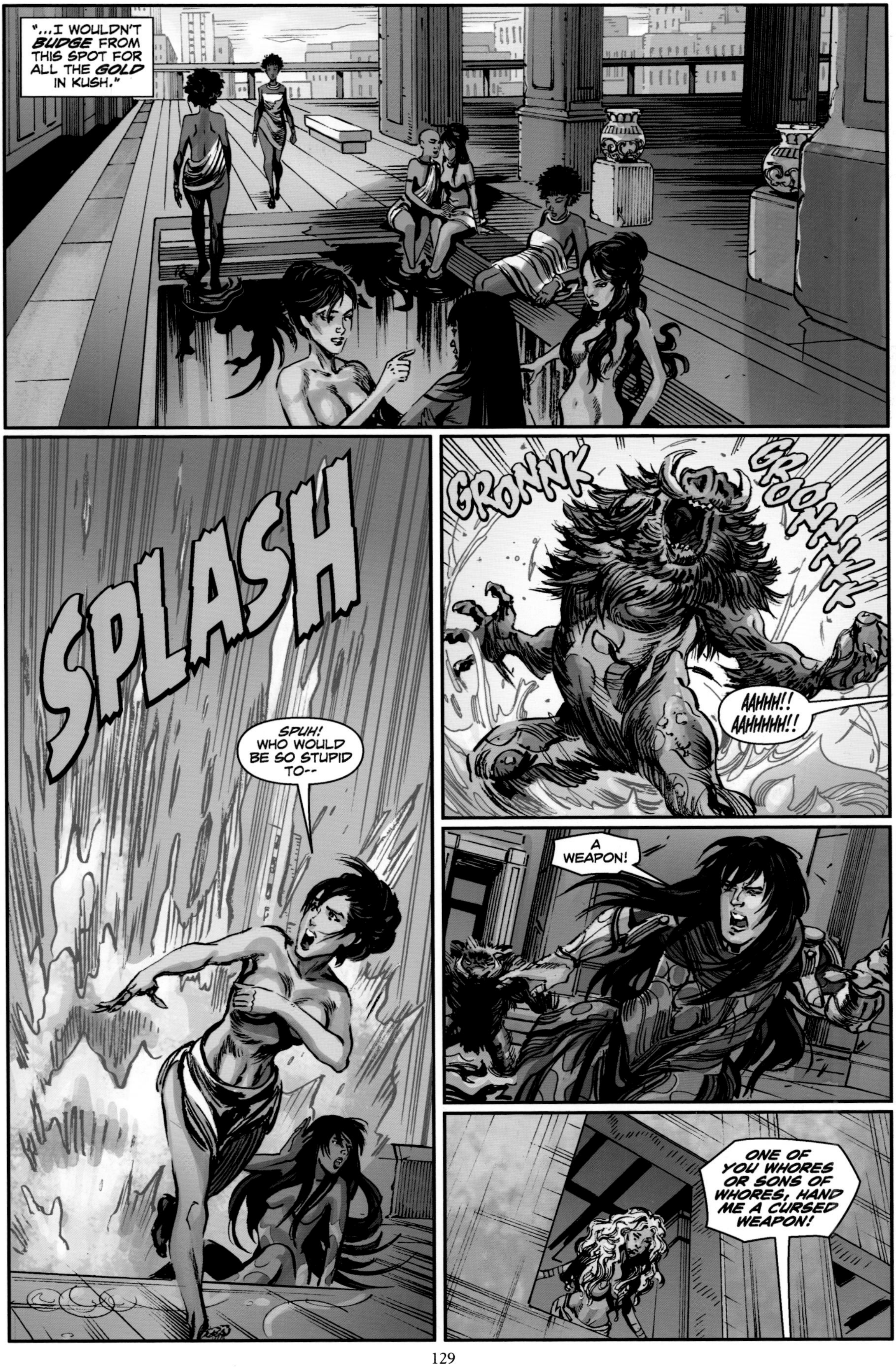
"...I WOULDN'T BUDGE FROM THIS SPOT FOR ALL THE GOLD IN KUSH."
SPLASH
SPUH! WHO WOULD BE SO STUPID TO--
GRONNK
GROONNNKK
AAHHH!! AAHHHHH!!
A WEAPON!
ONE OF YOU WHORES OR SONS OF WHORES, HAND ME A CURSED WEAPON!

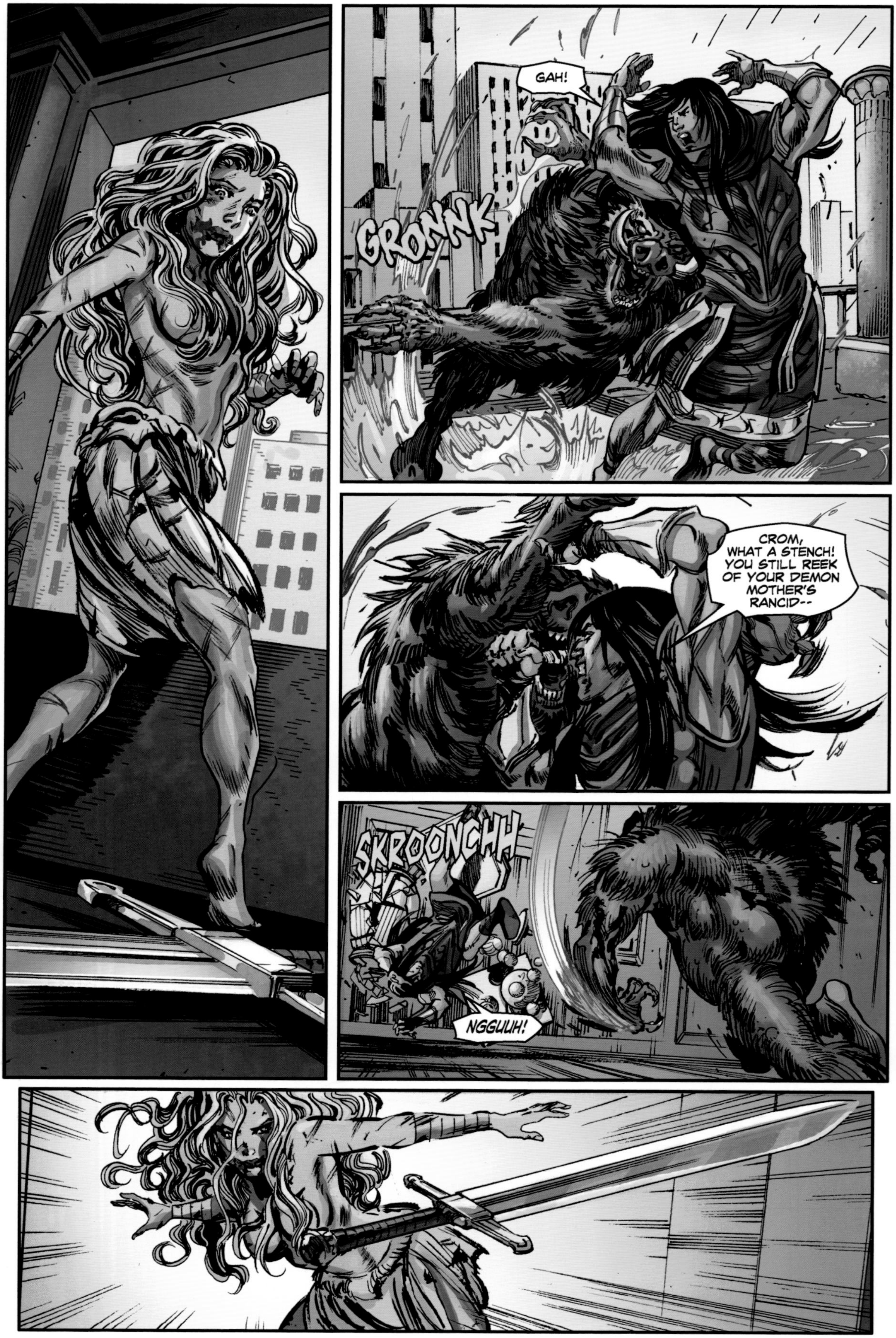
GAH!
GRONNK
CROM, WHAT A STENCH! YOU STILL REEK OF YOUR DEMON MOTHER'S RANCID--
SKROONCHH
NGGUUH!

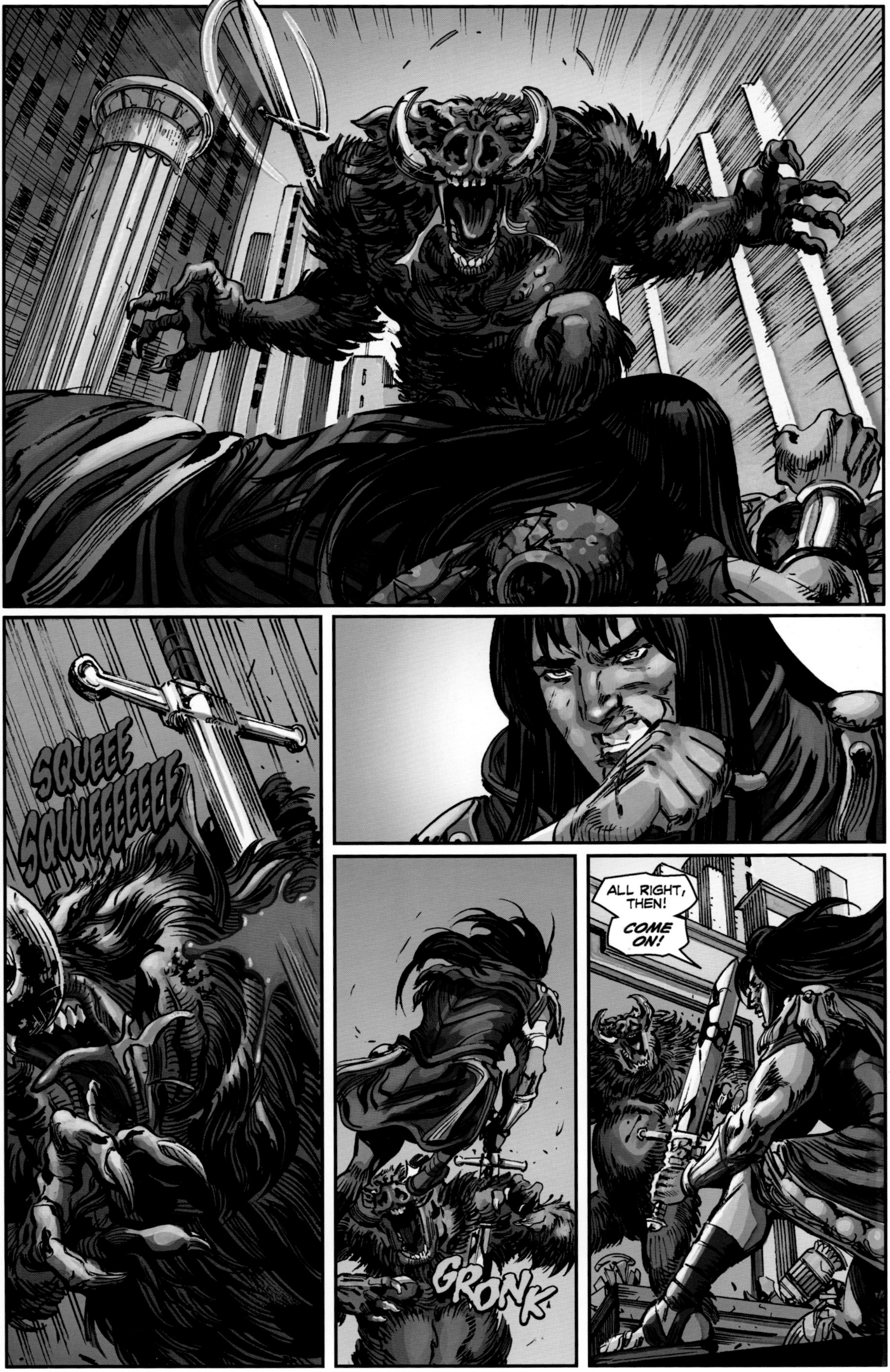
SQUEEE SQUEEEEEEEE
GRONK
ALL RIGHT, THEN! COME ON!

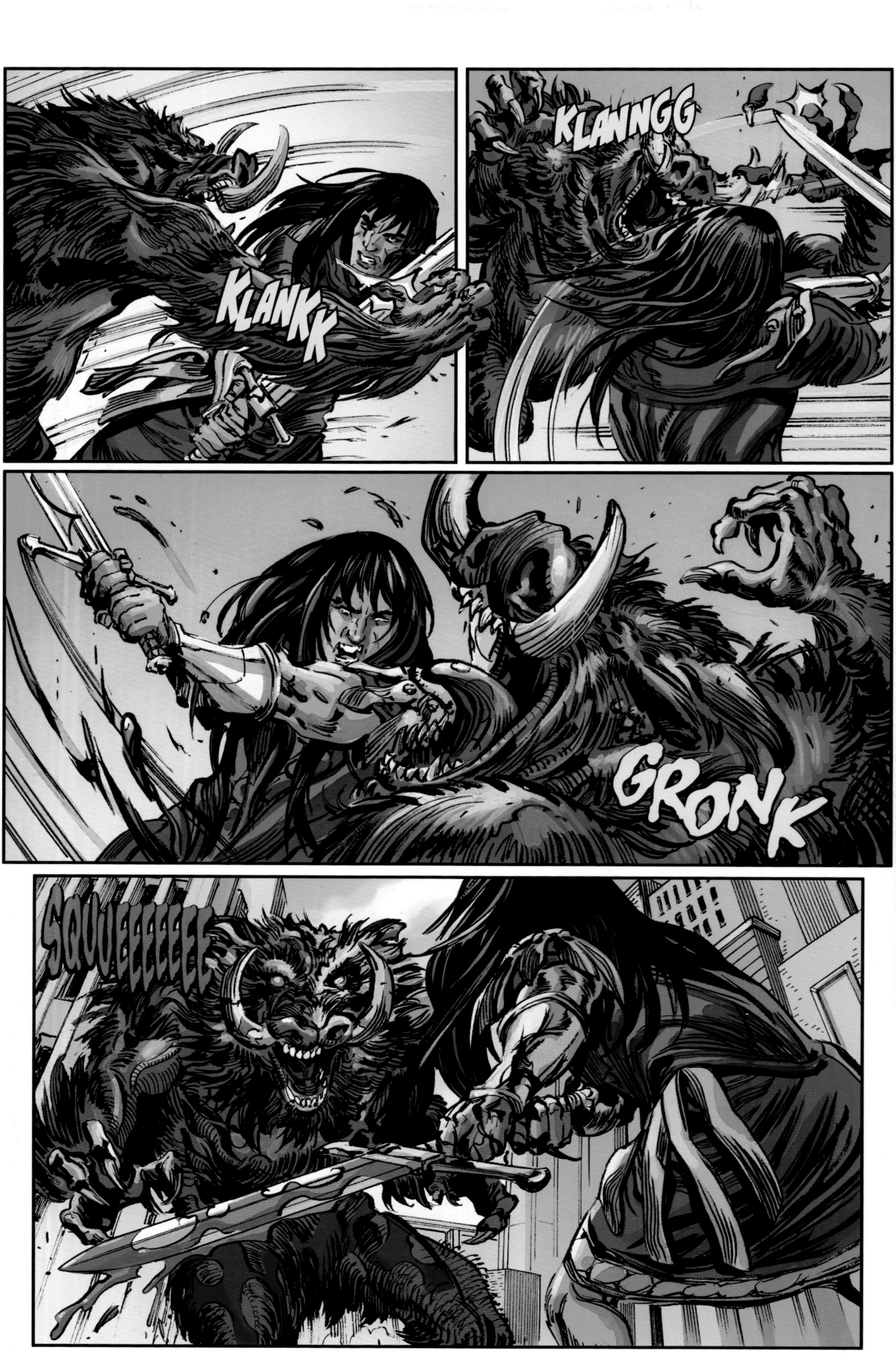
KLANKK
KLANNGG
GRONK
SQUEEEEEEE

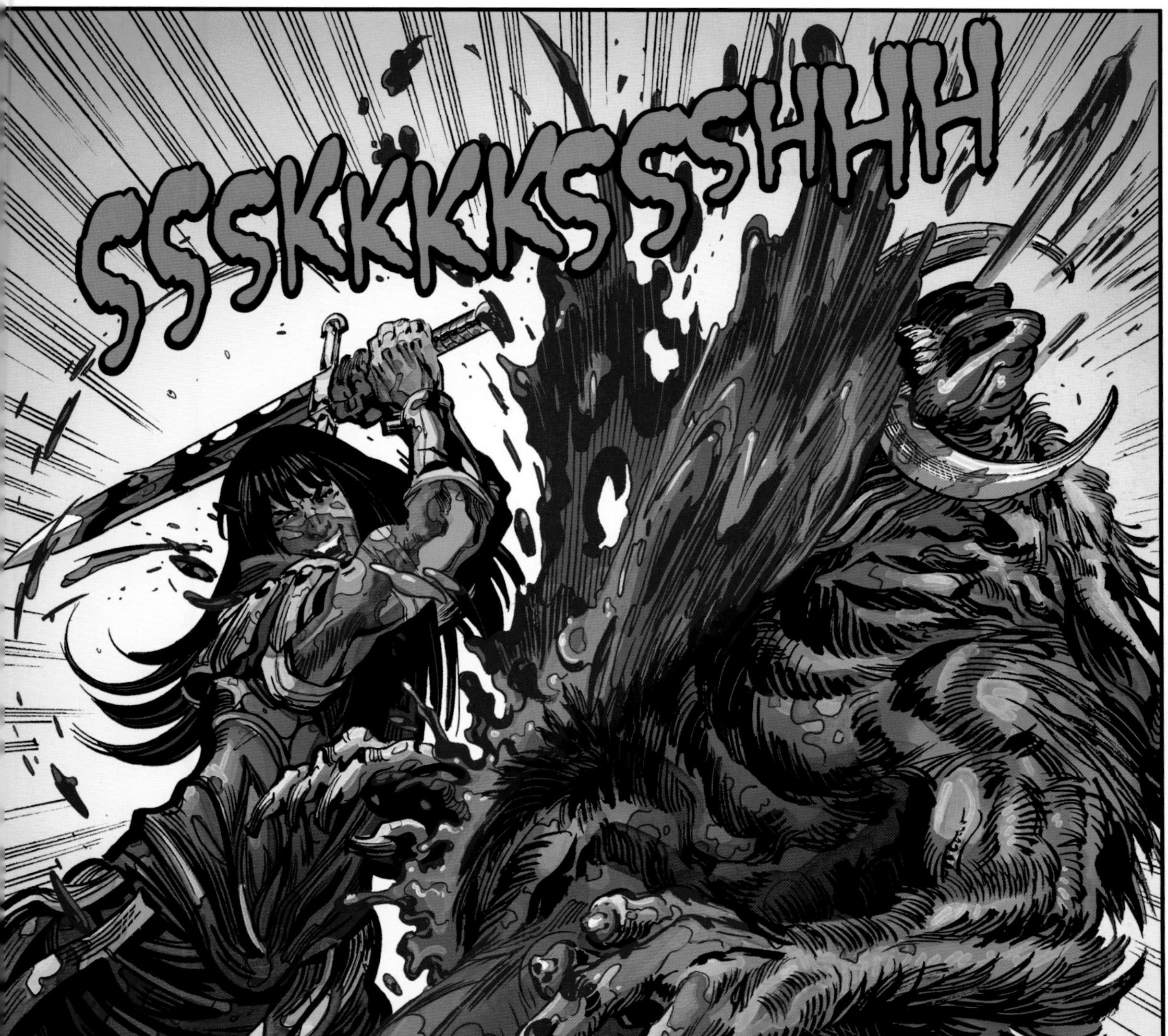
SSSKKKKSSSHHH

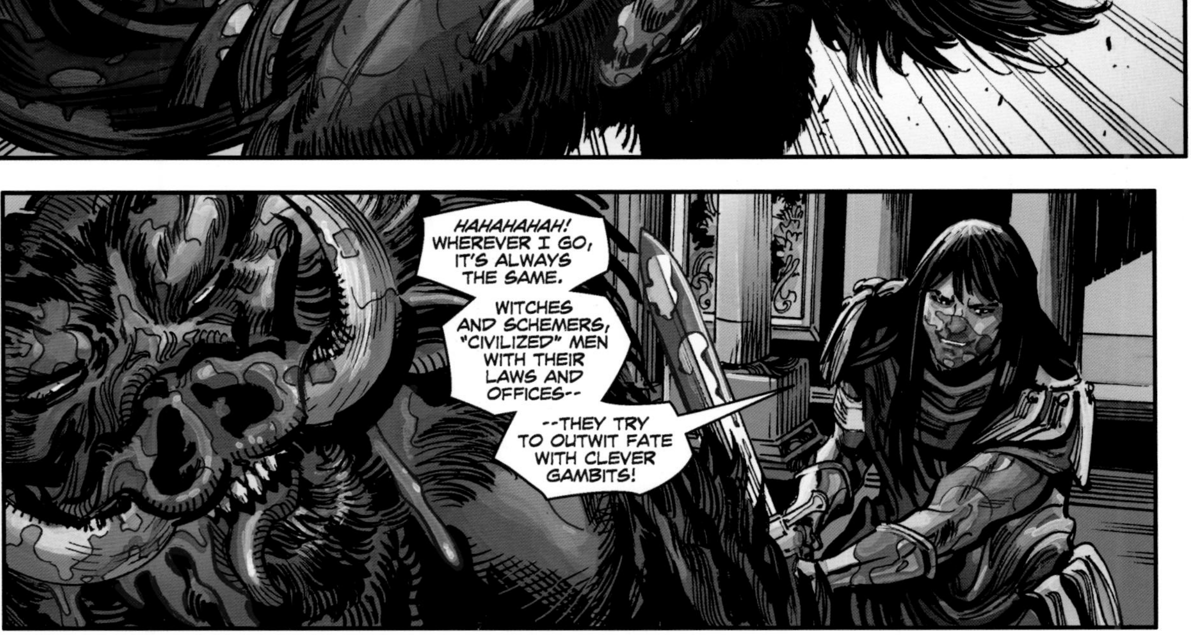
HAHAHAHAH! WHEREVER I GO, IT'S ALWAYS THE SAME.
WITCHES AND SCHEMERS, "CIVILIZED" MEN WITH THEIR LAWS AND OFFICES--
--THEY TRY TO OUTWIT FATE WITH CLEVER GAMBITS!

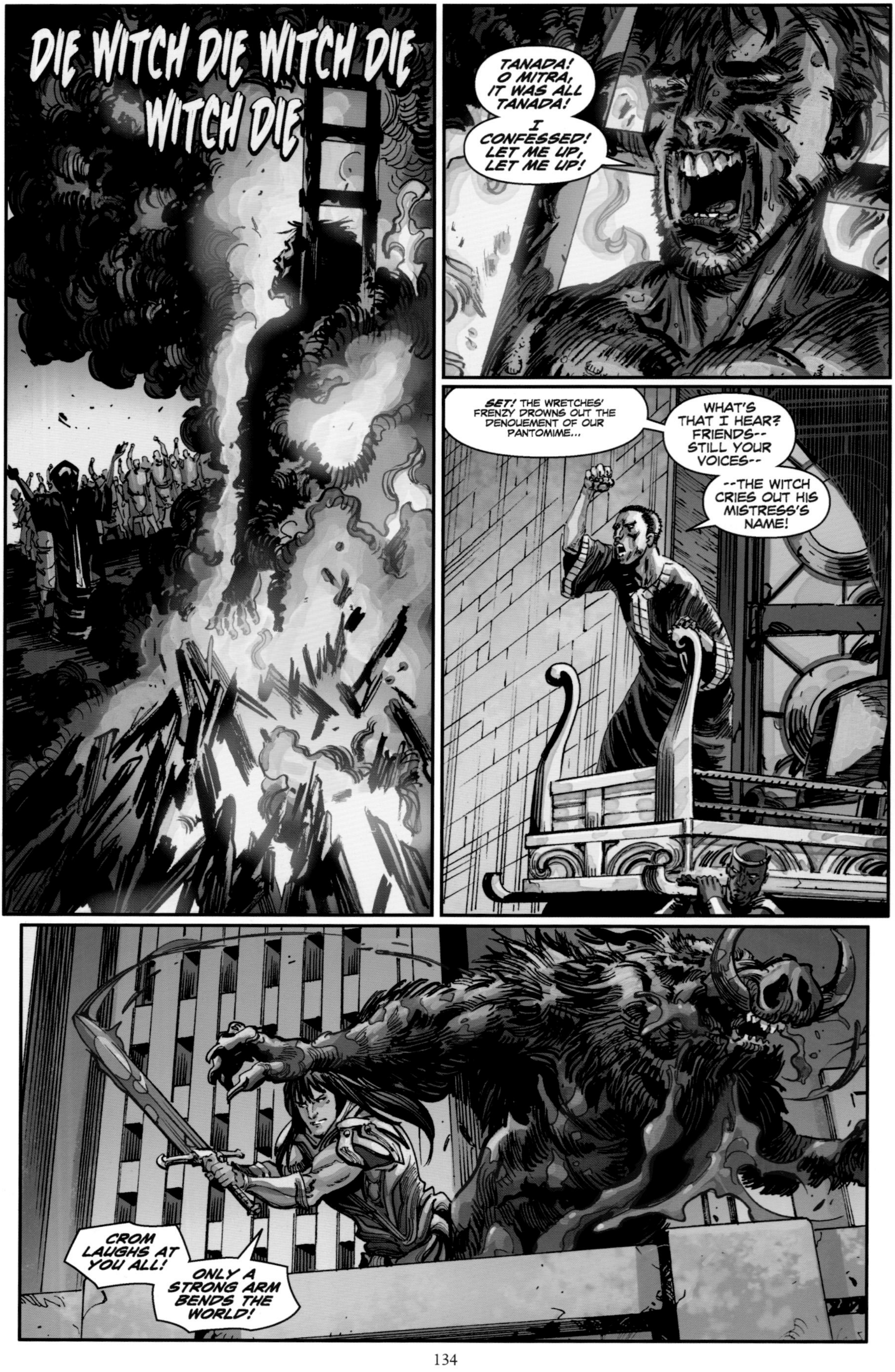
DIE WITCH DIE WITCH DIE WITCH DIE WITCH DIE
TANADA! O MITRA, IT WAS ALL TANADA!
I CONFESSED! LET ME UP, LET ME UP!
SET! THE WRETCHES' FRENZY DROWNS OUT THE DENOUEMENT OF OUR PANTOMIME...
WHAT'S THAT I HEAR? FRIENDS-- STILL YOUR VOICES--
--THE WITCH CRIES OUT HIS MISTRESS'S NAME!
CROM LAUGHS AT YOU ALL!
ONLY A STRONG ARM BENDS THE WORLD!

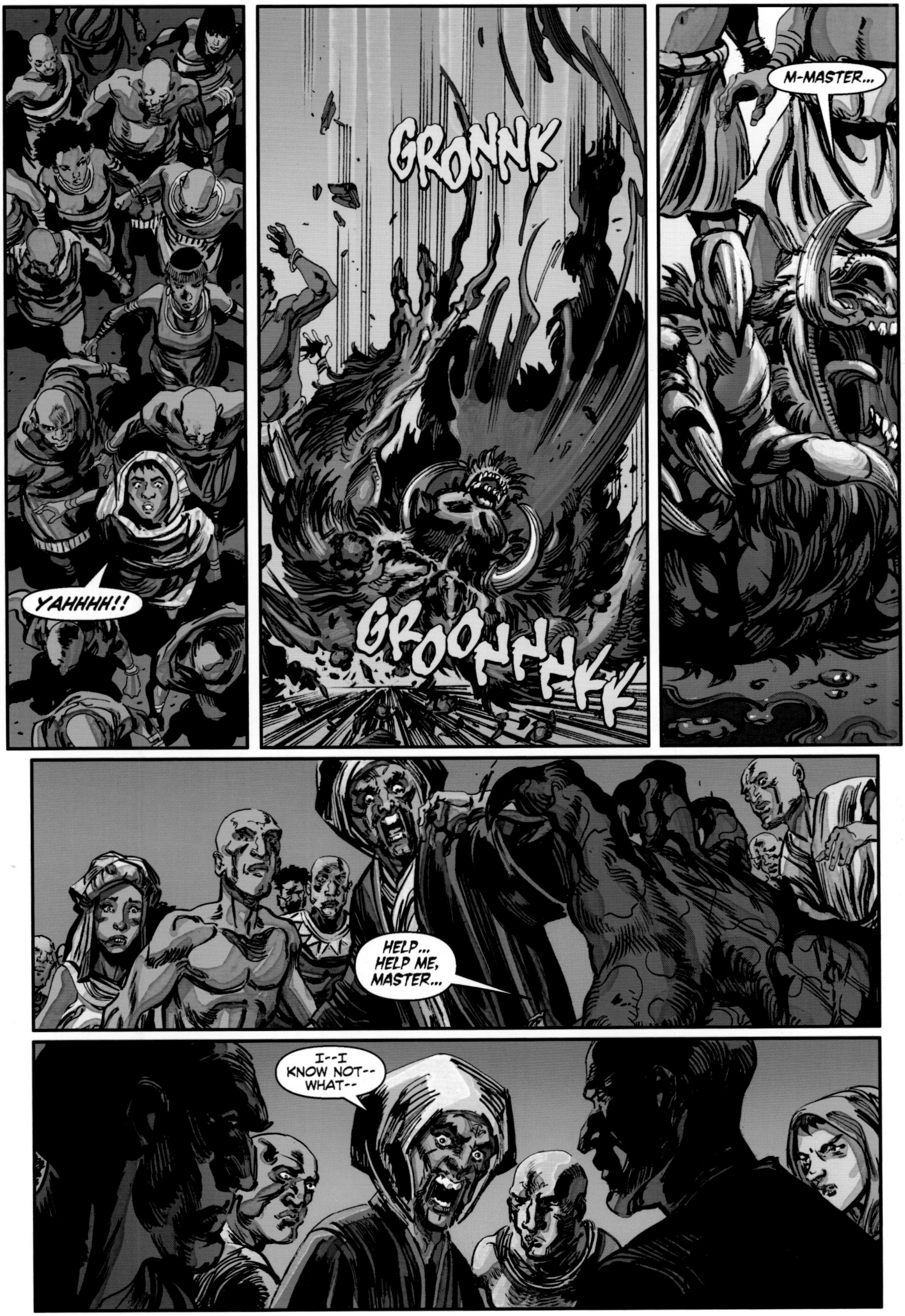
YAHHHH!!
GRONNK
GROONNKK
M-MASTER...
HELP... HELP ME, MASTER...
I--I KNOW NOT-- WHAT--

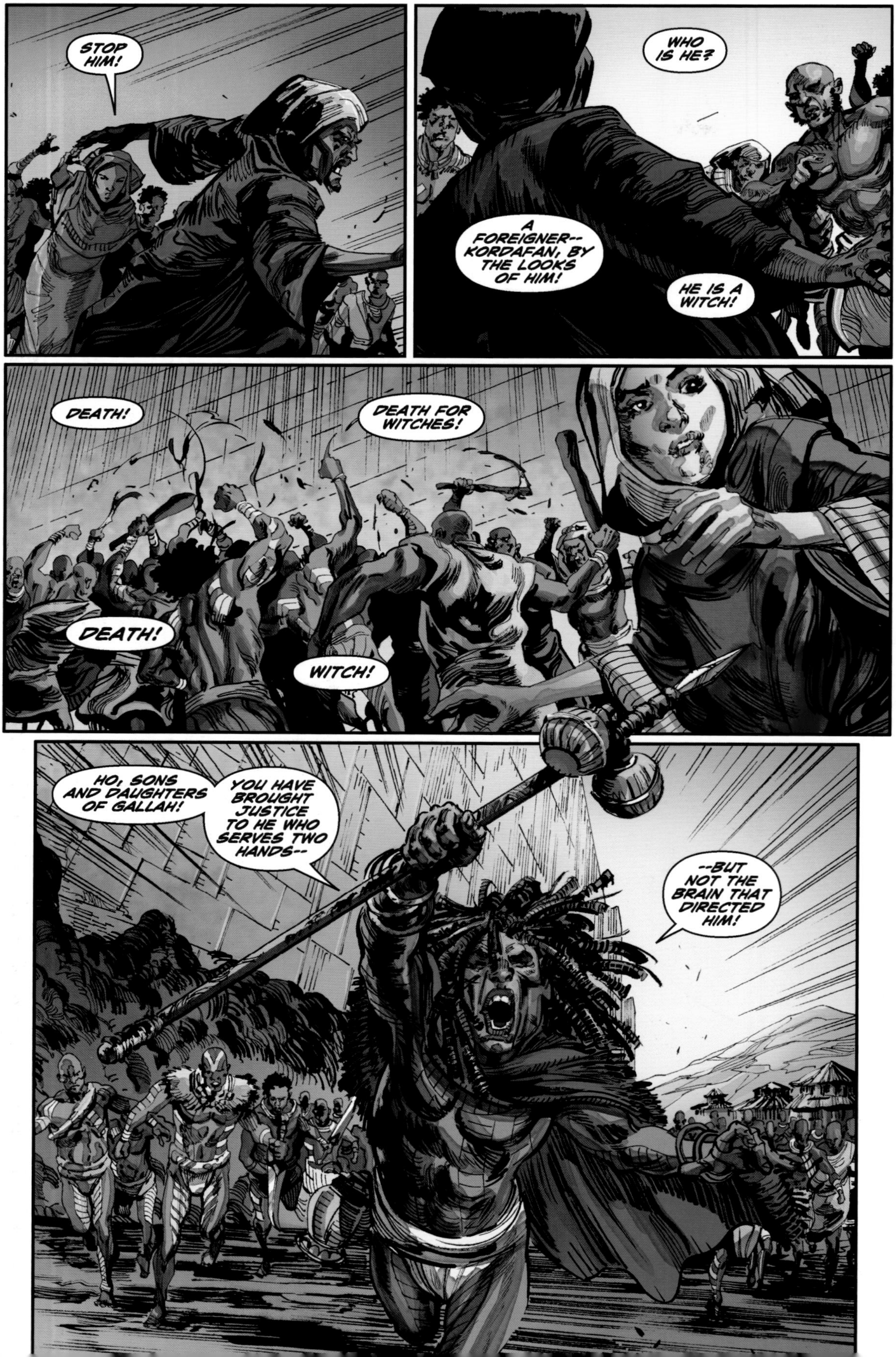
STOP HIM!
WHO IS HE?
A FOREIGNER-- KORDAFAN, BY THE LOOKS OF HIM!
HE IS A WITCH!
DEATH!
DEATH FOR WITCHES!
DEATH!
WITCH!
HO, SONS AND DAUGHTERS OF GALLAH!
YOU HAVE BROUGHT JUSTICE TO HE WHO SERVES TWO HANDS--
--BUT NOT THE BRAIN THAT DIRECTED HIM!

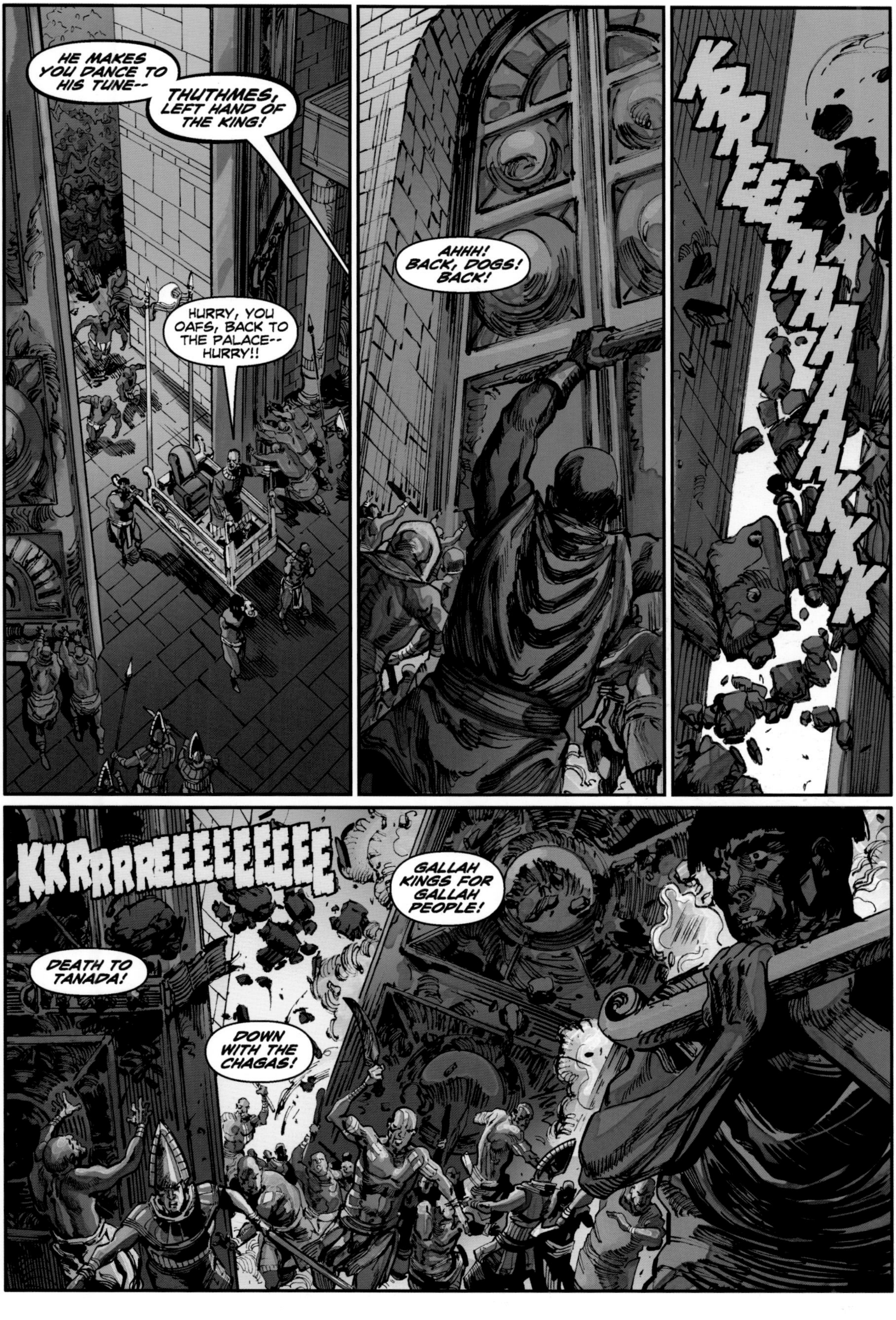
HE MAKES YOU DANCE TO HIS TUNE--
THUTHMES, LEFT HAND OF THE KING!
HURRY, YOU OAFS, BACK TO THE PALACE-- HURRY!!
AHHH! BACK, DOGS! BACK!
KRREEEAAAAAKKK
KKRRRRREEEEEEEEE
GALLAH KINGS FOR GALLAH PEOPLE!
DEATH TO TANADA!
DOWN WITH THE CHAGAS!

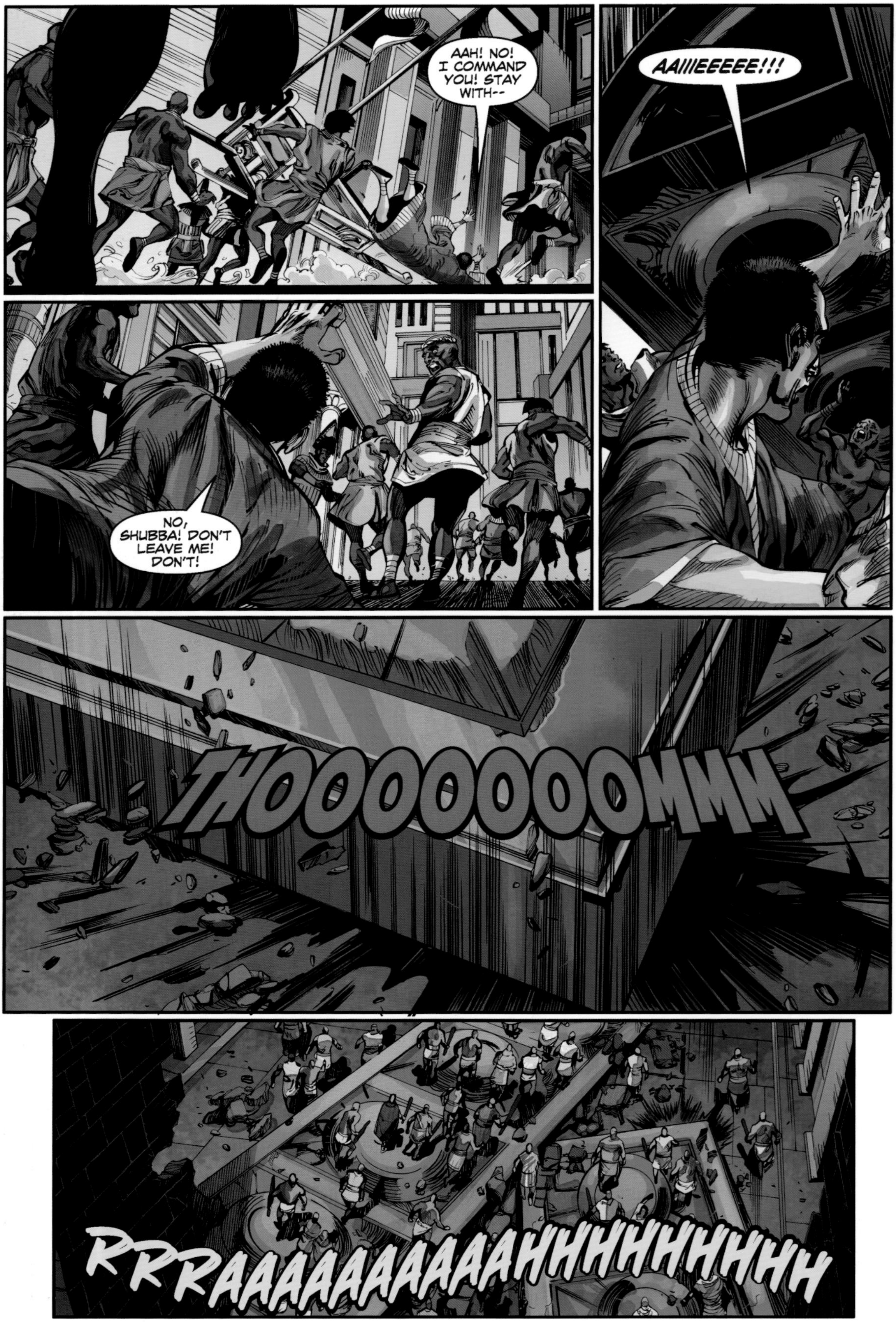
AAH! NO! I COMMAND YOU! STAY WITH--
AAIIIEEEEE!!!
NO, SHUBBA! DON'T LEAVE ME! DON'T!
THOOOOOOOMMM
RRRAAAAAAAAAAHHHHHHHHH

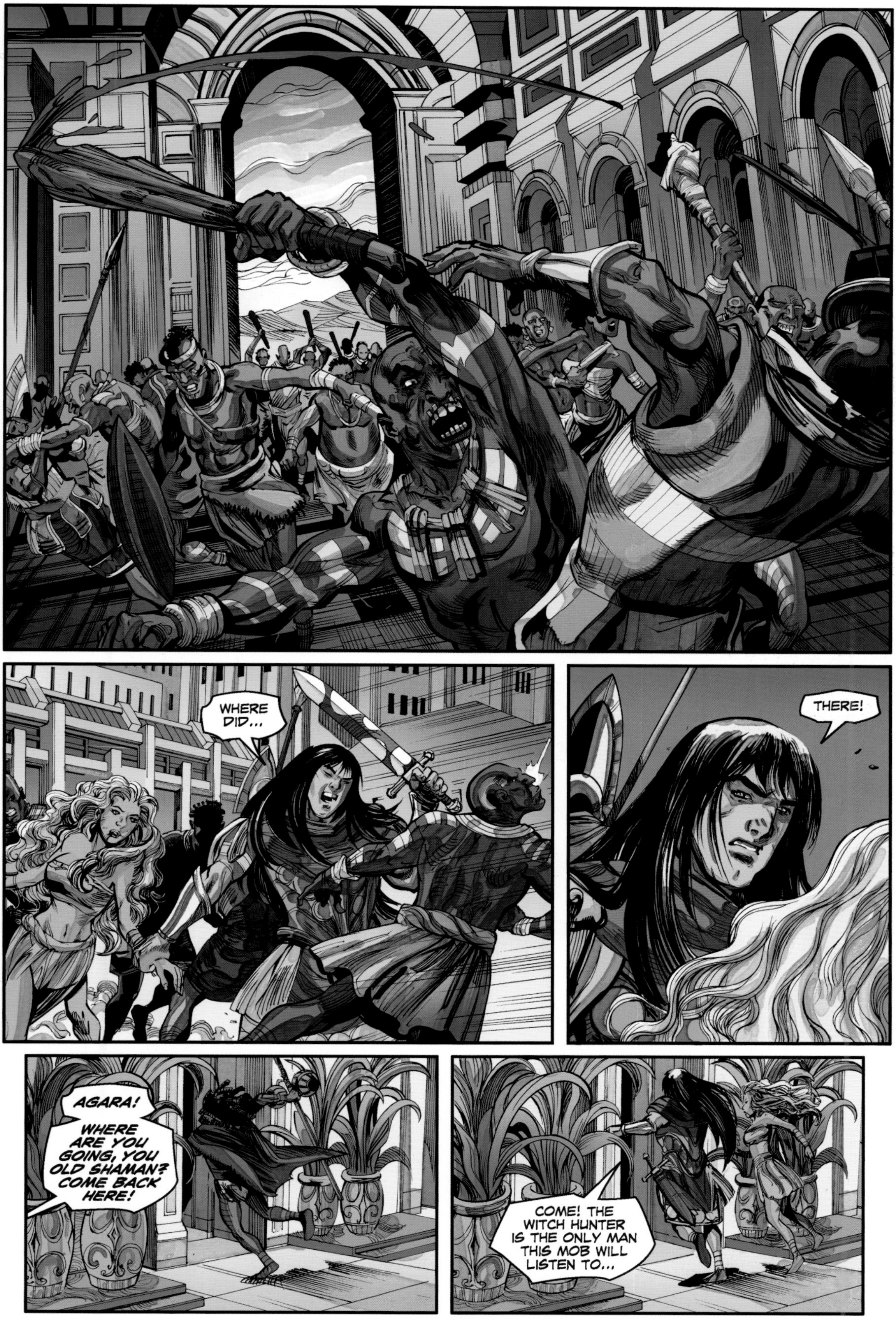
WHERE DID...
THERE!
AGARA!
WHERE ARE YOU GOING, YOU OLD SHAMAN? COME BACK HERE!
COME! THE WITCH HUNTER IS THE ONLY MAN THIS MOB WILL LISTEN TO...

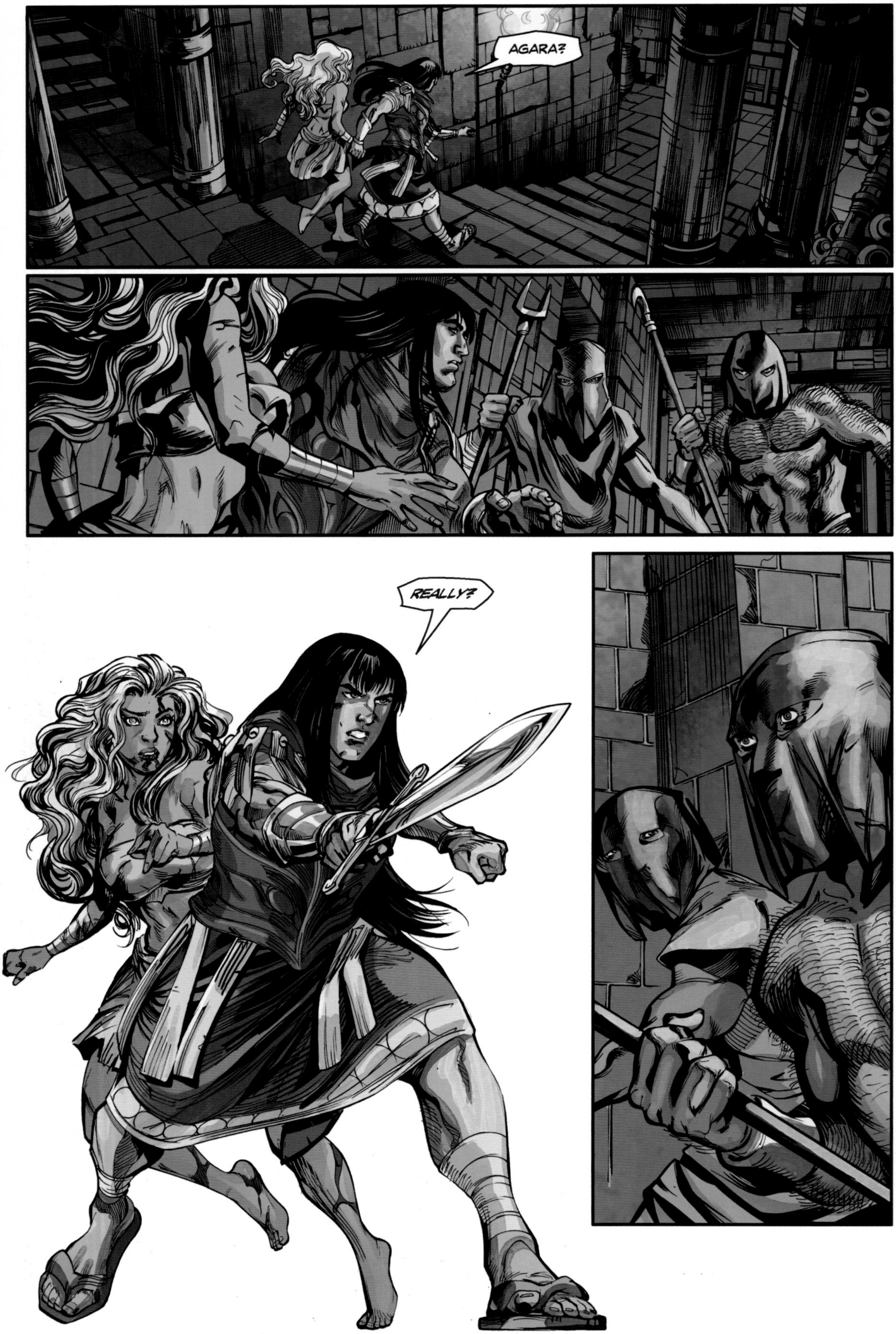
AGARA?
REALLY?

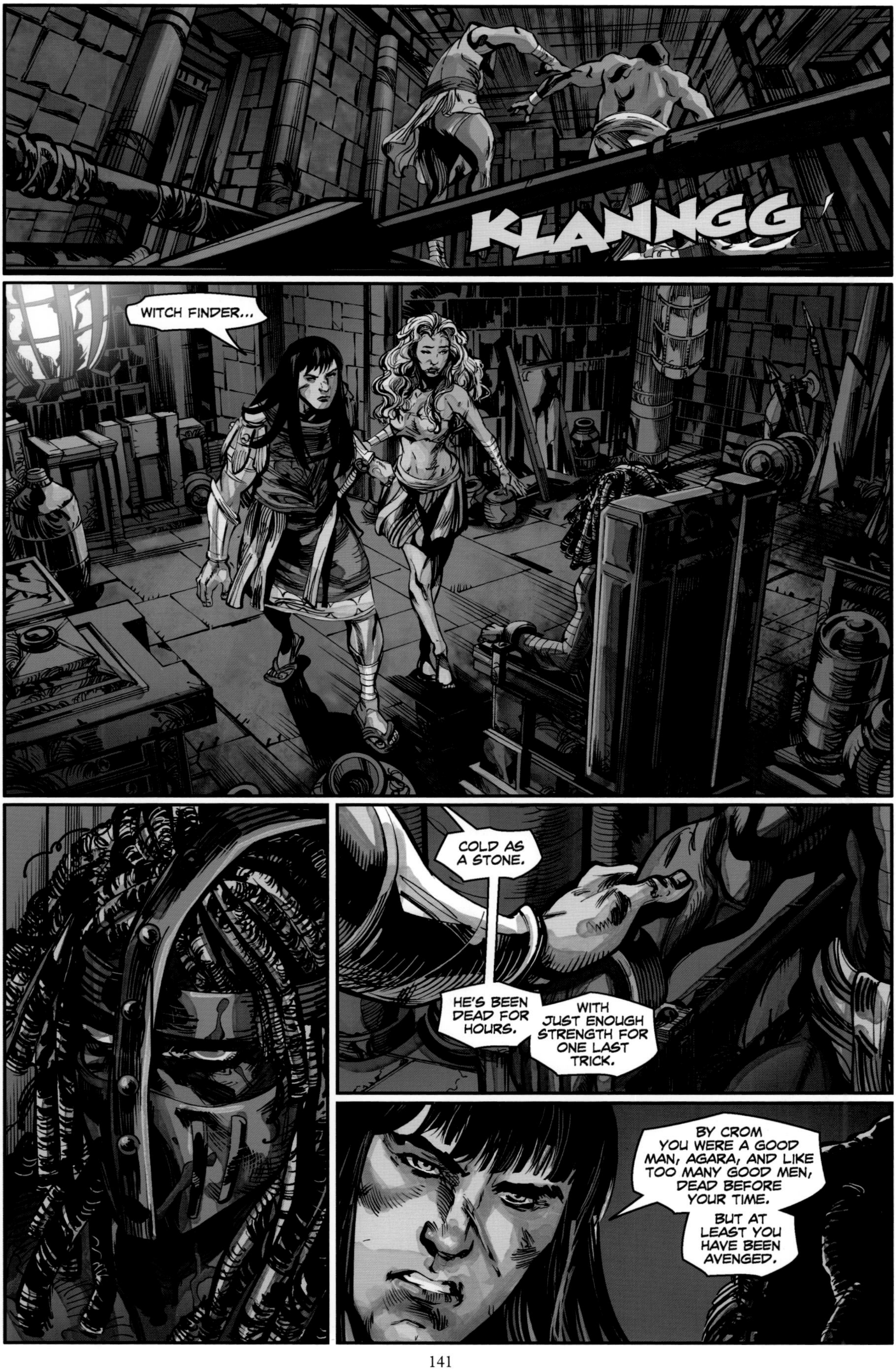
KLANNGG!
WITCH FINDER...
COLD AS A STONE.
HE'S BEEN DEAD FOR HOURS.
WITH JUST ENOUGH STRENGTH FOR ONE LAST TRICK.
BY CROM YOU WERE A GOOD MAN, AGARA, AND LIKE TOO MANY GOOD MEN, DEAD BEFORE YOUR TIME.
BUT AT LEAST YOU HAVE BEEN AVENGED.

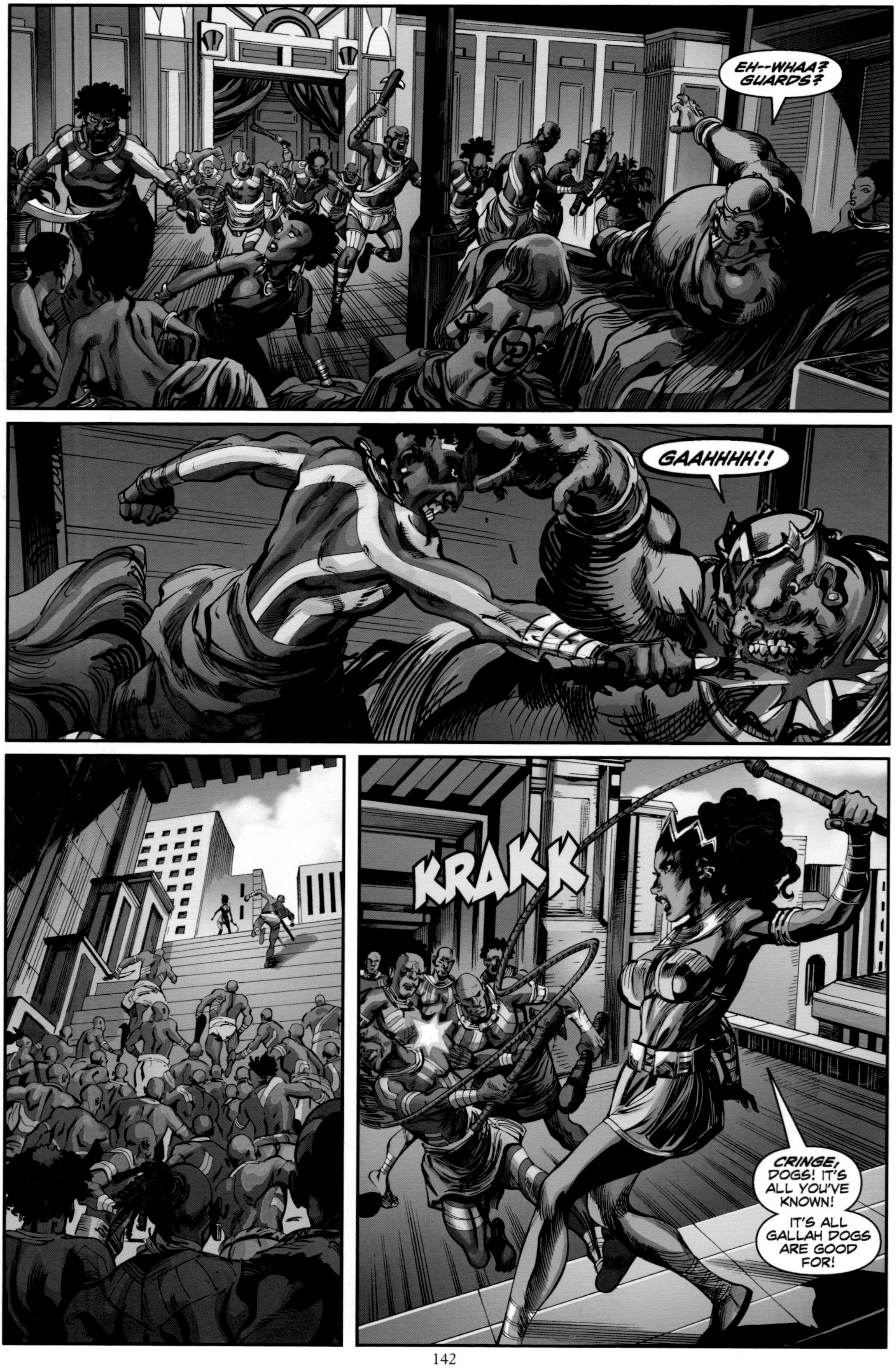
EH--WHAA? GUARDS?
GAAHHHH!!
KRAKK
CRINGE, DOGS! IT'S ALL YOU'VE KNOWN!
IT'S ALL GALLAH DOGS ARE GOOD FOR!

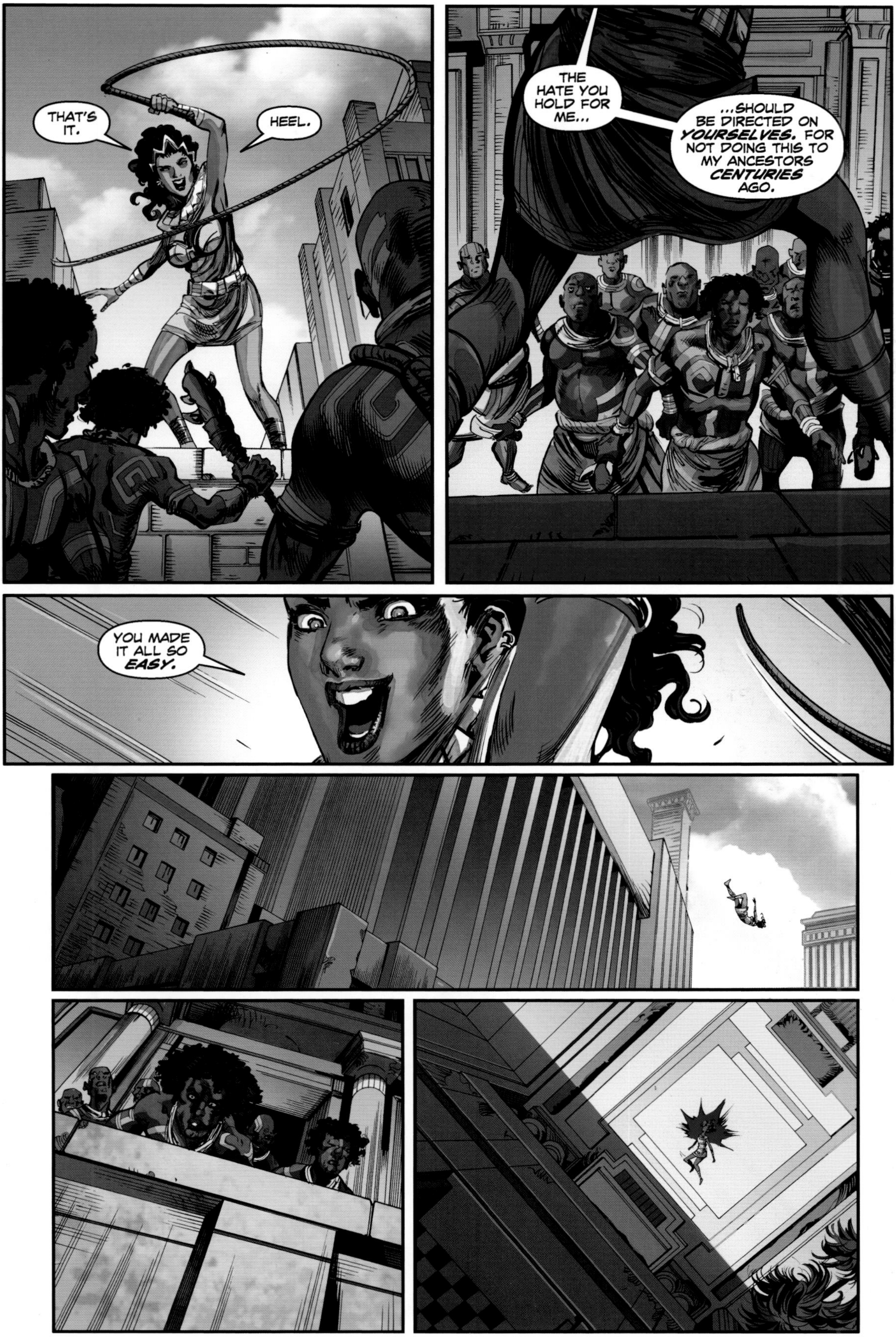
THAT'S IT.
HEEL.
THE HATE YOU HOLD FOR ME...
...SHOULD BE DIRECTED ON YOURSELVES. FOR NOT DOING THIS TO MY ANCESTORS CENTURIES AGO.
YOU MADE IT ALL SO EASY.

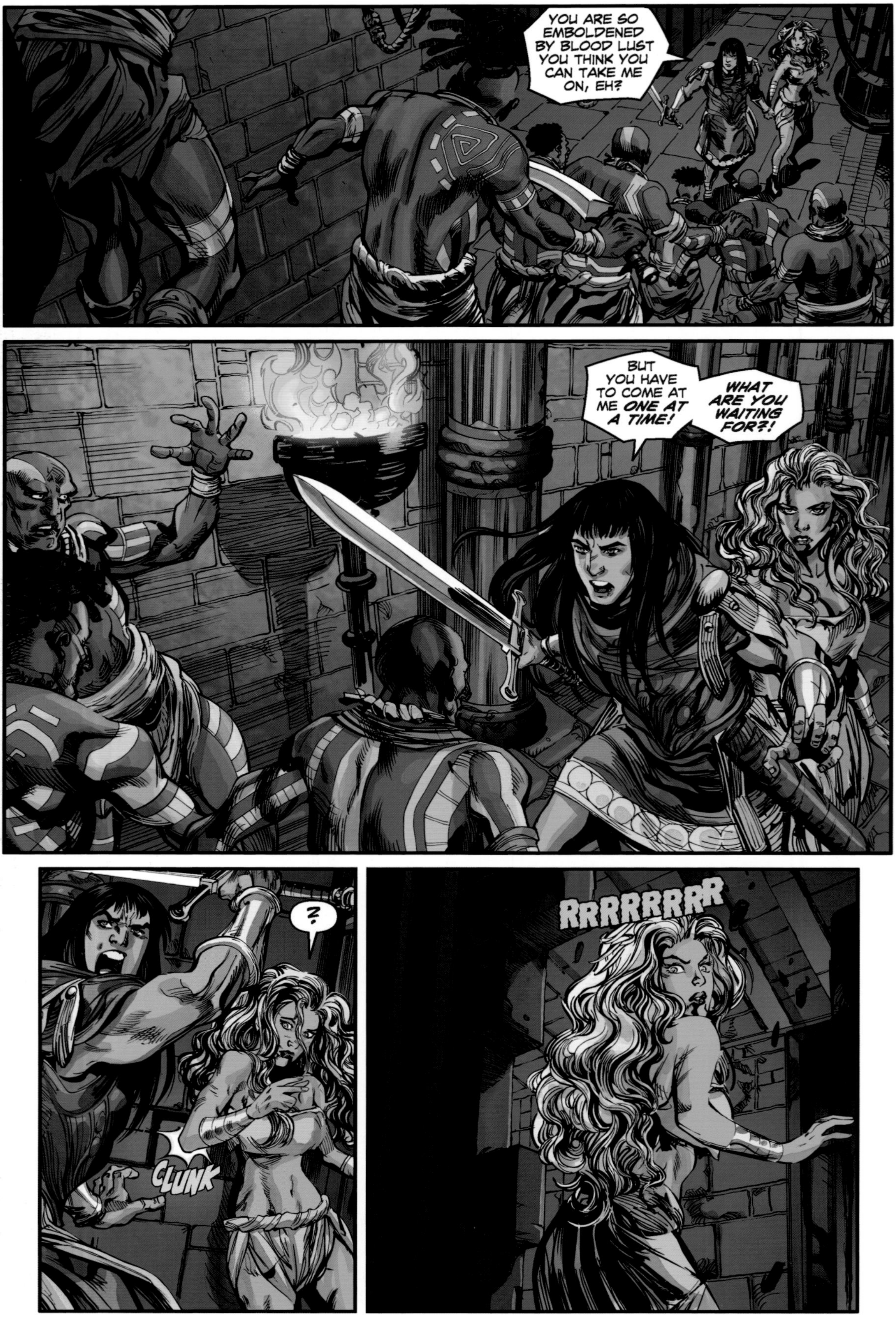
YOU ARE SO EMBOLDENED BY BLOOD LUST YOU THINK YOU CAN TAKE ME ON, EH?
BUT YOU HAVE TO COME AT ME ONE AT A TIME!
WHAT ARE YOU WAITING FOR?!
?
CLUNK
RRRRRRRR

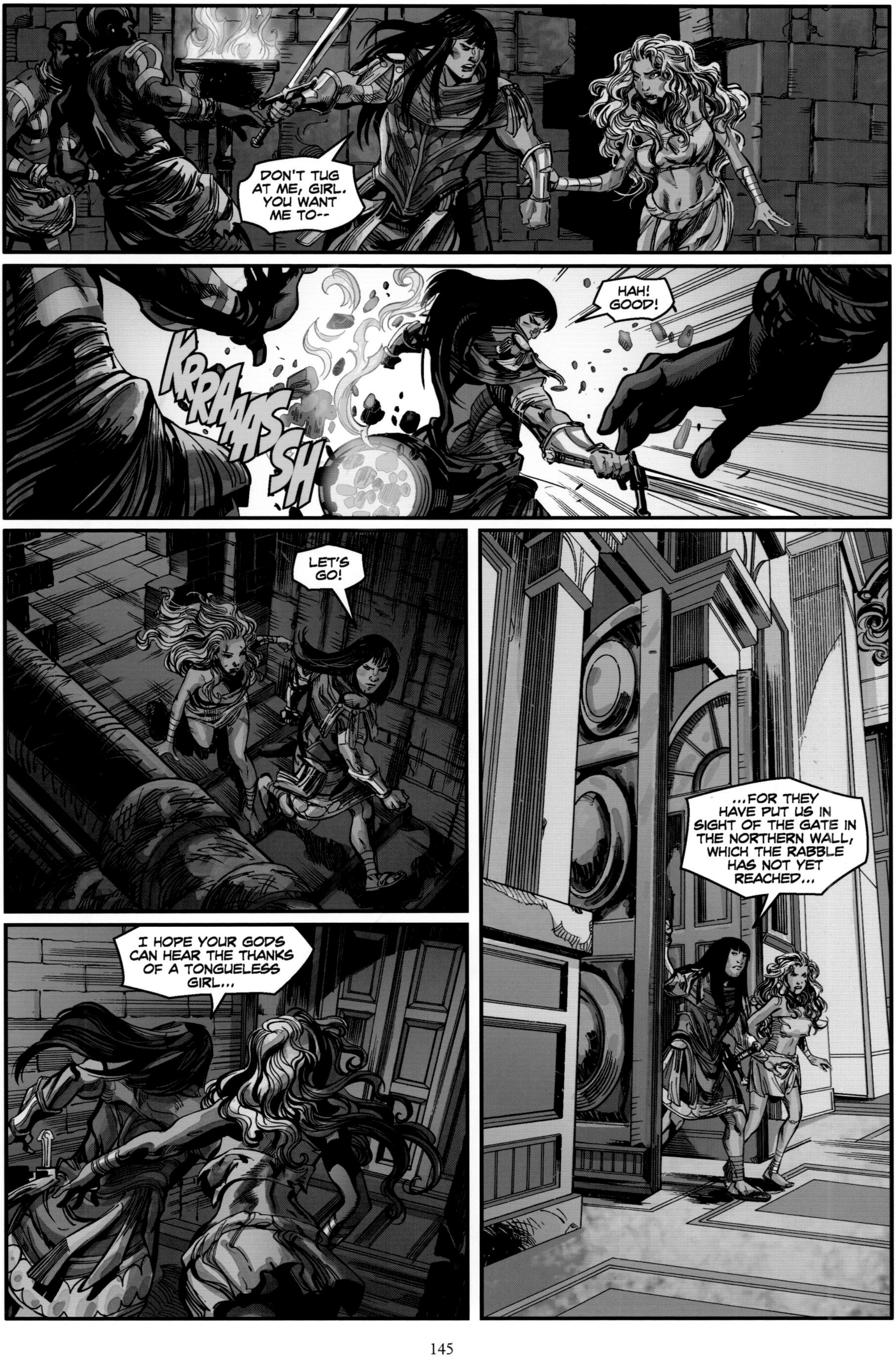
DON'T TUG AT ME, GIRL. YOU WANT ME TO--
KRRAAASSH
HAH! GOOD!
LET'S GO!
I HOPE YOUR GODS CAN HEAR THE THANKS OF A TONGUELESS GIRL...
...FOR THEY HAVE PUT US IN SIGHT OF THE GATE IN THE NORTHERN WALL, WHICH THE RABBLE HAS NOT YET REACHED...

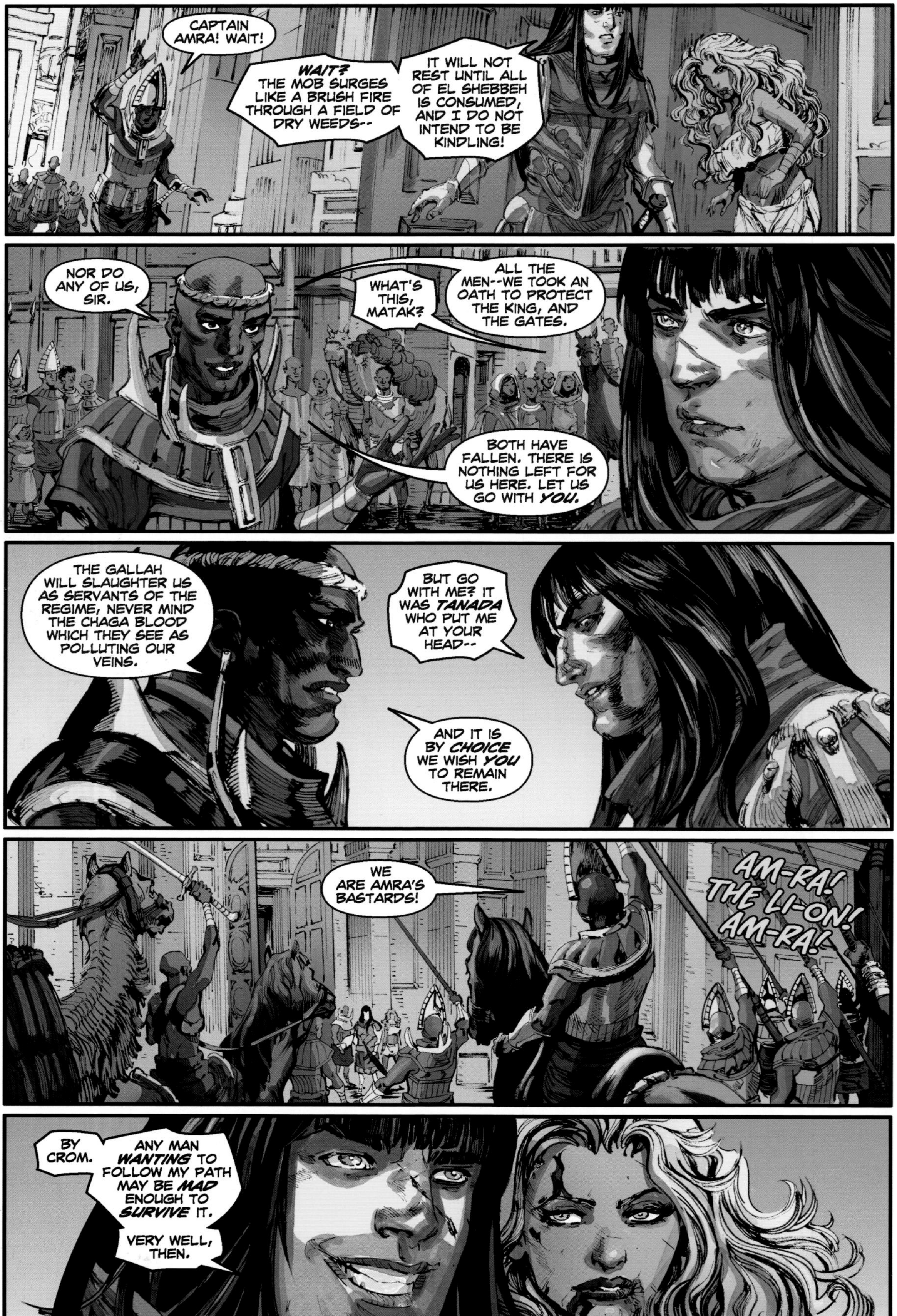
CAPTAIN AMRA! WAIT!
WAIT? THE MOB SURGES LIKE A BRUSH FIRE THROUGH A FIELD OF DRY WEEDS--
IT WILL NOT REST UNTIL ALL OF EL SHEBBEH IS CONSUMED, AND I DO NOT INTEND TO BE KINDLING!
NOR DO ANY OF US, SIR.
WHAT'S THIS, MATAK?
ALL THE MEN--WE TOOK AN OATH TO PROTECT THE KING, AND THE GATES.
BOTH HAVE FALLEN. THERE IS NOTHING LEFT FOR US HERE. LET US GO WITH YOU.
THE GALLAH WILL SLAUGHTER US AS SERVANTS OF THE REGIME, NEVER MIND THE CHAGA BLOOD WHICH THEY SEE AS POLLUTING OUR VEINS.
BUT GO WITH ME? IT WAS TANADA WHO PUT ME AT YOUR HEAD--
AND IT IS BY CHOICE WE WISH YOU TO REMAIN THERE.
WE ARE AMRA'S BASTARDS!
AM-RA! THE LI-ON! AM-RA!
BY CROM.
ANY MAN WANTING TO FOLLOW MY PATH MAY BE MAD ENOUGH TO SURVIVE IT.
VERY WELL, THEN.

KINGS NEED
MERCENARIES.

LOOT NEEDS
PLUNDERING.

AND THIS GIRL,
HERE, BELIEVES SHE
KNOWS WHERE LIES A
HOARD BEYOND
IMAGINATION.

ALL I
NEED ARE A FEW
STRONG SPEARS
TO SEIZE IT.

SO WHAT
ARE WE WAITING
FOR, MEN!
LET'S GO!

RAAHHHHHH!!

It had been a long time
since he had a command
of his own, with no
officer or nobleman or
chief above him but
Crom in his brooding
mountaintop abode.

He felt himself
again in a way he
had not for years.

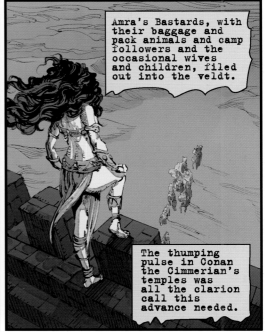

Amra's Bastards, with
their baggage and
pack animals and camp
followers and the
occasional wives
and children, filed
out into the veldt.

The thumping
pulse in Conan
the Cimmerian's
temples was
all the clarion
call this
advance needed.

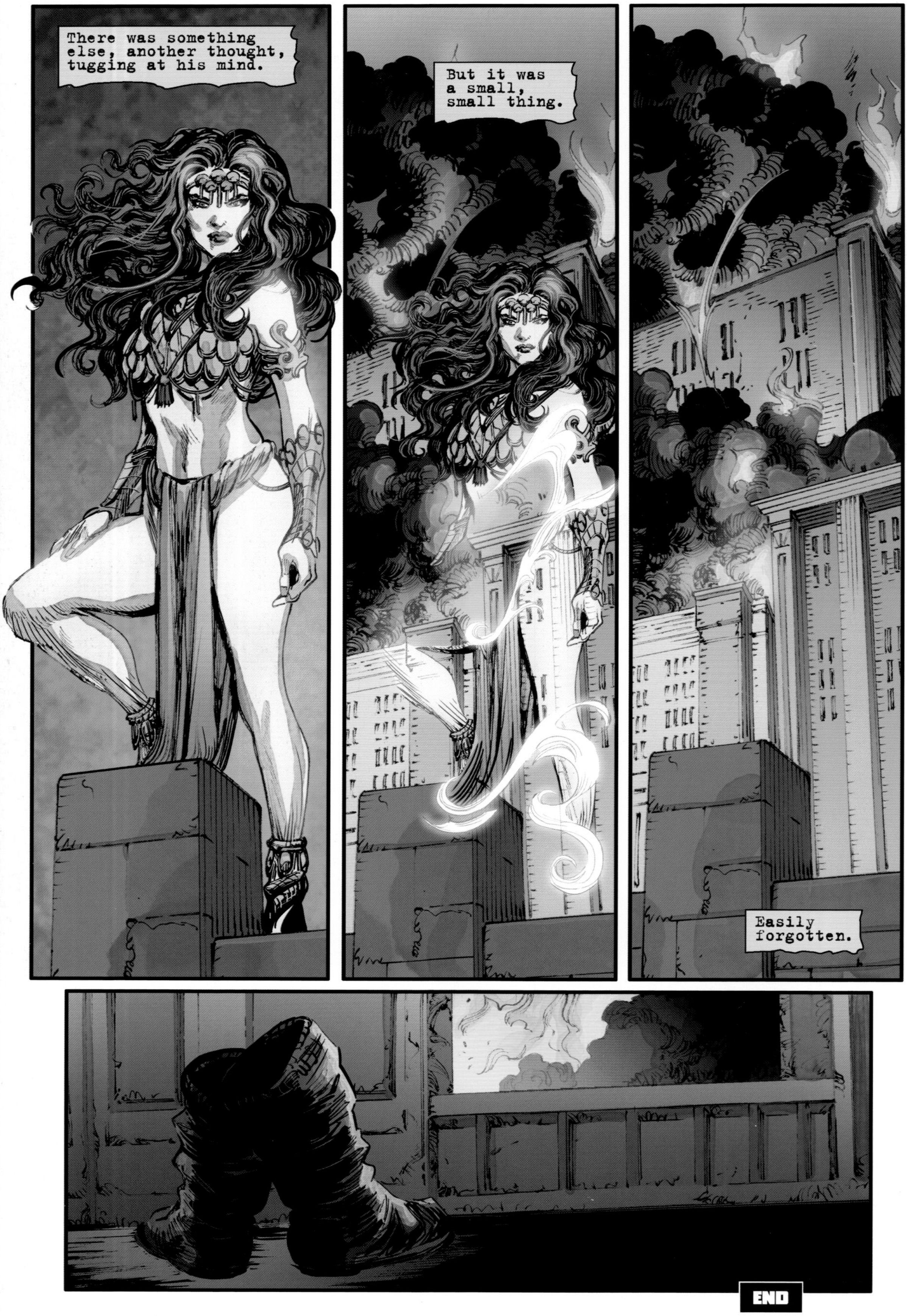
There was something else, another thought, tugging at his mind.
But it was a small, small thing.
Easily forgotten.
END

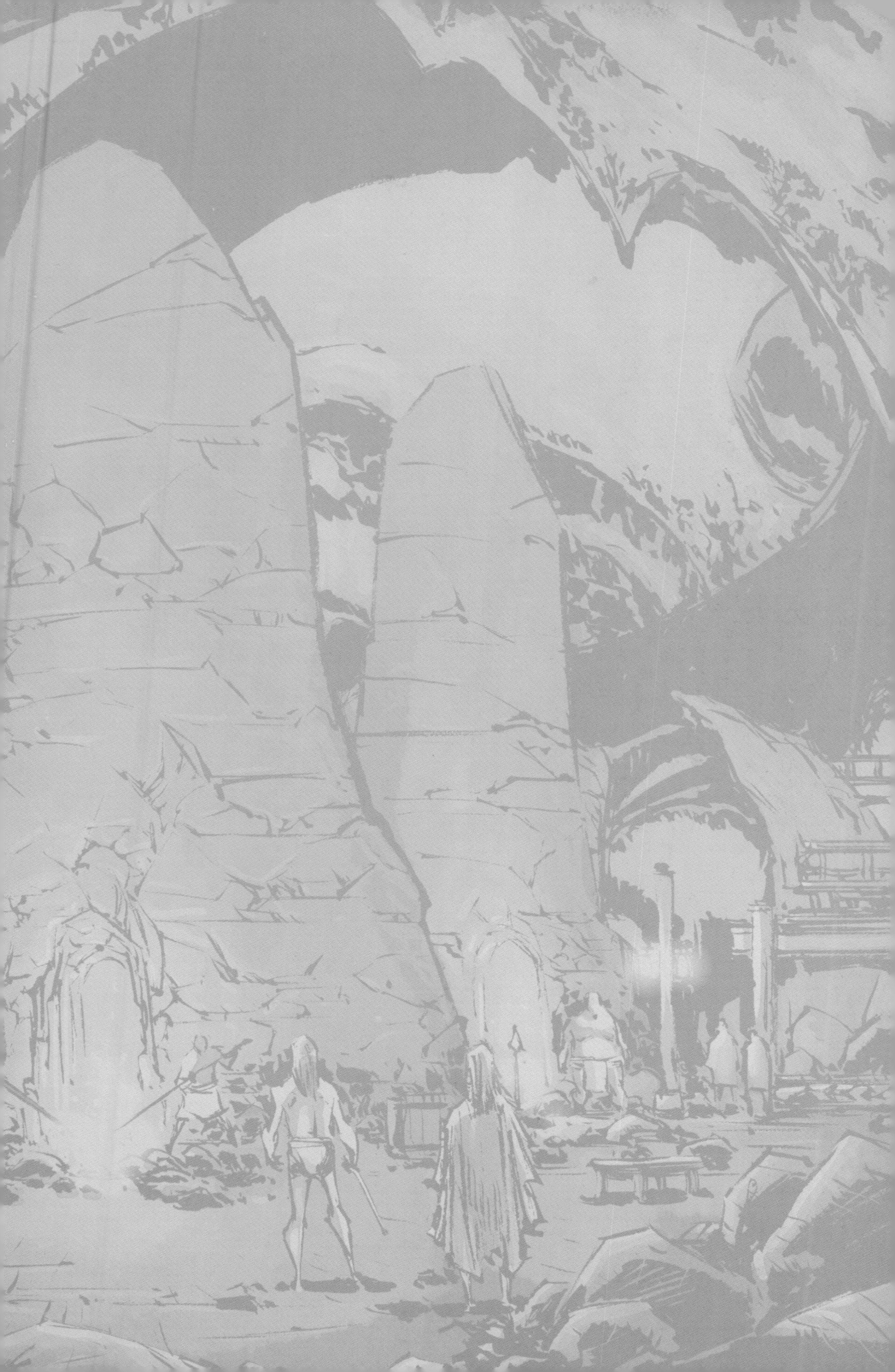

President and Publisher
MIKE RICHARDSON

Executive Vice President
NEIL HANKERSON

Chief Financial Officer
TOM WEDDLE

Vice President of Publishing
RANDY STRADLEY

Vice President of Book Trade Sales
MICHAEL MARTENS

Editor in Chief
SCOTT ALLIE

Vice President of Marketing
MATT PARKINSON

Vice President of Product Development
DAVID SCROGGY

Vice President of Information Technology
DALE LAFOUNTAIN

Senior Director of Print, Design, and Production
DARLENE VOGEL

General Counsel
KEN LIZZI

Editorial Director
DAVEY ESTRADA

Senior Books Editor
CHRIS WARNER

Executive Editor
DIANA SCHUTZ

Director of Print and Development
CARY GRAZZINI

Art Director
LIA RIBACCHI

Director of Scheduling
CARA NIECE

Director of Digital Publishing
MARK BERNARDI

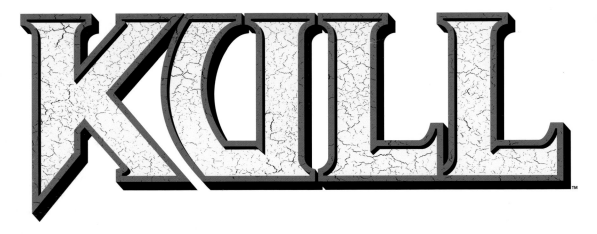

KULL